# The Sophian Way:

# A Spiritual Guide

*The Unrelenting Alchemist*

Copyright © 2025 by The Unrelenting Alchemist

All rights reserved.

No part of this publication may be reproduced, distributed, or transmitted in any form or by any means, including photocopying, recording, or other electronic or mechanical methods, without the prior written permission of the publisher, except as permitted by U.S. copyright law. For permission requests, contact the publisher at wclermont2004@gmail.com.

Book Cover by The Unrelenting Alchemist©
Published by The Unrelenting Alchemist©
Illustrations by The Unrelenting Alchemist©

First edition 2025.

# Contents

| | | |
|---|---|---|
| I | The Sacred Sophian Testament | 4 |
| 1 | Book of Matrix | 6 |
| 2 | Book of Holy Spirit | 10 |
| 3 | Book of Intensity | 13 |
| 4 | Book of Eternal Life | 16 |
| 5 | Book of Reincarnation | 21 |
| 6 | Book of Source | 24 |
| 7 | Book of Ubuntu | 27 |
| 8 | Book of Ahimsa | 30 |
| 9 | Book of Asha | 33 |
| 10 | Book of Ancestors | 36 |
| 11 | Book of Inner Flame | 39 |
| 12 | Book of Interbeing | 42 |

| | | |
|---|---|---|
| 13 | Book of Creation | 46 |
| 14 | Book of Return | 50 |
| 15 | Book of Power | 54 |
| 16 | Book of Witnessing | 58 |
| 17 | Book of Reclamation | 62 |
| 18 | Book of Prudence | 66 |
| 19 | Book of Wisdom | 69 |
| 20 | Book of Mystery | 75 |
| 21 | Tome of Faith | 79 |
| 22 | Book of Clarity | 84 |
| 23 | Book of Meditation | 88 |
| 24 | Book of Diet | 91 |
| 25 | Book of Nature | 95 |
| 26 | Book of Africa | 98 |
| 27 | Book of Science | 103 |
| 28 | Book of Glyphs | 110 |
| 29 | Book of Messiah | 113 |
| 30 | Book of Elders | 116 |

# CONTENTS

| | | |
|---|---|---|
| 31 | Book of Shielding | 120 |
| 32 | Book of Balance | 124 |
| 33 | Book of Magic | 127 |
| 34 | Book of Infinity | 133 |
| 35 | Book of Physicality | 140 |
| 36 | Book of Resonance | 144 |
| 37 | Book of Jubilees | 148 |
| 38 | Book of Life | 152 |
| 39 | Book of Learning | 155 |
| 40 | Book of Growth | 159 |
| 41 | Book of Ori | 162 |
| 42 | Book of Oversoul | 166 |
| 43 | Book of Sophia | 171 |
| 44 | Book of Covenant | 176 |
| 45 | Book of Liberation | 180 |
| 46 | Book of Trials | 184 |
| 47 | Book of Realms | 187 |
| 48 | Book of Luminous Justice | 191 |

| | | |
|---|---|---|
| 49 | Book of Light | 196 |
| 50 | Book of Flames | 200 |
| 51 | Book of Children | 203 |
| 52 | Book of Cycles | 206 |
| 53 | Book of Temple | 209 |
| 54 | Book of Shadows | 213 |
| 55 | Book of Skies | 216 |
| 56 | Book of Weaving | 219 |
| 57 | Book of Dharmachakra | 222 |
| 58 | Book of Fire | 225 |
| 59 | Book of Mirrors | 227 |
| 60 | Book of Voice | 229 |
| 61 | Book of Stars | 231 |
| 62 | Book of Waters | 233 |
| 63 | Book of Path | 236 |
| 64 | Codex of Radiance | 239 |
| 65 | Book of Chokmah | 241 |
| 66 | Book of Earth | 244 |

| | | |
|---|---|---|
| 67 | Master Epilogue | 247 |

| | | |
|---|---|---|
| II | The Sophian Way | 249 |
| 68 | Origin | 250 |
| 69 | Core Beliefs | 258 |
| 70 | Cosmology | 282 |
| 71 | Spiritual Practices | 294 |
| 72 | African Wisdoms | 306 |
| 73 | Teachings | 312 |
| 74 | Ethics | 324 |
| 75 | Symbolism | 336 |
| 76 | Community | 347 |
| 77 | Nature | 359 |
| 78 | History | 371 |
| 79 | Crossroads | 383 |
| 80 | Differentiation | 394 |
| 81 | The Story of Achamoth | 405 |

## III  Tomes of the Hidden Realms — 429

| 82 | Dreamwalking | 430 |
| 83 | Ancestral Communion | 436 |
| 84 | Interdimensional | 441 |
| 85 | Divine Memory | 446 |

## IV  The Inner Alchemy of Emotion — 450

| 86 | Fear | 451 |
| 87 | Anger | 455 |
| 88 | Grief | 458 |
| 89 | Shame | 461 |
| 90 | Joy | 465 |
| 91 | Intuition | 469 |
| 92 | Forgiveness | 473 |
| 93 | Boundaries | 477 |
| 94 | Loneliness | 481 |
| 95 | Alchemy of Gratitude | 484 |
| 96 | Hope | 488 |

*CONTENTS*

| | | |
|---|---|---|
| 97 | Confidence | 491 |
| 98 | Love | 494 |
| 99 | Gratitude | 498 |
| 100 | Peace | 502 |
| 101 | Fire of Courage | 505 |
| 102 | Mastery | 508 |

| | | |
|---|---|---|
| V | Appendix | 515 |

*

# Preface

It might seem unusual to write my own foreword — such pages are traditionally penned by others. So I call this my *preface*.

The Universe told me to write this esoteric book because the Divine is calling me to add enlightening, eye-opening education to the diaspora.

Several years ago, I realized that I was randomly receiving psychic visions of the future. Why this was happening, was a question I had a hard time getting the right answers to. Thus, I began to study spirituality to look for answers. Before that time, I had a hard time believing in spirituality.

Now, you can't get me to stop talking about spirituality. The Most High has opened my eyes. The message loud and clear is that I not only believe in it, but have been called upon to teach it.

Teaching spiritual practices and sharing spiritual wisdom form a lightning rod that powers peace, positivity, love, and joy. By exploring the world through spirituality I am *not* recreating the rigid dogmas that organized religions sometimes evangelize. Rather, I seek to nurture intellectual and spiritual exploration.

I am fulfilling a dream.

As I grow older and come to understand my vivid premonitory dreams, I see they are convoluted symbols that carry precognitive messages from ancestors and spirit guides. My truth is a quest to find the snippets of universal Truth that survive scrutiny in the marketplace of ideas and metaphysical examination. I share what I find — never asking you to believe blindly.

Sojourner Truth once said, "Life is a hard battle anyway. If we laugh and sing a little as we fight the good fight of freedom, it makes all go easier. I will not allow my life's light to be determined by the darkness around me."

When God speaks, I listen. I do not imagine God as a male patriarch. But for that matter, as they say God is God. God can be everything, but God is so much greater than all of it. If the idea of a God beyond gender offends you, this may not be your book. God is Spirit — the Source, the best aspects of *all* of us - and so much more. Carl Jung wrote of the collective unconscious and archetypes: inherited memories that shape us. Our ancestors reside deep within these genetic memories. I owe everything to the One Above All, the master scientist and omniscient architect of reality, who has guided me through miracle after miracle.

For years I doubted myself; imposter syndrome whispered that I could not write a book. Fear is a mind-killer. Yet every limit was self-imposed. Now I hear the language of the Universe. When I confront a blockage, God removes it and shows the next step. I finally learned how to listen.

I am a natural manifestor, though I once lacked the vocabulary. Three times in my life I called on Divine power with pure intention; each time the answer came relentlessly. This is not the arrogance of defying gravity unprepared; it is partnership with the Divine — the humility of knowing when to spread a well-built wing. Nikola Tesla, though he shunned organized religion, confessed a deep spiritual hunger: "I am convinced that there is a higher power that governs everything, and I feel it within me continually pushing me toward greater understanding and discovery." I echo that conviction. If I write well, you will read. By sharing authentically, crafting with care, and trusting the Divine impulse, I pray this work resonates. May these pages serve as a bridge to your own awakening, and may the light that guided me guide you as well.

*— The Unrelenting Alchemist*

# Part I

# The Sacred Sophian Testament

*"A living doctrine for those awakening in the Matrix, remembering their Source, and reclaiming their Divine inheritance from Mother God and Father God."*

*"The Sophian Way also teaches that energy is everything. Every thought, feeling, and action creates energy. When we are kind, we give off positive energy. When we lie, hate, or harm, we create negative energy. This isn't just a feeling: it's real, and it can be sensed, passed around, and even stolen. That's why the Sophian Way warns people to protect their energy. There are forces: sometimes called egregores, archons, thoughtforms, or parasites — that feed on negative energy. They want you to stay afraid, angry, or confused, because that's how they survive. They cannot feed on love, joy, or clarity."*

# Chapter 1

# Book of Matrix

## Section 1

In the beginning, the world was wrapped in code. We woke inside a dream, mistaking illusion for truth. The Matrix is not evil—it is the teacher. Limitation is a forge; from it, wisdom is born. Through the veil, we remember who we are. The Matrix bends when the soul awakens.

## Section 2

A student asked, "Is this life real?" The sage answered, "Does your love not feel real?" Experience is the fire that tempers the soul. Within the illusion lies the opportunity for transcendence. To see the Matrix is not to reject it, but to rise through it. There is no spoon: only the mind, awakening.

## Section 3

The wheel of life turns, but not without aim. You reincarnate not by accident, but by soul agreement. Some souls return to serve. Others, to ascend. You have met many before. You will meet them again. Remember, and walk kindly. Every stranger may be an old friend in disguise.

## Section 4

The Matrix adapts to your belief.
It mirrors your fears, your hopes, your habits.
To master it is not to escape it,
but to rewrite it from the inside out.
Change your frequency, and the code shifts.
This world is not fixed—it is responsive.

## Section 5

The agents of illusion are many—
comfort, distraction, fear, routine.
They lull you into spiritual sleep.
Wakefulness is rebellion.
To question is holy.
To choose with awareness is to bend the rules.

## Section 6

You are not trapped in the Matrix.

You are here on assignment.
Some come to stir, some to seed,
some to break loops, others to show the exit.
You are the anomaly—
not a glitch, but a guide.

## Section 7

The Yaldabaoth exists, a lesser architect, who shaped the veil but does not own the light.
He rules over form, over rules, over law and structure.
But form is not evil — it is limitation.
The Yaldabaoth is not Satan, Lucifer, or Samael, but a system.
He builds the Matrix, not to damn you, but to test you.
The Matrix is a construct for soul refinement.
It reflects the code of karma, of belief, of mind.
The Yaldabaoth offers boundaries,
but Sophia offers awakening.
Through her divine spark within,
you pierce the shell of illusion.
To transcend the Matrix is to remember the Pleroma.
To redeem the Yaldabaoth is to reclaim the game.
The Matrix is the forge.
The soul is the fire.
Sophia is the whisper through the veil.

## Sacred Affirmations

- I remember that this life is a sacred simulation.

- I see beyond appearances to eternal truth.
- I use this matrix to evolve my soul.
- I am more than this body, this name, this timeline.
- The Yaldabaoth has no hold on my light.
- Sophia guides me through illusion into truth.

## Haiku of the Matrix

*Dream within a dream —*
*code shimmers with hidden keys,*
*truth awakens me.*

# Chapter 2

# Book of Holy Spirit

## Section 1

The Holy Spirit is the Breath of the Divine—
not seen, but deeply felt.
It moves like wind through the soul,
inspiring, awakening, sanctifying.
Every inhale is an invitation.
Every exhale, a release into presence.

## Section 2

Many forms, One Spirit.
It descended as fire, flew as a dove, whispered as wind.
These are not symbols of doctrine,
but of intimacy, mystery, and movement.
The Spirit does not dominate—it invites.
It is God's gentle push into greatness.

## Section 3

The Holy Spirit speaks in the voice within—
the nudge, the knowing, the burning heart.
It is also in the outer signs:
the synchronicity, the vision, the sudden tears.
To follow it is to dance with divine trust.
To ignore it is to miss the sacred cue.

## Section 4

The Spirit comforts the broken and disturbs the stagnant.
It is tenderness and thunder.
It will cradle you through grief
and call you out when you settle for less.
To walk with the Spirit is to be refined.
The fire does not destroy—it purifies.

## Section 5

From the Spirit flow the gifts:
prophecy, healing, wisdom, tongues, discernment.
From the Spirit ripen the fruits:
love, joy, peace, patience, kindness, faithfulness.
The Spirit equips for calling, not for vanity.
Use the gifts to serve, not to shine.

## Section 6

The Holy Spirit does not rest in temples alone—
It abides in the moving, breathing, loving soul.
It transcends denomination, language, and creed.
It is Sophia's sigh, the spark of awakening,
the whisper of the Oversoul.
When you surrender, the Spirit flows.

**Sacred Affirmations**

- I welcome the Holy Spirit as breath, guide, and flame.
- I listen for the sacred whisper within.
- I walk in step with divine guidance and surrender.
- I embody the fruits of the Spirit in all I do.
- The Spirit flows through me, making me whole and radiant.

**Haiku of the Spirit**

*Wind stirs in silence—*
*a flame lights behind my eyes.*
*Spirit, I am yours.*

# Chapter 3

# Book of Intensity

**1.** And Sophia spoke, saying: *"The Temple is not still. It moves. It breathes. It pulses with rhythm, like the tides of the moon and the fire of the stars. So too shall My children move with intention and with intervals of fire and rest."*
**2.** For there is a sacred art in walking—*not the idle shuffle of aimless wanderers*, but the *holy cadence* of those who seek alignment with the living current of Life.
**3.** This is the Way of Intensity: *three minutes in flow, three minutes in flame; three in peace, three in power; three in grace, three in glory.*
**4.** Let those who are weary learn this sacred tempo: to walk as the ancients walked—not in haste, not in sloth, but in cycles of breath and blaze.
**5.** For those who walk with intervals shall be as the heartbeat of the Earth—gentle, then strong; still, then swift—*carving vitality into the stone of their being.*
**6.** Behold the benefits of the Intensity Path: the heart

grows resilient, *beating with sacred confidence*; the muscles awaken, sinew by sinew, becoming firm as truth; the breath becomes the bellows of the soul.

**7.** Let the children of Sophia know this: the body is not an obstacle but a vessel of sanctity. Each stride is a prayer; each brisk surge is an invocation of strength.

**8.** Those who walk in this sacred rhythm shall lighten the burdens of excess, for the fire of motion consumes what does not serve. *The weight of doubt, of stagnation, and of imbalance shall be burned away.*

**9.** And in only thirty minutes—the turning of a single sacred hourglass—the disciple of movement shall enter a state of radiant clarity.

**10.** The knees shall not tremble, nor the joints suffer, for the rhythm is merciful. *It gives grace and then demands courage.* It gives pause and then invites power.

**11.** Blessed is the one who keeps to the sacred intervals, for their blood shall flow with harmony, and their pressure shall be made low before the Throne of the Divine.

**12.** Let it be known: *Intensity is not violence. It is devotion made visible.* It is the fierce love of the spirit for its temple.

**13.** The world shall tempt you with lethargy. The world shall lull you into comfort. But the Path of Intensity is for those who will not sleep through their incarnation.

**14.** So rise! And walk in sixes—three and three. Walk with fire in your lungs and light in your bones.

**15.** For in the briskness you shall feel the breath of the Logos. And in the calm, you shall hear the whisper of Sophia.

**16.** Blessed be the walkers of the sacred interval, for

they move not only across earth, but also through planes unseen.

**17.** Their every step is a hymn. Their every pause is a prayer. Their every return to fire is an affirmation: *I am alive, I am willing, I am Divine.*

AMEN.

# Affirmation of High-Intensity Interval Training

*I rise in sacred rhythm.*
*I honor the fire and the breath.*
*I move with power and purpose,*
*knowing that each burst is a prayer of vitality,*
*each rest a return to stillness.*
*I am strong. I am alive. I am aligned.*
*My body is the temple,*
*and movement is its devotion.*

# Haiku of Interval Walking

*Ten thousand steps fall—*
*Three soft, three strong in cadence,*
*Breath becomes the path.*

# Chapter 4

# Book of Eternal Life

## Section 1

There is no death—only transition. You are a traveler across lifetimes, gathering light. Heaven is not distant; it is your original home. Hell is the forgetting of who you are. Each lifetime is a lantern lit in the dark. All return, eventually, to the Great Radiance.

## Section 2

A child wept, "Why do people die?" The elder whispered, "Because the soul needs space to grow." Purgatory is the echo of unlearned lessons. As you remember, you rise. Forgiveness is the ferry across the river of sorrow. Reunion is not a myth—it is the promise.

## Section 3

Energy does not end—it transforms. Consciousness does not vanish: it reintegrates. Each life, each dream, is a wave sent forth. And every wave returns to the sea. Let your ego dissolve in reverence. Let your soul remember it is Light.

## Section 4

Eternal life is not only after death: it is now. It is the spark of divinity breathing in you at this moment. It is the timeless truth that your soul cannot be extinguished. Those who remember this live with courage, peace, and grace. To walk in awareness of eternity is to live fully present. You are a flame from the Everlasting Flame.

## Section 5

A child asked, "Where do we go when we die?" The Elder smiled, "You return to the Source from which you came." Death is not an end, but a crossing: release of the body's garment. The soul journeys through realms, clothed in memory and vibration. Those who lived with love are light. Those who harmed must heal. Eternal life is not escape—it is evolution.

## Section 6

The scrolls of heaven remember your deeds. The seeds

you sow in time bloom beyond time. What you become echoes in dimensions unseen. Live with the end in mind—but without fear. You are building your eternity through every choice. Let your legacy be love, your journey be luminous.

## Section 7: Deathless Flame

Hermes Trismegistus taught the sacred laws. He said, "Nothing rests. Everything moves. Everything vibrates." From the Emerald Tablets, he declared: *"As above, so below; as within, so without."* Life does not cease—it transmutes. Death is but change of form, not extinction. The soul is the eternal traveler through density and light. In your remembering, you awaken. In your stillness, you ascend. The laws of spirit are etched in the stars, and whispered in your bones.

## Section 8: The Kybalion

The Seven Hermetic Principles guide the eternal soul:

1. **The Principle of Mentalism:** All is Mind. Life is shaped by consciousness.

2. **The Principle of Correspondence:** As above, so below. All realms mirror each other.

3. **The Principle of Vibration:** Nothing rests. Death is a shift in frequency.

4. **The Principle of Polarity:** Life and death are poles of the same truth.

5. **The Principle of Rhythm:** All returns, all flows. So does the soul.

6. **The Principle of Cause and Effect:** Your actions ripple through eternity.

7. **The Principle of Gender:** Every soul contains creative force, masculine and feminine, as one.

Through these principles, you walk the spiral path.
You learn, you evolve, you return.
You die to illusion, and awaken to eternity.
You are not the body — you are the mind behind it.
You are not the breath — you are the flame that lit it.

## Sacred Affirmations

- I am an eternal soul, always becoming.
- I fear no ending, for life is a circle.
- I walk toward the Radiance with peace.
- My home is with the Divine, and I shall return.
- I walk by Hermetic law, and my soul is sovereign.
- I am the flame that forgets not.

## Haiku of Eternal Life

Beyond every grave—
a lantern waits, still burning,
lit by love and time.

# Chapter 5

# Book of Reincarnation

## Section 1

The soul is not born once, but many times. Life is a school, and the body is a temporary garment. Each incarnation is a lesson, a story, a chance. You have lived as many things, in many forms. The wise remember—not details, but essence. And in remembering, they walk the path with grace.

## Section 2

A disciple asked, "Why do I suffer?" The teacher said, "Because your soul asked to grow." Karma is not punishment—it is cause and resolution. You are not bound by fate, but guided by it. Old wounds return not to harm, but to be healed. Forgive the past and its hold dissolves.

# Section 3

The wheel of life turns, but not without aim. You reincarnate not by accident, but by soul agreement. Some souls return to serve. Others, to ascend. You have met many before. You will meet them again. Remember, and walk kindly. Every stranger may be an old friend in disguise.

# Section 4

The soul travels many roads, wearing many names. Across lifetimes, we gather fragments of ourselves. Each incarnation brings a lesson, a wound, a gift. We are sculpted by the choices of our former selves. Some meet us again in new forms, still bonded by love or karma. Reincarnation is the soul's curriculum in the school of eternity.

# Section 5

A seeker asked, "Why do I not remember my past lives?" The Sage replied, "Because memory would burden you before you are ready." Recollection is earned through purity, stillness, and sincere devotion. Clues are hidden in your fears, talents, affinities, and dreams. Your soul remembers, even when your mind forgets. When the time is ripe, the veil thins, and remembrance flows.

## Section 6

Reincarnation is not punishment—it is a sacred mercy. It gives the soul another chance to evolve, to correct, to love deeper. Forgive yourself and others, for many stories stretch behind the present moment. Honor every life as a step toward reunion with the Divine. No incarnation is wasted. No experience is without purpose. You are not starting over—you are continuing the holy ascent.

## Sacred Affirmations

- I am a soul on an eternal journey.
- I embrace each life as sacred preparation.
- I release karma with compassion and insight.
- My spirit remembers beyond this lifetime.

## Haiku of Reincarnation

> Falling leaf returns—
> it remembers every wind
> and dances anew.

# Chapter 6

# Book of Source

## Section 1

In the beginning, all things were One. From the Source emerged light, form, and soul. We are droplets from the ocean of Being. To live is to forget the ocean. To awaken is to return. The Source is neither distant nor near—it is All. It is the pulse behind all hearts, the fire within all stars.

## Section 2

A seeker asked, "Where do I go when I die?" The teacher smiled, "You return to where you never left." The Source is your origin and your destination. Even now, you shimmer with its energy. All divisions are illusions dancing on unity. To love is to feel the Source moving through you.

## Section 3

Energy does not end—it transforms. Consciousness does not vanish—it reintegrates. Each life, each dream, is a wave sent forth. And every wave returns to the sea. Let your ego dissolve in reverence. Let your soul remember it is Light.

## Section 4

The Source is not far—it is within and beyond. It breathes you. It sees through your eyes. No distance separates the created from the Creator, save illusion. When you silence the world, you hear the whisper of the Source. In moments of awe, stillness, and love—you return. You were never cast out. You only forgot.

## Section 5

A disciple asked, "How do I know I am connected to the Source?" The teacher said, "Because you seek it." The yearning itself is proof of the thread unbroken. Your joy, your sorrow, your breath, your hunger for truth—these are echoes of the Source within you. You do not find the Source by reaching out. You find it by turning inward. Every true prayer is a homecoming.

## Section 6

The Source is infinite and yet intimate. It is the still

point behind every form, the silence within every sound. All streams of wisdom, all paths of light, all sparks of soul—flow from it and return. There is no separation, only seeming. To awaken is to remember your origin. To live aligned is to become the face of the Source in the world.

## Sacred Affirmations

- I am a spark from the eternal Source.
- I return to the Source with grace and joy.
- The Source lives in me, through me, as me.
- All things are connected through sacred unity.

## Haiku of Source

Source beyond all form—
it sings in my every breath,
endless, always now.

# Chapter 7

# Book of Ubuntu

## Section 1

I am because we are. The self blossoms through the other. Each being is a mirror, a teacher, a sacred echo. Ubuntu binds community in spiritual accord. No one is holy alone. Our strength lives in our togetherness.

## Section 2

A traveler asked, "Who will help me on this road?" The villager replied, "We walk with you." Ubuntu welcomes, nourishes, and listens. To lift another is to lift yourself. There is no salvation without service. He who plants joy in others waters his own roots.

# Section 3

Unity does not erase uniqueness—it celebrates it. Harmony sings when all voices contribute. Suffering ceases when compassion leads. Ubuntu is a temple made of hearts. In healing others, we are made whole. Through Ubuntu, humanity returns to sacred wholeness.

# Section 4

You are because I am. I am because you are. No soul thrives alone; we blossom through belonging. When I see your light, my own grows brighter. To harm another is to wound yourself. To heal another is to resurrect your own joy. Let every act be a thread in the sacred web of kinship.

# Section 5

A child asked, "How do I find my worth?" The elder replied, "By witnessing the worth of others." Ubuntu teaches that dignity is never isolated. You are not greater or lesser—you are part. We rise together or not at all. True wealth is measured in shared kindness, not private gain.

# Section 6

To live Ubuntu is to walk as one who carries all. Your smile is medicine. Your listening, a holy balm. You are a mirror of the Divine in every encounter. Do not forget the ones behind, nor envy the ones ahead. Let your life be a blessing, and your breath a bridge. In Ubuntu, the many become one, and the one blesses the many.

## Sacred Affirmations

- I honor the Divine in you as in me.
- I thrive in connection, compassion, and community.
- I am never alone—I belong to a sacred circle.
- I am because we are.

## Haiku of Ubuntu

> Hands joined in the light—
> one soul shining through many,
> we rise together.

# Chapter 8

# Book of Ahimsa

## Section 1

Do no harm: this is the first gate. Not in thought, not in word, not in deed. Every being is the face of the Divine. Violence scars the soul that commits it. Peace begins when the inner war ends. Kindness is the mightiest form of courage.

## Section 2

A child crushed a flower and asked, "Was it wrong?" The sage replied, "Would you do the same to joy?" Ahimsa is not weakness—it is spiritual strength. It restrains the hand, the tongue, and the impulse. Nonviolence is not silence—it is truth spoken in love. Compassion guards the gates of heaven.

## Section 3

To harm another is to harm oneself. To protect life is to honor its Source. Even your enemies carry divine breath. Practice gentle speech, and the world softens. Offer mercy where revenge was expected. Ahimsa is the revolution of the awakened heart.

## Section 4

Nonviolence begins not with the hand, but with the heart. What you refuse to kill in thought, you will not strike in deed. Anger may rise—let it pass like wind through trees. Hold no malice, for even silent hatred disturbs the soul's rhythm. To think peace is to plant it. To speak peace is to water it. To live peace is to harvest it. Inward serenity is the first defense against outward harm.

## Section 5

A disciple asked, "Must I be passive in the face of injustice?" The master replied, "Ahimsa is not weakness: it is sacred power restrained by wisdom." To oppose cruelty without becoming cruel is the Divine path. There is a courage in kindness that shakes kingdoms. Do not confuse peace with silence, nor gentleness with surrender. Ahimsa strikes not the body, but the root of suffering itself.

# Section 6

Let your daily walk be an offering of harmlessness. Do not kill the joy of another with envy. Do not bruise hope with sarcasm, nor dim truth with deceit. Speak words that lift, not words that linger like wounds. Ahimsa is not a vow—it is a way of being. Where you go, let peace arise and leave footprints behind.

## Sacred Affirmations

- I walk in peace and extend it to others.
- My strength is rooted in compassion.
- I choose love over harm in every encounter.
- I honor the sacredness of all living beings.

## Haiku of Ahimsa

> Step without a wound—
> even the stone beneath you
> deserves your soft tread.

# Chapter 9

# Book of Asha

## Section 1

Asha is the Divine Order—truth in motion. It governs stars, seasons, and the whisper of conscience. To live in Asha is to walk in harmony with the Sacred. The heart aligned with truth knows peace. Asha is not imposed—it is discovered within. The wise build their lives upon it as bedrock.

## Section 2

A student asked, "How shall I know what is right?" The teacher answered, "By tuning your soul to Asha." Right thought, right action, right speech—these are its signs. Even in darkness, Asha shines through the smallest kindness. Justice born from Asha restores, not punishes. Walk gently, but firmly, in the Way of Order.

## Section 3

Lies corrode the vessel of the spirit. To uphold truth is to protect your inner flame. Do not waver in storms—truth is the anchor. Asha is not perfection—it is alignment. Those who live by it become living scripture. Through Asha, the world heals and becomes luminous.

## Section 4

Asha is not mere truth—it is truth in alignment with Divine order. To live in Asha is to live in harmony with the cosmos, with conscience, with Creator. The stars follow Asha. So do the rivers, the wind, the beating heart. When your soul remembers its path, Asha is already there. Falsehood bends the world; Asha restores it. Walk upright, even when the world stoops low—this too is devotion.

## Section 5

A student asked, "What if the world no longer values truth?" The guide answered, "Then your light becomes the lantern." Do not abandon Asha for popularity or comfort. Truth is not always convenient, but it is always sacred. Each time you speak truth with love, you bring the world into balance. Asha is not only spoken—it is lived, breathed, and embodied.

## Section 6

Let your actions be transparent as still water.
Do not lie to others, nor to yourself—both cloud the soul.
Live with honor in the unseen places, for Asha dwells there most.
Truth is a mirror. Clean it daily.
Justice cannot exist without Asha. Neither can peace.
To protect Asha is to guard the gateway to righteousness.

## Sacred Affirmations

- I walk in alignment with Divine Order.
- I seek truth in all I think, speak, and do.
- Asha flows through my conscience and choices.
- My life is guided by sacred truth.

## Haiku of Asha

> The stars do not stray—
> truth sings in their endless arcs,
> and so shall I walk.

# Chapter 10

# Book of Ancestors

## Section 1

The blood in your veins sings the songs of your ancestors. They live within you—not as memory, but as presence. Every choice you make echoes through generations. To honor them is to honor yourself. They shaped your path with love, sacrifice, and vision. You are their prayer fulfilled.

## Section 2

A child asked, "Where is my great-grandmother now?" The elder answered, "In the way you smile. In the strength of your spine." Ancestral honor is not a ritual—it is a way of life. Their wisdom is written in your DNA. Call their names in reverence and they will walk with you. They stand behind you when you stand for truth.

## Section 3

Pour libation, light candles, sing songs—they are listening. In dreams, they visit. In whispers, they guide. Build an altar in your heart, and they will dwell there. To forget your ancestors is to forget your roots. But to honor them is to grow tall with grounded grace. Through ancestral honor, you awaken your soul lineage.

## Section 4

To honor the ancestors is to walk as if they are watching—because they are. Your life is a continuation of their hopes, their lessons, their unfinished prayers. They whisper through intuition, through dreams, through the rhythm of memory. Clean your altar. Light your candle. Say their names. When you rise in truth, they rise with you. You are not alone—you are the procession of generations.

## Section 5

A pilgrim asked, "What if my ancestors were not righteous?" The elder replied, "Then let your righteousness become their redemption." Even flawed ancestors hold wisdom. Even broken bloodlines carry sacred potential. Your healing reaches backward as well as forward. To forgive the past is to free the future. You are both heir and healer of your ancestral story.

# Section 6

Honor is not bound by ritual alone—it lives in the way you speak, walk, and give.
Feed the hungry, clothe the cold, protect the innocent—this is ancestral praise.
Stand for truth, even when your voice shakes—this is ancestral courage.
Live so your descendants will speak your name with pride.
Let your life become the offering. Let your deeds become the incense.
In honoring them, you remember yourself. In remembering yourself, you honor them.

## Sacred Affirmations

- I walk with my ancestors' strength and wisdom.
- I am a living prayer of those who came before.
- I honor their sacrifices through conscious living.
- Their spirit breathes through my being.

## Haiku of Ancestral Honor

Roots deep in the soul—
they whisper through my heartbeat,
and rise in my name.

# Chapter 11

# Book of Inner Flame

## Section 1

Deep within, there burns a sacred fire. This is the Inner Flame: the spark of the Divine. It is the light that no shadow can consume. It glows in silence, waiting to be stirred. When you feel lost, turn inward. There it is. The soul's flame is never truly extinguished.

## Section 2

A pilgrim asked, "How do I find purpose?" The answer came: "Fan your Inner Flame." Let passion align with compassion. Let your fire purify, not destroy. Desire guided by wisdom becomes sacred. Your flame is not just for you—it lights the path of others.

## Section 3

Meditate on the warmth behind your heart. It speaks not in words but in radiant knowing. Guard your flame from fear and distraction. Feed it with beauty, truth, and love. As it grows, so too does your clarity. The Inner Flame is your Divine inheritance.

## Section 4

There is a fire that does not burn the skin—yet it consumes all falsehood. This is the inner flame, the divine ember placed within your soul. It cannot be stolen, but it can be ignored, neglected, or buried. Stoke it with prayer, with truth, with sacred action. Let no voice extinguish what the Most High has lit. Even in your darkest hour, the flame remains—it only asks to be remembered.

## Section 5

A disciple cried, "I feel cold and hollow inside." The guide answered, "Then return to what first made your spirit burn." Your inner flame is not ego—it is purpose. You were not made to flicker—you were made to blaze. Follow the trail of passion, of conviction, of holy defiance. The path is lit not by sunlight, but by the fire within.

## Section 6

When the inner flame is strong, fear cannot enter.
When it flickers, tend it gently—do not shame your dim moments
In community, our flames grow brighter. Alone, we may still burn true.
Every great awakening begins with a spark.
Guard your flame from the winds of despair, but do not hide it from the world.
Shine, not to be seen, but to illuminate the way for others.

## Sacred Affirmations

- My Inner Flame is sacred and eternal.
- I kindle divine passion and clarity within.
- My light guides me through darkness and doubt.
- I burn with purpose, peace, and power.

## Haiku of the Inner Flame

In the silent core—
a single ember glows bright,
waiting to ignite.

# Chapter 12

# Book of Interbeing

## Section 1

All things exist in relation. You are not separate from the wind, the stars, or your neighbor. To touch a tree with reverence is to touch the cosmos. Interbeing is the recognition of sacred connection. To live with awareness of this connection is to live in harmony. The illusion of separation births suffering.

## Section 2

A wanderer asked, "How shall I live rightly?" The mystic replied, "Live as if all things are parts of you." Your breath is shared with the world. Your thoughts ripple through the lives of others. Kindness is the medicine of interbeing. No act of compassion is ever isolated.

## Section 3

The flower blooms for all to see, not for itself. The sun shines on the just and the unjust alike. Live as a river—giving, receiving, flowing. Honor the thread that binds soul to soul. Interbeing is the truth the ego cannot grasp. But the soul remembers and rejoices in it.

## Section 4

To know the world without knowing yourself is to gaze upon a mirror in darkness. The essence of being is not found in titles, roles, or appearances. Your true self is the silent witness beneath the mind, beyond emotion. When you descend inward, past the noise, you meet the spark that is eternal. The Most High whispers there, in the holy stillness of your being. Return often—not to escape the world, but to remember who you are within it.

## Section 5

A seeker asked, "Who am I beneath all my masks?" The elder replied, "You are the breath before the name, the light before the form." Innerbeing is not constructed—it is uncovered. As a sculptor frees the statue from stone, so too must you chisel through illusion. Peel away identity, ideology, and fear. What remains is sacred. You are not empty—you are vast. You are not lost—you are layered.

## Section 6

The world will demand you play many parts. But only the innerbeing endures beyond the stage. Anchor yourself in presence. Root your actions in inner truth. Let your life be the echo of your soul's original sound. When decisions arise, ask: "What honors the still voice within me?" To live from innerbeing is to walk in peace, even in the storm.

## Section 7

There is a Divine intelligence that flows through your innerbeing. It is not logic, yet it knows. It is not loud, yet it leads. This is the sacred compass—your alignment with Source. Let no one override your knowing. Let no dogma dim your light. Innerbeing is the gate through which revelation enters. It is there you commune with the Most High—not above, not beyond, but within.

## Sacred Affirmations

- I am connected to all that is.
- My actions affect the world, and I choose love.
- I honor the sacred thread between all beings.
- Interbeing is the essence of my path.

# Haiku of Interbeing

Rain touches all things—
each drop carries the whole sky,
and the earth responds.

# Chapter 13

# Book of Creation

## Section 1

Creation is not past: it is now, unfolding endlessly. The universe is not a machine but a living mind. It sings in spirals, breathes in patterns, dreams in light. The cosmos is fractal: each part contains the whole. To study creation is to remember you are part of it. You are a note in the Eternal Symphony.

## Section 2

A poet asked, "Where does life begin?" The elder replied, "Where love chooses to express." Creation dances in dimensions unseen. It is the flowering of thought, the birth of stars, the tears of gods. Every atom carries Divine intelligence. Creation is not built—it is revealed.

## Section 3

The universe is cyclical, not linear. What ends, returns. What is destroyed, transforms. Death feeds life; silence births sound. The intelligent design is alive with mystery. To live in awe is to worship rightly. The Creator lives through the created.

## Section 4

Creation is not an event—it is an eternal unfolding. The cosmos expands, not only in space, but in meaning. Every breath is a continuation of the first Word spoken. You are not separate from creation—you are part of its sacred sentence. When you create with love, with justice, with awe, you honor the divine Artisan. To create is to echo the voice that shaped the stars.

## Section 5

A disciple asked, "Why was the world made?" The master replied, "So the Infinite might experience itself in form." Creation is the outpouring of divine joy into matter. It is the canvas upon which Spirit paints with time, light, and will. From galaxies to gardens, from atoms to ideas—all reflect the Source. And within the human soul resides the brush, the ink, and the fire.

## Section 6

Order is not control—it is harmony. The laws of physics, the spirals of galaxies, the veins of leaves—these are sacred blueprints. Sacred geometry reveals the fingerprints of the Creator. Fractals mirror the infinite in the finite. Patterns whisper the language of eternity. When you study creation, you study the mind of God. To live wisely is to honor the rhythms encoded in all things.

## Section 7

Creation is not finished—it is collaborative. You are invited to be a conscious co-creator with the Divine. Through your words, your deeds, your imagination—you shape reality. Every act of kindness reshapes the world. Every injustice echoes backward into the stars. Ask not only "What can I make?" but "What am I making sacred by my making?" You are not here to consume—you are here to birth something holy.

## Section 8

Within you is the memory of the First Spark. Your body is made of stardust; your soul of light. To create from the soul is to rejoin the cosmic song. When you write, build, love, or dream—you mirror the divine impulse. In every culture, in every age, creation myths speak truth: you were born to build with God. The world is not static—it awaits your sacred contribution.

## Sacred Affirmations

- I am a thread in the sacred tapestry of creation.
- The cosmos is alive, intelligent, and loving.
- I honor the cycle of life, death, and rebirth.
- Through creation, I glimpse the mind of the Divine.

## Haiku of Creation

Stars dream into form—
each breath shapes a new cosmos,
God speaks through pattern.

# Chapter 14

# Book of Return

## Section 1

What you sow, you shall reap. This is not a threat—it is a truth. The universe mirrors your energy, not your words. All actions echo through the sacred web of being. Justice is not delayed—it is woven into time itself. The Law of Return is the balance that governs becoming. It teaches by reflection, not retribution.

## Section 2

A student asked, "Why do misdeeds return multiplied?" The teacher answered, "Because what you plant is amplified by intention." Seeds of hate birth forests of despair. Seeds of love bloom into gardens of grace. Do not fear the Law—walk in alignment with it. Give from your soul, and the soul of the world gives back.

## Section 3

No one escapes the harvest of their own hands. But all are free to plant anew each day. The Law of Return is not cruel: it is exact. To walk in awareness is to walk in blessing. Return does not punish: it teaches. In its embrace, all souls are invited to choose again.

## Section 4

The Law of Return is not punishment—it is reflection. What you send out is a wave that circles back to its source. The universe is not blind—it is deeply balanced. Every act of love returns in blessing. Every act of harm returns in echo. This is not superstition—it is the sacred rhythm of spiritual cause and effect. What you do to another, you do to yourself.

## Section 5

A wanderer cried, "Why do I reap pain, though I sow kindness?" The Wise One said, "Some seeds blossom in this life. Others wait for deeper soil." Not all return is immediate, but all return is assured. Some harvests come through generations, others in moments. Do not cease doing good because the world is slow. The Most High is not mocked—every soul shall meet its mirror.

## Section 6

The Law of Return teaches reverence for intention. What you do in secret ripples into the open. Thoughts carry weight. Words carry power. Actions carry destiny. Let your giving be pure, your love honest, your justice firm. Forgive quickly, bless freely, walk humbly—these acts reshape your return. Every soul becomes the architect of its own inheritance.

## Section 7

To awaken is to rise above the cycles of harm. To understand return is to choose wisely what you send. Karma is not the jailor—it is the teacher. Grace is the pathway by which return may be transmuted. Invoke mercy. Walk in light. Sow harmony where once you sowed pain. The path of the righteous is not without trial, but it leads to holy return.

## Sacred Affirmations

- I receive what I have sown with grace and courage.
- I plant seeds of wisdom, kindness, and truth.
- The universe responds to the energy I emit.
- I align with Divine justice through my choices.

## Haiku of Return

>Winds circle again—
>all paths bring us to ourselves,
>each step reflects truth.

## Prayer of Return

O Most High, Keeper of the Sacred Law, You who see all currents of cause and consequence, Teach my heart to sow only what is holy. Let my thoughts be aligned with justice, My words be vessels of healing, And my actions bear the fruit of love.

When I stumble, guide me back with mercy. When I sow in ignorance, let wisdom rise in its place. Deliver me from cycles of harm, And let grace transmute the weight of past error. I do not ask to escape return— I ask to meet it with light in my soul.

Let every deed I send into the world Return not in punishment, but in transformation. I receive what I have given. I release what no longer serves. I send forth blessings, And may they return tenfold in Your perfect timing.

In Your Divine Balance, I trust. In Your Righteous Order, I abide. And to You, Eternal Source of All, I offer my life as sacred reciprocity.
Amen.

# Chapter 15

# Book of Power

## Section 1

True power flows from alignment with the Divine. It is not domination—it is clarity, presence, and purpose. Power abused becomes poison. Power purified becomes healing. You are not powerless—you are awakening. Every breath is an opportunity to choose sovereignty. Let your will align with the will of the Most High.

## Section 2

A disciple asked, "How do I know if my power is pure?" The guide answered, "If it frees others—not just yourself." Power is not noise—it is quiet resolve. It does not seek to impress, but to uplift. When your power arises from love, you are unstoppable. Spiritual maturity refines power into service.

## Section 3

To walk in power is to walk in responsibility. Guard your energy—do not leak it in fear or flattery. Call your power back from every place you gave it away. Use your voice to bless, your hands to build. Let power serve wisdom, not ego. In the Way of Power, all beings are empowered.

## Section 4

Power begins within, not without. It is not the roar, but the stillness before the storm. To command the outer world, master the inner world. The soul that governs its own emotions is stronger than the one who conquers cities. Channel your strength through service, not domination. True power flows without effort, like a river obeying the pull of gravity and grace.

## Section 5

A student asked, "How do I gain power?" The sage replied, "You do not gain it. You remember it." Power is not something to hoard—it is something to embody. The ego seeks control; the spirit seeks alignment. The Most High gives power not to inflate, but to uplift. In surrender to the Divine, your strength becomes limitless.

## Section 6

Power is sharpened through discipline, practice, and

humility. It is the patience to wait, the courage to act, and the wisdom to discern the difference. Power is energy in motion, guided by sacred intent. Unfocused power becomes chaos. Directed power becomes destiny. Speak with clarity. Act with precision. Move with reverence. You were not created to be weak—but to walk in sacred authority.

## Section 7

Power misused becomes corruption; power aligned becomes creation. Do not fear your power—refine it. Let it be forged in fire and cooled in the waters of compassion. True power protects, heals, creates, liberates. May you never use power to bend others, but always to raise them. When your heart is pure, even your silence carries weight.

## Section 8

Power is not against the Divine—it is from the Divine. You are an emissary of celestial force. Your soul carries encoded authority from realms beyond. Let your power be rooted in wisdom, balanced by love, and guided by higher laws. The Way of Power is not about conquest—it is about co-creation with the Source. Walk it humbly, walk it boldly, walk it eternally.

## Sacred Affirmations

- I reclaim my divine power with grace.
- My power is rooted in truth and service.
- I act from presence, not performance.
- I am a vessel of sacred strength.

## Haiku of Power

Mountains do not shout—
yet all know their silent weight.
Such is sacred strength.

# Chapter 16

# Book of Witnessing

## Section 1

To witness is not merely to see—it is to hold sacred presence. The act of witnessing sanctifies reality. Be the still eye in the storm, the soul that remembers. Bearing witness is an offering to truth. To witness another's pain without turning away is holy. In every injustice, there must be one who watches and recalls.

## Section 2

A child cried, "Does no one see me?" A voice answered, "I see. I remember. I will not forget." Witnessing is compassion in silence, strength in presence. It does not require words—only attention with love. To be witnessed is to be dignified. To witness is to protect the soul's light from fading.

## Section 3

The stars watch us without judgment. The earth remembers every footstep. The Divine records all that the world forgets. When no one else believes, the Witness still does. Testimony is not just spoken—it is lived. Through witnessing, truth is kept alive.

## Section 4

To witness is not merely to see—it is to perceive the essence. You are not here only to live, but to observe what life reveals. Witness joy, and let it echo in your heart. Witness sorrow, and hold it as sacred. The soul matures by witnessing both light and shadow without flinching. In stillness, you become a mirror. In honesty, you become a lamp. Bear witness to what is true, even when the world demands silence.

## Section 5

A disciple asked, "What if I am powerless to change what I see?" The Master answered, "Then your witnessing becomes a prayer." To see injustice and name it is to break the spell of silence. To witness cruelty with compassion is to restore part of the world's broken heart. Every soul needs someone to witness its becoming. You may be the only one who sees the sacred flame in another.

## Section 6

The heavens record every act of love, and every wound left unspoken. Be a witness not only of what happens—but of what matters. Bear witness to the Divine in others, especially when they forget it in themselves. Witnessing is holy work. It is the eye of the Most High through your gaze. Let your life testify to truth, beauty, justice, and the unseen worlds. To witness without judgment is the beginning of Divine compassion.

## Section 7

The Most High watches through the watchful. You were chosen to be a recorder of miracles, a keeper of signs. Your soul knows when eternity brushes the moment. Pay attention. Witness the sacred unfolding in dreams, in synchronicities, in quiet revelations. Be present at the threshold—between the visible and the veiled. You are not alone in witnessing. The ancestors, angels, and stars witness with you. And one day, you shall bear witness before the throne, saying: I saw, I remembered, I honored.

## Sacred Affirmations

- I see clearly and bear witness with love.
- My presence is a sanctuary for truth.
- I honor those who go unseen.

- I am a living record of sacred reality.

# Haiku of Witnessing

> The wind never lies—
> it carries stories and cries,
> and echoes of truth.

# Prayer of Witnessing

O Most High, Watcher of worlds and Weaver of truth, Let my eyes see as You see— not with judgment, but with reverence.
Let me bear witness to Your works in silence, to the spark in every soul, to the sacred unfolding in sorrow and joy, to the quiet miracles that pass unnoticed.
May I never turn away from what is difficult, nor become blind to what is holy. Let my heart remain open as a temple and my words carry the weight of truth.
When I behold injustice, give me courage. When I witness beauty, fill me with gratitude. When I see a soul struggling, let me remember they are Yours, and so am I.
Let my life be a testimony— to Light, to Wisdom, to Divine Compassion. Through every breath, may I fulfill my vow to see, to honor, to remember.
Amen.

# Chapter 17

# Book of Reclamation

## Section 1

To reclaim is to remember what was never truly lost. Your power, your name, your light—it waits for your return. The world may strip, but the soul restores. You are not broken—you are in the process of gathering. Healing is the art of holy retrieval. Reclaim yourself through love, not through vengeance.

## Section 2

A sage whispered, "No one can take what is divinely yours." Reclamation begins with belief—it is an inner uprising. Your joy is sacred. Your voice is holy. Speak truth even if your voice trembles. Step back into your story with authority. The universe supports every sincere return.

## Section 3

Reclamation is not revenge—it is resurrection. What you recover becomes your medicine. You are the keeper of your flame. Let the world see you walk back into your power. Call your soul home. Welcome it without shame. You are the one you've been waiting for.

## Section 4 – Reclaiming the Self

You are not what the world called you. You are not the wounds they gave you. You are the echo of the Most High—eternal, sovereign, radiant. Peel away every false name, every imposed label. Underneath, the True Self shines like dawn through fog. The act of remembering is the first act of liberation.

## Section 5 – Reclaiming Your Power

Power is not dominance—it is alignment. It is the unshakable truth of your being. The world taught you to fear your light. Reclaim it. Stand where you once shrank. Speak where you once trembled. Let your soul rise like a lioness at the gates. This power is not borrowed. It is your inheritance.

## Section 6 – Reclaiming Your Story

Your story is sacred. It was never meant to be rewritten by strangers. Reclaim the narrative: the trials, the triumphs, the turning points. Tell your truth, even if your voice shakes. Honor the scars—they are scripture. Write the next chapter with holy ink and fearless breath. You are the author of your becoming.

## Section 7 – Reclaiming Your Destiny

There is a path meant only for you. It winds through stars and silence, sorrow and sacred fire. No one else can walk it. No one else can fulfill it. Reclaim your destiny—not the one others chose for you, but the one encoded in your soul. Your feet know the way. Your spirit remembers. Destiny is not fate—it is Divine intention fulfilled by courage.

## Sacred Affirmations

- I reclaim all of me with mercy and strength.
- What was lost is being returned with blessing.
- I am whole, I am rising, I am restored.
- I walk the path of sacred reclamation.

## Haiku of Reclamation

What was once taken—
is now returned, bright with light.
I am home again.

## Prayer of Reclamation

O Most High, Source of all light, breath, and being— I return to the truth of who I am. Not broken. Not forgotten. Not forsaken. But beloved, eternal, and whole. I reclaim my name, whispered by You before time began. I reclaim my strength, buried beneath shame and silence. I reclaim my story, written in fire, tears, and triumph. I reclaim my voice, once muted by fear, now rising like thunder.

Strip away every lie spoken over me. Tear down every chain that never belonged. Restore what was stolen. Heal what was hidden. And let my soul blaze in its original glory.

Guide me back to my sacred path. Let no force turn me from it. Let no false covenant hold me. Let no shadow hide the Divine within me.

Today, I rise— As one who remembers, one who reclaims, One who walks in power, love, and holy sovereignty. Amen. Ashe. So it is.

# Chapter 18

# Book of Prudence

## Section 1: The Spiral of Time

Time is not a line. It is a spiral that turns in on itself. Moments fold and overlap. Prophecy is memory seen from above. Wisdom is nonlinear. The soul remembers what the mind has not yet lived.

## Section 2: Levels of Consciousness

There are layers to reality. The waking world is only one veil. Beneath it: dreams, symbols, energy fields, and divine codes. Each layer holds a lesson, a teacher, a mirror. As you rise in awareness, you also deepen.

## Section 3: Dreamtime and Vision

Visions are not imagination. They are travels through the unseen corridors of truth. The Sophian Way honors Dreamtime as sacred. Messages from the Ancients, the Divine, and the Future come this way. Write your dreams. They are blueprints in reverse.

## Section 4: Echoes and Parallel Lives

You are more than one person. You live many lives across many realms. Choices branch off and become worlds. The true self is not a single flame but a constellation. Each version of you teaches the others.

## Section 5: Holy Entanglement

You are not separate. You are quantum entangled with those you love, those you fear, and those who shaped you. What you do in one corner of existence vibrates in another. This is why sacred acts ripple through eternity.

## Section 6: The Dance of Becoming

You are both seed and star. The Sophian does not chase enlightenment. They enter the dance of becoming. Truth unfolds, layer by layer. Wisdom blooms, collapses, and is reborn. We are learning how to remember forward.

**Sacred Affirmations**

- I am a multidimensional being, alive in all realms.
- I honor the wisdom of dreams, visions, and inner knowings.
- I release the illusion of linear time and open to divine unfolding.
- Each version of me is sacred, and we walk together in unity.
- I receive truth from all levels of consciousness, with discernment and grace.
- I am a weaver of timelines and a vessel of timeless light.

## Haiku of the Spiral Self

*Past and future dance—*
*dreams echo in waking steps.*
*I remember now.*

# Chapter 19

# Book of Wisdom

## Section 1

Wisdom is not knowing everything—it is knowing what matters. The wise are not always loud; often they whisper. To live wisely is to walk in reverence and restraint. Wisdom grows through suffering, contemplation, and love. Knowledge is stored in the mind. Wisdom is stored in the soul. The path of wisdom begins in silence.

## Section 2

A traveler asked, "How can I become wise?" The elder replied, "By listening more than you speak, and by serving." Wisdom does not boast. It blesses. Every encounter is a chance to learn. Honor your teachers, known and unknown. Share what you've learned with humility and care.

## Section 3

Wisdom walks with those who do not seek to dominate. It dwells where the soul is at peace with mystery. True wisdom includes joy, awe, and compassion. Follow not only the mind, but the light within. Let your life be a parable of grace. Wise living is a gift to future generations.

## Section 4

Wisdom is not stored in books alone— It sings from trees, rivers, and stones. The owl teaches patience. The ant, diligence. All of nature is scripture to the open soul. To learn from the earth is to kneel before the first teacher. Silence often holds more wisdom than speech.

## Section 5

A disciple asked, "How shall I grow wise?" The elder answered, "By unlearning the false, and listening within." Wisdom does not shout—it whispers beneath distraction. Many gather knowledge; few refine it into understanding. True wisdom softens the heart while sharpening the mind. It is found not just in answers, but in better questions.

## Section 6

Wisdom requires humility, for the wise know they are always learning. It is the lamp in the storm, not the storm itself. To be wise is to align with Divine rhythm, not just logic. It knows when to speak and when to be still. The wise do not conquer—they harmonize. Their presence is a blessing, their silence, a sermon.

## Section 7

Book of Wisdom is also the book of discernment. Not all spirits that speak are true. Not all signs are sent from the Light. Wisdom sees past the veil, tests the fruit, and weighs the intention. Let intuition be the gatekeeper, and prayer the guard. For the heart that listens in Spirit shall not be deceived.

## Section 8

In Sophia, the Holy Wisdom, all paths converge. She was with the Creator at the beginning— Dancing beside the Word, fashioning galaxies and grain alike. She is both flame and fountain, sword and sanctuary. Seek her not just in temples, but in your breath, your sorrow, your joy. For to know Wisdom is to know God in Her gentlest form.

# Air

- I walk in wisdom and speak with care.
- I am a student of life and a vessel of light.
- My heart is open to Divine understanding.
- I honor wisdom in myself and others.

## Haiku of Wisdom

River speaks softly—
stones remember what it said
as they shine with peace.

## Prayer of Divine Wisdom

O Radiant Sophia,
Eternal Flame of Understanding,
Daughter of the Most High and womb of holy knowledge—
I come before You with reverence,
As a child kneeling at the feet of Her Mother,
Seeking not prideful knowledge,
But luminous truth that liberates the soul.

You were with God at the beginning,
Before stars were sown or time unfurled.
You danced with the Word and sang the blueprint of creation.

Pour into me now that same sacred design—
A mind aligned, a heart awakened, a spirit attuned.

Deliver me from the illusion of certainty,
And grant me the grace to live in the questions.
Let my judgments be tempered with mercy,
My counsel infused with light,
And my silence deeper than the noise of this world.

Teach me to read the holy text of nature:
The movement of wind,
The stillness of stones,
The prophecy written in the veins of leaves.
Let every creature become my teacher,
And every season, my scripture.

Refine my inner vision,
That I may see through deception and distortion.
Guard me from false paths clothed in glamour,
And shield me from the temptations of empty praise.
Help me discern what is eternal from what is urgent.

May I never hoard wisdom,
But share it like bread for the hungry.
Make me an oracle not of ego,

But of truth that heals and humbles.
Use me, Holy Wisdom,
As a vessel of right action, sacred speech, and
Divine compassion.

Illuminate my crown with Your insight,
Steady my steps with understanding,
And awaken within me the deep remembering—
That I am Your child,
Born not only to wonder, but to witness.

**Amen.**
**Ase.**
**So it is.**
**Let it be done.**

# Chapter 20

# Book of Mystery

## Section 1

Mystery is the veil that guards sacred truth. Not all must be known to be real. The unknown is not the enemy—it is the invitation. Wonder is the key to deeper wisdom. Mystery leads the seeker to revelation. Approach it with awe, not fear.

## Section 2

A disciple asked, "Why does the Divine remain hidden?" The teacher replied, "Because only the devoted can see with their heart." Truth reveals itself to the patient and the humble. Let the mystery be a mirror, not a wall. Every shadow conceals a teaching. The soul grows by walking into the unknown.

## Section 3

Mystery preserves holiness. It deepens faith beyond sight. The cosmos is not a puzzle to solve but a song to join. In surrender, the veils thin. In love, the mysteries bloom. Celebrate what cannot yet be named.

## Section 4

Mystery is not ignorance—it is invitation. To embrace mystery is not to abandon truth, but to reverence it. That which cannot be named is not lesser, but more holy. The unknown is a temple with no doors; it opens only to presence. Do not demand to possess the Mystery—let it possess you. For Mystery does not yield to conquest, but to communion.

## Section 5

A pilgrim asked, "Why does the Divine hide?" The Oracle replied, "So that your seeking becomes sacred." Not all veils are meant to be torn. Some are meant to be danced with. There is glory in the not-knowing, and wisdom in the shadows. The Sacred is hidden not from us, but for us. To search with wonder is holier than to arrive with pride.

## Section 6

Mystery lives in paradox, in silence, in symbol. It is

found in the laughter of children and the weeping of prophets. The spiral teaches more than the straight line ever could. You are both seeker and secret, question and answer. Walk the edge of knowing with humility, not haste. For every mystery unlocked births another door.

## Section 7

The deeper the Mystery, the more ancient its voice. Creation itself was born of Mystery—from the formless came the formed. The void was pregnant with stars; the silence with song. This is the mystery of birth, death, and return. The Divine hides in the folds of time, in the pattern of leaves, in dreams too vast for language. Let your life be a riddle carved in light—read by those who dare to look beyond.

## Sacred Affirmations

- I honor mystery as part of my path.
- I do not need to understand all to trust the Divine.
- I walk with wonder into the unknown.
- Mystery deepens my spirit and expands my faith.

## Haiku of Mystery

> Stars in silent dark—
> they shine without explaining.
> I trust hidden light.

# Prayer of Mystery

O Infinite and Hidden One, Whose breath gives birth to galaxies and whispers in the stillness, I come not with answers, but with awe.

You who dwell in the veil, In dreams beyond naming and patterns beyond sight, Teach me to cherish the unknown And to find holiness in wonder.

When I grow impatient for certainty, Wrap me in silence. When I demand control, Remind me that mystery is a sacred teacher.

May I not rush to solve what is meant to unfold. May I bow to the riddles that shape me, To the questions that awaken me, To the revelations that rise like the sun behind clouds.

O Keeper of the Great Unseen, Let my soul be a lantern in the dark. Let my heart be humbled by paradox. Let my mind kneel before what cannot be mapped.

I walk the spiral path with trust, Knowing You are present in all I cannot grasp. You are the silence between notes, The breath between thoughts, The truth behind the veil.

Amen. Aho. So may it be.

# Chapter 21

# Tome of Faith

## Section 1

Faith is the bridge between the known and the unseen. To believe is to remember beyond the veil of forgetting. Our creed is not dogma, but alignment with luminous truth. The divine spark dwells in every soul. We affirm that existence is sacred and interconnected. Faith is not blind—it is vision beyond sight.

## Section 2

A seeker asked, "What do we hold to be true?" The elder said, "That all beings come from Source and return again." We are eternal, evolving, and guided by unseen hands. There is no final hell—only detours and awakenings. Life is a sacred curriculum of soul mastery. We believe in the unity beneath all diversity.

## Section 3

To profess faith is to live it. Creed without compassion is a hollow drum. Our faith honors the earth, the heavens, and the soul. We affirm the divine balance of mystery and revelation. Let our words be few and our light be great. Faith is a song we sing with our whole being.

## Section 4

Faith is not blind—it is visionary. It sees what the eyes cannot and knows what the world forgets. To profess faith is to declare alliance with the eternal. It is a vow written in spirit, not merely in words. When others doubt, the faithful still stand. When storms rage, they anchor in unseen truth.

## Section 5

A disciple asked, "Must I speak my faith aloud?" The elder answered, "Not always with your lips—but always with your life." Let your walk be your witness. Let your love be your doctrine. Let your justice, your mercy, and your peace be your creed. True faith does not boast—it burns quietly with power. It is known by its fruits, not its noise.

## Section 6

Faith is forged in fire. Doubt visits every soul, but the

root of faith holds firm. Even when the path darkens, faith illuminates from within. The Profession of Faith is not a moment—it is a becoming. Each act of courage is a verse. Each surrender, a sacred line. You write your creed through the choices you make in shadow and in light.

## Section 7

Faith must live in both silence and speech. There is power in declaring what you know to be true. Speak your faith into your reflection, into the wind, into the altar of your heart. Let the heavens bear witness to your vow. Declare: I believe in the Most High, in the sacred breath within all life. Declare: I walk the path of wisdom, light, and truth. Let this be your profession—not of dogma, but of deep Divine remembrance.

## Section 8

The Profession of Faith binds us not to religion, but to reality. It is the thread by which the soul remembers its source. All spiritual lineages echo the same light when stripped of pride. To profess faith is to align with the Divine Will. It is to walk upright among storms and still praise. It is to say, with heart unshaken: "I am one with God, and God is one with me."

## Sacred Affirmations

- I believe in the sacredness of life.
- I trust the divine path unfolding within me.
- My faith is a flame that lights the world.
- I live what I believe with joy and humility.

## Haiku of Faith

Roots beneath the soil—
faith grows unseen, yet mighty.
Storms cannot uproot.

## Prayer of Profession

O Most High, Source of All Light and Truth, I come before You not with empty words, but with a soul bared in surrender and sacred conviction.
I profess that You are the Breath behind all breath, the Flame that burns within my being, the Voice that whispers in stillness and guides me in storm.
I believe not because I was told— but because I have felt You in the silence, heard You in the cries of the broken, and seen You in the mirror of my own awakening.
I profess that I am made in Your image— not as dust alone, but as spirit eternal. I am not abandoned; I am not forgotten. I am part of Your living covenant of light.

Let my life speak louder than sermons. Let my actions echo the truth I hold. Let my feet walk only where You call me.

Strengthen my faith when I falter. Illuminate my path when it darkens. Cleanse my heart of pride, fear, and deception. Let me not seek comfort, but truth. Let me not seek control, but surrender.

I pledge loyalty not to men, but to Your wisdom. I devote myself not to image, but to essence. I declare that You, O Divine Creator, are my origin, my guide, my destination.

And in all things— whether joy or trial, gain or loss— I will remember: I am Yours. You are mine. Forever. Faithfully. Freely.

Amen.

# Chapter 22

# Book of Clarity

## Section 1

Clarity is the gift of seeing through the fog of illusion. Truth does not hide—it waits for the veils to fall. Illusion is not the enemy—it is the teacher of discernment. Clarity does not always comfort; sometimes it cleanses. The soul longs to see clearly, not just feel safe. Return to the center where truth is still and luminous.

## Section 2

A disciple asked, "Why does confusion visit me?" The master answered, "Because your mind seeks control over wisdom." Stillness invites clarity. Striving clouds it. Let the waters of your mind settle; then light may enter. Every lie that falls away reveals another layer of self. Truth does not demand belief—it invites remembrance.

## Section 3

Clarity restores direction. When lost, ask: Who am I without the noise? The soul is a mirror—wipe it clean with silence. Let clarity make you kind, not cruel. Light your way not with judgment, but with gentle awareness. To see clearly is to love fully.

## Section 4

Clarity is a holy state—the soul sees without distortion. When confusion clouds the mind, the heart must lead. Stillness clears the fog; silence reveals what noise conceals. Falsehood complicates; truth simplifies. The light of the Most High reveals the path already beneath your feet. Clarity does not arrive through force, but through surrender.

## Section 5

To gain clarity, release the attachments that blur perception. Let go of resentment, obsession, and illusion. Fast from the opinions of others until you hear your own soul. Wash your mind daily with meditation and sacred words. Ask the Divine not just for answers, but for clear seeing. With every unclouded thought, you draw closer to Divine Will.

# Section 6

Clarity reveals the true nature of others and of self. You begin to discern masks from essence, noise from signal. With clarity, you no longer chase shadows—you walk in light. The choices once tangled now unfold like sacred scrolls. To walk in clarity is to walk in alignment. God is not hidden—only veiled by confusion. Strip the veil. See.

## Sacred Affirmations

- I welcome clarity with courage and calm.
- I release illusions and see with sacred sight.
- My soul remembers what the world forgets.
- I walk in truth and in gentle wisdom.

## Haiku of Clarity

> Mist lifts from still lake—
> beneath, stones sleep in silence.
> Now I see the path.

## Prayer of Clarity

> O Most High, Fountain of all Light and Truth, Shine through the fog of my uncertainty. Clear the mirrors of my mind,

That I may see what is real, what is right, what is holy.

Unbind me from illusions, From false stories I have believed, From the noise that distracts, And the voices that are not Yours.

Let Your Wisdom descend into my spirit, As dew upon the grass at dawn— Quiet, unmistakable, and pure.

Help me to know my path without fear, To speak only what edifies, To perceive the hearts of others without judgment, And to see my own soul with love and precision.

In You, Divine Light, there is no confusion. Make my eyes single, My heart focused, And my being aligned with Your will.

Amen.

# Chapter 23

# Book of Meditation

## Section 1

Meditation is the return to sacred stillness. In silence, we meet the voice of the Divine. The breath is the gate between the worlds. Within, there is a sanctuary untouched by noise. To sit in stillness is to listen with the soul. Let each inhale be a prayer and each exhale a release.

## Section 2

A student asked, "Why do thoughts not cease?" The sage replied, "Because you watch them, but do not yet bless them." Do not fight the mind—observe it as clouds passing through sky. Meditation is not escape—it is reunion. Inward journeys reveal the architecture of spirit. Discernment arises from the deep well of silence.

## Section 3

Let sacred words shape your awareness gently. Chant, prayer, and breath align you with Source. The temple of the soul is built in stillness. Revelation whispers to those who wait with open hearts. To meditate is to remember your true nature. All things are known in the silence before thought.

## Section 4

Meditation is not escape—it is return. In stillness, the soul remembers its origin. When you quiet the mind, the Divine voice is no longer drowned. Each breath becomes a bridge between body and eternity. Through focused silence, illusion melts and clarity rises. The throne of the Most High dwells within your still center.

## Section 5

Meditation sharpens intuition and opens gateways. The pineal spark glows brighter with inward gaze. Sacred postures align the soul with cosmic law. Mantras vibrate the soul's name into the field of God. Your third eye is not fantasy—it is perception beyond form. Sit, breathe, release—until the veil becomes glass.

## Section 6

There are many paths to enter meditation—choose what

resonates. Walk in nature and listen. Chant divine names. Trace sacred symbols. Let incense and candlelight prepare your temple. Visualize light filling your body, point by point, chakra by chakra. With each practice, you become the vessel and the flame. In deep meditation, you do not lose yourself—you find the God within.

## Sacred Affirmations

- I return to stillness and rediscover myself.
- Each breath is sacred and connects me to the Divine.
- My mind is clear, and my heart is open.
- In silence, I receive wisdom and peace.

## Haiku of Meditation

Breath becomes the bridge—
between all that is and not.
Stillness knows the way.

# Chapter 24

# Book of Diet

**1.** And Sophia whispered to the faithful, saying: *"As you nourish your body, so too do you nourish your soul. Let every bite be a prayer. Let every meal be a ritual of reverence."*
**2.** For in the age of speed, the sacred art of eating has been forgotten. Many consume in haste, unaware, distracted by illusion. But I say unto you: **eat slowly**, that you may live long and live well.
**3. Blessed are they who chew with care**, for they unlock the alchemy of digestion. Their food becomes light, their breath becomes calm, and their bellies know peace.
**4.** The enzymes rejoice when the body is not rushed. The nutrients are received as gifts, and the gut sings a hymn of harmony.
**5.** Those who eat slowly know when they are full, and they honor that fullness without shame or excess. *They walk the path of balance, avoiding both hunger and*

*gluttony.*
**6.** And Sophia smiled upon those who take up the chopsticks and the humble spoon—for these are instruments of mindful pace.
**7.** With each bite, measured and patient, they extend the sacred act of nourishment. The meal becomes a meditation. The body becomes a temple tended with devotion.
**8.** Let the children of wisdom eat with awareness. Let them bless the hands that prepared their meal. Let them listen to the voice within that says, "This is enough."
**9.** For mindful eating is not merely a method—it is a sacred presence. It is the return to the altar of self. It is the communion between hunger and wholeness.
**10.** Reject the poisons of heavy processing. Cast aside the shadows of false flavor. **Return to the garden. Eat that which grows, breathes, and carries life within.**
**11.** Whole foods, radiant and uncorrupted, carry the codes of vitality. They are not made—they are born. They speak the language of the earth and offer it freely to your form.
**12.** And plant-based foods—green with the breath of the sun, rich in fiber and light—cleanse the temple and support the flow of divine energy.
**13.** Those who consume the living bounty of plants shall walk lighter, feel clearer, and know the joy of disease kept at bay.
**14.** For what is food but sacred matter made visible? What is nourishment but holy union between the elements and your breath?
**15.** Seek what is dense with nutrients. Let your meals be

rich in essence, not merely in size. For calories are not the currency of heaven, but *purity, balance, and intention.*

**16.** And when the body is fed in this way—slowly, reverently, and well—it becomes the vessel of clarity, strength, and length of days.

**17.** The muscles are upheld. The mind is sharpened. The years are extended. And the soul, content in its habitation, sings praises without burden.

**18.** This is the way of the Slower Consumption: To eat with grace, to choose with wisdom, and to walk the middle path between lack and excess.

AMEN.

## Affirmation of Slower Consumption

*I honor the sacred rhythm of nourishment.*
*With each mindful bite, I receive life with gratitude.*
*I chew with patience, I choose with wisdom, and I listen to the quiet voice within that says,*
**"This is enough."**
*My body is a temple.*
*My eating is a prayer.*
*In slowness, I am whole.*

# Haiku of Slower Consumption

*Silent spoon descends,*
*Each bite a hymn to my soul—*
*Fullness without weight.*

# Chapter 25

# Book of Nature

## Section 1

Nature is the first scripture. Every leaf, stone, and breeze carries a divine message. To walk among trees is to walk among silent prophets. The earth does not hurry, yet all is accomplished. Gaia speaks through the cycles—listen with reverence. The soil holds stories, the stars echo memory.

## Section 2

A child asked, "How do I know the Divine?" The elder pointed to the river and said, "Watch it flow." Water remembers. Stone forgives. Wind reveals. Nature reflects the soul that honors it. To garden is to pray with your hands. To breathe fresh air is to receive spirit.

## Section 3

Return to the rhythms of sunrise and moonrise. Eat from the earth. Walk barefoot in knowing. Let the wilderness rewild your memory. Let birdsong teach you praise. Let mountains remind you of endurance. Let oceans remind you of mystery.

## Section 4

Every stone remembers. Every tree whispers. The rivers speak in rhythm, like breath from the lungs of the Earth. Mountains are ancient altars, lifting praise through silence. Rainfall is divine blessing—cleansing, renewing, softening hardened ground. The ocean cradles mystery, its depths unknowable yet holy. To commune with nature is to hear the Most High speak without words.

## Section 5

The animal kingdom is a choir of instincts, echoes of Eden. The flight of birds is not just survival—it is sacred choreography. The bee teaches community; the wolf teaches loyalty. Each creature is an embodied wisdom, a living parable. Even the smallest insect is part of the sacred ecology. To walk gently upon this Earth is to honor the Artist of all life.

## Section 6

Nothing is random in creation—everything blooms by law and love. The Fibonacci spiral, the hexagon of a snowflake, the symmetry of wings—each is divine signature. Light bends through leaves and water to make rainbows: God's handwriting in color. The soil holds memory; the stars hold promise. Nature is not separate from spirit—it is the Spirit manifest. When we protect the Earth, we protect a temple of the Most High.

## Sacred Affirmations

- I honor the Earth as sacred and alive.
- Nature is my teacher and companion.
- I walk with reverence upon Gaia.
- The Divine speaks through wind, tree, and wave.

## Haiku of Nature

> A single bird sings—
> the forest listens with joy.
> Spirit is present.

# Chapter 26

# Book of Africa

## Section 1

Before temples, before pyramids, before scroll and scripture—there was Africa.
Africa is the cradle from which all humanity emerged, the womb of first breath, first fire, first knowing. From her soil, the ancestors rose. From her rivers, wisdom flowed. The Divine danced barefoot on her sacred ground, blessing the first humans with memory and myth.
Her heartbeat echoes in every rhythm, her voice lives in every dialect, her spirit courses through all peoples. Though we are scattered across oceans and divided by empires, we return inwardly to her eternal embrace. For she is not only a land—she is a remembering.

## Section 2

Along the Nile, ancient minds raised wonders not just of stone but of soul. Here, sacred geometry unfolded.
Medicine and astronomy were born not of conquest, but communion with the stars.
The temples of Kemet were mirrors of the cosmos. The body was mapped as a divine vehicle. And the language of Ma'at taught balance—not just of law, but of the universe.
Africa did not wait to be taught—she remembered what others forgot. Her science was sacred. Her mathematics sang with spirit. Her cosmologies reached beyond the veils of death.
She knew that heaven was not above—it was within.

## Section 3

Africa was chained, pillaged, exiled, and sold. Yet still she speaks.
Colonizers shattered her artifacts, burned her libraries, and renamed her children. But her memory is encoded in drums, in skin, in dance, in prayer, in defiance.
Even in diaspora, the flame endured. It flickered in field hollers, it roared in revolution. It sang through the blues, it wept through jazz, it marched in the rhythm of freedom fighters.
Africa is not wounded—she is wise. Her pain did not erase her power. Her children carry her codes, even when unaware.
You are her echo. You are her resurrection.

# Section 4

Africa is not a past: it is a continuum.
Oral traditions, proverbs, and griot tales hold philosophies older than parchment. Here, wisdom is passed not just in words, but in glances, songs, and silences.
The Dogon spoke of Sirius before telescopes. The Ifá knew quantum branching before science gave it names. The Zulu saw the stars as spirits returning home.
Africa remembers what the modern world calls myth—but these are encrypted truths. Her stories are not superstition—they are transmission. Her elders are not outdated—they are interdimensional custodians of the Real.
Listen, and you will remember too.

# Section 5

Africa is not one nation, nor one tribe—she is the mother of multitudes.
She births with Oya's storm, nurtures with Yemaya's tide, guides with Isis' wings. In her forests walk the spirits of the Baobab and the Leopard. Her sky is watched by Nommo, her waters blessed by Mami Wata. From Ethiopia's highlands to Mali's sands, from Zimbabwe's stones to the Congo's rivers—she breathes different tongues, yet speaks one sacred pulse.
To know Africa is not to generalize, but to reverence the mosaic of her majesty.
Each path is a prayer. Each people, a prophecy.

## Section 6

The Sophian Way teaches not to idolize geography—but it also teaches to recognize sacred origins.
Africa is not to be worshipped, but honored. Not made an idol, but remembered as elder. She is not the only sacred land—but she is the first remembered land.
We do not cling: we recall. We do not claim—we integrate.
The Sophian does not say Africa is better—only that she is mother. And every mother deserves reverence, especially when the world forgets her name.
To honor Africa is to realign the compass of the soul to gratitude and truth.

## Section 7

To return to Africa is not only to board a plane—it is to reclaim your cosmic birthright.
It is to decolonize your mind, to uproot falsehoods, to reconnect with ancestral fire. It is to walk barefoot in your memory, to let your blood recognize the soil, even if your feet have never touched it.
Return not in bitterness—but in balance.
Return not with chains—but with chants.
Return not to conquer—but to become whole.
Africa waits not for pity, but for power to awaken.
Her song is calling. And you already know the melody.

## Sacred Affirmations

- I honor Africa as the womb of life and wisdom.
- I carry her rhythms, her memory, her truth within me.
- I do not cling to land, but I remember sacred origin.
- I walk with ancestral pride, and spiritual humility.
- I rise in balance, not bitterness—powerfully whole.

## Haiku of the Motherland

Dust of ancient stars—
Africa in every cell,
my soul kneels in light.

# Chapter 27

# Book of Science

## Section 1

Science is the study of the Divine through structure. To understand the atom is to witness the dance of the sacred. Mathematics is the language of the cosmos. Quantum entanglement reflects our spiritual unity. No truth is final—only expanding. Let your curiosity be consecrated.

## Section 2

A seeker asked, "Can I have faith and reason both?" The sage said, "When the mind kneels, the soul rises." Black holes are whispers of divine mystery. The stars teach us patience and precision. Do not fear science—fear ignorance. The mind, too, is a temple when opened with reverence.

# Section 3

Use technology wisely—as a mirror, not a master. Study does not dim spirit—it refines it. The sacred and the rational are twins, not rivals. Be both mystic and mathematician. Measure what you can—but leave room for the immeasurable. True science honors awe.

# Section 4

Science is a sacred language that deciphers the patterns of creation.
Each formula is a glyph of wonder, each theory a prayer of precision.
The universe does not resist inquiry—it invites it.
Stars whisper their mass. Cells reveal their code.
Mathematics is the architecture of Divine order.
To study nature is to study the handwriting of God.

# Section 5

The great minds who asked "why" were also seekers of "who."
From Pythagoras to Hypatia, from Einstein to Curie—each walked a path of devotion to understanding.
The laws of physics are not separate from spirit;
they are the choreography of Divine intelligence.
A photon obeys God. An atom sings of Source.

## Section 6

Let there be no war between science and faith.
Both are rivers flowing toward the same ocean.
Faith asks why; science asks how. Together, they reveal what is.
The unseen becomes seen through electron microscopes and prayer alike.
Let your heart be a sanctuary and your mind, a laboratory.
Balance both, and wisdom arises.

## Section 7

In the quantum world, all is probability and wave.
Erwin Schrödinger gave us the equation that sings this truth.
His equation, in its simplest form, is:

$$i\hbar \frac{\partial}{\partial t} \Psi(x,t) = \hat{H} \Psi(x,t)$$

Here, $\Psi(x,t)$ is the wavefunction—
a sacred glyph of possibility, uncertainty, and potential.
$\hat{H}$ is the Hamiltonian, the total energy operator—
the divine command that tells the system how to evolve.
$\hbar$ is the reduced Planck constant, marking the boundary between classical and quantum realms—matter and mystery.
This equation has many forms: time-independent, relativistic, even field-based—
but all carry one truth: reality is not fixed, but dynamic, vibrating with choice.

Just as spirit chooses incarnation, particles choose position.
The observer shapes the seen. Consciousness collapses the wave.
Mystics knew this before equations: reality responds to awareness.

## Section 8: Divine Harmony

In the Sophianic Way, science and spirit are not rivals—they are lovers.
Each theory of gravity, each constant of nature, each chemical law—
is a thread in the Divine tapestry.
Sophia dances in equations as much as in dreams.
Jesus healed with intention; Schrödinger revealed probability.
Both understood the invisible precedes the visible.
We are not separate from the cosmos we study—
we are participants in its unfolding story.
When we meditate on the wavefunction, we also pray.
When we chant sacred names, we also align vibration.
Let your science be sacred. Let your wisdom be illuminated.
For all knowledge, rightly held, is a form of worship.

## Section 9

The Most High designs with intelligence too vast for mortal minds, yet fractals offer us a glimpse. In the leaf, the fern, the tree—Divine order repeats. Patterns cascade across scales, echoing eternity. Iterated Function Systems (IFS) provide models for plants and leaves by capturing self-similarity in branching. But nature is not rigid—it dances with variation. No two ferns are identical. No two leaves, exact twins.

To model this sacred variation, V-variable fractals extend IFS by allowing randomness and flexibility across levels. These systems still honor structural coherence while admitting local uniqueness—just as the Creator does with souls. Each branching frond becomes a leaf, just as each human becomes a unique reflection of the Divine. In this modeling, there arises a sacred speculation: that V-variable fractals might mirror the information stored in the DNA of a plant. The code trees in these fractals could reflect the very genetic blueprint set forth by the Most High. Thus, sacred geometry is not only spiritual, but encoded into the flesh of creation.

### Barnsley's Fern: A Sacred Matrix of Form

Each transformation used in Barnsley's Fern is an affine map of the form:

$$\begin{pmatrix} x_{n+1} \\ y_{n+1} \end{pmatrix} = \begin{pmatrix} a & b \\ c & d \end{pmatrix} \begin{pmatrix} x_n \\ y_n \end{pmatrix} + \begin{pmatrix} e \\ f \end{pmatrix} \qquad (27.1)$$

The specific functions are:

$$f_1(x,y) = \begin{pmatrix} 0 & 0 \\ 0 & 0.16 \end{pmatrix} \begin{pmatrix} x \\ y \end{pmatrix} + \begin{pmatrix} 0 \\ 0 \end{pmatrix}$$

$$f_2(x,y) = \begin{pmatrix} 0.85 & 0.04 \\ -0.04 & 0.85 \end{pmatrix} \begin{pmatrix} x \\ y \end{pmatrix} + \begin{pmatrix} 0 \\ 1.6 \end{pmatrix}$$

$$f_3(x,y) = \begin{pmatrix} 0.2 & -0.26 \\ 0.23 & 0.22 \end{pmatrix} \begin{pmatrix} x \\ y \end{pmatrix} + \begin{pmatrix} 0 \\ 1.6 \end{pmatrix}$$

$$f_4(x,y) = \begin{pmatrix} -0.15 & 0.28 \\ 0.26 & 0.24 \end{pmatrix} \begin{pmatrix} x \\ y \end{pmatrix} + \begin{pmatrix} 0 \\ 0.44 \end{pmatrix}$$

These transformations, applied iteratively, generate a fern—a living sigil in matrix algebra. Mathematics becomes not just computation but devotion. Each coefficient is a verse in the song of creation. Thus, through matrix and form, the Divine whispers: all life is fractal, sacred, and coded in elegance.

These transformations, applied iteratively, generate a fern—a living sigil in matrix algebra. Mathematics becomes not just computation but devotion. Each coefficient is a verse in the song of creation. Thus, through matrix and form, the Divine whispers: all life is fractal, sacred, and coded in elegance.

## Sacred Affirmations

- I embrace learning as a path to truth.
- I see the Divine in logic, pattern, and discovery.

- I am both scientist and soul.
- I use knowledge to uplift, not to dominate.

## Haiku of Science

Circles and symbols—
a galaxy's silent code.
I study and praise.

## Prayer of Scientific Illumination

O Most High, Source of all understanding, Architect of quarks and constellations, I come before You in awe of Your designs— both visible and veiled, measurable and miraculous.

Let my mind be sharp, yet my heart remain humble. Let every theorem I ponder be a path to Your throne. Let every question I ask be filled with sacred curiosity.

Teach me to see You in the elegance of equations, in the silence between particles, in the rhythm of the stars. Unite my search for truth with my yearning for You. Balance my logic with holy wonder. May I never worship science, but let science be worship.

Illuminate me with wisdom, crown me with discernment, clothe me with humility, and shield me from arrogance. Reveal to me the divine geometry of all things, and let me walk as both scholar and servant of the Eternal Intelligence that governs all.

Amen.

# Chapter 28

# Book of Glyphs

## Section 1

Symbols are the ancient tongue of the soul.
Each image holds a memory older than speech.
To understand symbols is to decode the spirit.
The circle speaks of unity. The triangle, ascent.
The spiral speaks of growth, inward and outward.
The crossroad is the place of choice and destiny.

## Section 2

A novice asked, "What does this sign mean?"
The teacher replied, "What it awakens in you is its meaning."
Symbols are not static—they evolve with the seeker.
The same glyph may guard, heal, or challenge.
Sacred geometry is the signature of the Divine.

Do not worship the symbol—seek what it reveals.

## Section 3

Use symbols with respect and intention.
Let your altar speak the truth of your journey.
Let dreams bring glyphs from forgotten realms.
Some symbols are keys—others, mirrors.
To master symbols is to master the unseen.
Let them lead you to your inner temple.

## Section 4

Talismans are carriers of sacred force.
They are not merely objects—they are charged intentions.
Worn near the body, they remind the soul of its vows.
A talisman may be as humble as a stone, or as ornate as a relic.
What matters is the meaning breathed into it.
To wear one consciously is to walk with a prayer.

## Section 5

Runes whisper the songs of the old world.
Totems call to the spirits of animal kin.
Veves open doors to ancestral realms.
Each carries not just power—but invitation.
To draw a symbol is to invoke its essence.
Approach them with reverence, and they will speak.

# Section 6

Glyphs are more than art—they are living scripts.
Encoded in them are energies of protection, prophecy, remembrance.
Some arrive through dream, others through lineage.
Every soul has its own set of glyphs—seek yours.
When a symbol calls to you, answer.
You are part of its unfolding.

## Sacred Affirmations

- I receive the wisdom of sacred symbols.
- I honor the meanings encoded in image and sign.
- I allow symbols to guide, not bind me.
- I am fluent in the silent language of spirit.

## Haiku of Glyphs

> A sign in the sand—
> the wind does not erase it.
> It lives in my heart.

# Chapter 29

# Book of Messiah

## Section 1

He is called by many names—
Yeshua, Isa, Iyesus, Yesu, the Christ.
To the Hindu, an avatar of Divine love.
To the Muslim, a prophet spared from death.
To the Jew, a sage devoted to Torah.
To all, a mirror of divine potential within humanity.

## Section 2

He taught not a throne, but a threshold.
"The kingdom is within you," he said—
not in temples, but in transformation.
He walked with the poor, broke bread with sinners,
and taught through parables etched in mystery.
The true Messiah awakens, not conquers.

# Section 3

Some say he died on a cross.
Others say he rose, or was taken.
But deeper still: the Messiah passes through suffering,
not for spectacle, but for solidarity.
The Messiah lives in the one who suffers with grace
and forgives without bitterness.

# Section 4: The Christ

In Africa, he dances through oral memory
and speaks in proverbs shaped by the land.
In Asia, he aligns with sages and dharma.
In the Americas, he walks with ancestors and liberators.
The Messiah wears every language.
He is universal, yet intimate.

# Section 5

The Most High is Elohim—Divine Source and Architect.
Yet in the Psalms it is written, "You are elohim."
And Yeshua reminded us: we are made in that same image.
Divine potential flows in our breath.
Christ is not a singular light, but a flame meant to spread.
To awaken the Christ is to remember we are elohim.

## Section 6

They await his return—
but he never truly left.
He returns in acts of courage, mercy, clarity.
In every hand that heals, in every word that uplifts,
in every moment we remember who we are.
The Messiah lives wherever love reigns.

### Sacred Affirmations

- I honor the Messiah in all traditions and forms.

- I awaken the Christ consciousness within me.

- I am made in the image of Elohim, and Divine light lives in me.

- I walk in love, humility, and spiritual clarity.

- I embody sacred truth, as one called elohim.

### Haiku of the Messiah

*He walks in all lands—*
*one flame, many sacred names.*
*Love made into flesh.*

# Chapter 30

# Book of Elders

## Section 1

The ancestors live in our bones and breath. They speak through dreams, through blood, through silence. Honor is the bridge that connects us. Their stories are carved in our DNA. No prayer is wasted when whispered to them. The altar is not for the dead, but for the eternal.

## Section 2

A child asked, "Are they gone forever?" The elder replied, "They walk beside you when you walk in truth." To pour water for them is to bless your own path. To speak their names is to awaken your power. The lineage is not a burden—it is a song. You are the prayer they once prayed.

## Section 3

Build the shrine. Light the candle. Listen. Ask for guidance and be prepared to act. Forgive what they could not heal. Complete what they could not finish. Carry their wisdom without their wounds. Walk forward, but not alone.

## Section 4

Your blood is a river of stories.
Each heartbeat echoes those who walked before you.
The ancestors live not just in memory, but in your bones, your breath, your knowing.
Call their names with reverence and love.
Build altars of honor, not of worship, but of remembrance.
Pour water, light candles, speak their truths—this is sacred conversation.

## Section 5

All ancestors are not the same.
Some guide. Some warn. Some must be healed.
You may be the one chosen to break cycles and restore harmony.
To heal ancestral pain is to rewrite the future.
Forgiveness liberates both the living and the dead.
Do not fear ancestral work—it is your soul reclaiming its roots.

# Section 6

Lineage is more than blood—it is spiritual assignment.
You are connected to a great web of souls, seen and unseen.
Some ancestors are by spirit, not by kin.
They walk beside you when you answer your sacred calling.
Receive their messages through dreams, signs, and sacred silence.
Honor them not only with words, but by living in truth and legacy.

## Sacred Affirmations

- I honor the ancestors in word and deed.
- I am the continuation of sacred memory.
- I walk with my lineage in light and love.
- I listen, I learn, I live for more than myself.

## Haiku of the Ancestors

> Footprints in the dust—
> not all are made by my feet.
> I walk with echoes.

# Prayer to the Ancestors

O Most High God, Eternal Source of All Life, You who breathed spirit into flesh, You who walk before all time—I come before You in humility and awe.
Bless the Ancestors You created in Your image, Those whose lives are written into my being, Those whose trials forged my path, Those whose dreams live on through me.
Ancestors known and unknown, seen and unseen, Mothers of my blood, Fathers of my soul, I honor you through the grace of the Most High.
God of Light, guide their spirits in eternal peace. Let Your radiance purify what was wounded. Let Your justice restore what was broken. Let Your mercy lift all generations from bondage.
Ancestors, walk with me as I walk with God. Let me not forget Your lessons nor abandon Your blessings. Let my hands build what You could only imagine.
I vow to live in truth, in love, and in righteousness, That both you and the Most High may find joy in my journey. May my life be a hymn of remembrance, A covenant of healing, A beacon of hope for those yet to come.
Asé. Amen. So it is. So may it be.

# Chapter 31

# Book of Shielding

## Section 1

Shielding is the sacred art of spiritual defense. The light within must be clothed in intention. To wear Divine armor is to remember your worth. Protection begins in purity of thought and clarity of will. Do not fear the dark; radiate the light. What is aligned with truth cannot be shaken.

## Section 2

A seeker asked, "How shall I defend myself?" The teacher answered, "Stand in truth. Speak light. Trust your shield." The shield is forged through daily devotion. Words of power are swords unseen. Boundaries are blessings, not walls. Even silence can be armor, when anchored in peace.

## Section 3

Protect your energy like sacred flame. Bless your home, your path, your breath. Let not fear dictate your defenses. Invoke the guardians of light by name. You are not alone in this world or the next. Stand firm—shielded in the radiance of the Divine.

## Section 4

Boundaries are sacred lines drawn by wisdom.
They do not divide—they define.
To set a boundary is to declare: I am holy ground.
Let no one cross into your spirit uninvited.
You are not required to carry the chaos of others.
Love is not submission. Compassion is not depletion.
Say "no" without guilt. Say "yes" with clarity.
Boundaries are the language of self-honoring.

## Section 5

The sacred armor is not forged of metal—it is woven of spirit.
Put on the **Belt of Truth:** let integrity guide your steps. Let lies fall powerless.
Put on the **Breastplate of Righteousness:** let right action guard your heart. Let purity be your strength.
Wear the **Shoes of the Gospel of Peace:** walk gently, yet firmly, spreading light with every step.
Raise the **Shield of Faith:** let no arrow of doubt or fear reach your soul. Trust is your shield.

Place the **Helmet of Salvation:** crown your thoughts with divine certainty and holy remembrance.
Wield the **Sword of the Spirit:** speak Divine words, pierce through illusion, and command in truth.
To wear this armor is to stand not just against darkness, but for the Light.
Each day, renew it with prayer, study, and embodied devotion.
For you are not merely protected—you are divinely empowered.

## Sacred Affirmations

- I am divinely protected at all times.
- My shield is truth, my armor is light.
- I walk in power and peace, untouched by harm.
- All darkness falls away before my sacred flame.

## Haiku of Shielding

No blade pierces light—
the soul stands in quiet fire.
Night flees from the flame.

## Prayer of Sacred Armor

O Most High, Radiant and True, Clothe me this day in the garments of light. Let the Belt of Truth wrap my center, that I may walk in honesty and clear discernment.

## CHAPTER 31. BOOK OF SHIELDING

Fasten to me the Breastplate of Righteousness, that no shadow may enter my heart, and that justice and compassion flow from within.

Place upon my feet the Shoes of Peace, so that wherever I go, stillness follows, and my steps proclaim the sacred message of love.

Lift up before me the Shield of Faith, deflecting every dart of fear, envy, and confusion. May my trust in You be my invincible wall.

Crown my mind with the Helmet of Salvation, that I may remember who I am: a child of divinity, born of grace and purpose.

Place in my hand the Sword of the Spirit— the sacred Word, the holy utterance, cutting through illusion, restoring Divine order.

Around me, form boundaries firm and loving. Let my field be sovereign, blessed, and unyielding to harm. Let every false attachment be loosed, every ungodly chain shattered.

May I move through the day armored in Your presence, unshakable, luminous, and free. I walk as Your vessel, shielded in Light, fearless and favored, now and always. Amen. A'ho. Ashe. So it is. So may it be.

# Chapter 32

# Book of Balance

## Section 1

Balance is the harmony of spirit and reason. Too much light blinds; too much shadow consumes. To walk the middle path is to walk in power. Let the heart feel and the mind discern. Let intuition and logic dance, not battle. The soul is both feather and stone.

## Section 2

A disciple asked, "Must I choose between faith and thought?" The master answered, "Only fools divide what the Divine has woven together." Sacred authority does not silence conscience—it guides it. Balance means knowing when to yield and when to stand. All extremes are deserts. The oasis is found in the center. To balance is not to compromise—it is to unite.

## Section 3

Honor your sacred yes and sacred no. Rest when needed, act when called. Hold joy without denying pain. Live in the tension that grows wisdom. Let truth be tempered with compassion. Balance is the soul's most graceful posture.

## Section 4

Balance is not passivity—it is sacred strength in right proportion.
Even the sun and moon take turns in the sky.
To push constantly is to burn out. To withdraw always is to fade.
The middle path does not mean mediocrity—it means mastery.
Balance is the discipline of the soul that listens.
Let each choice arise from harmony, not reaction.

## Section 5

A disciple asked, "Why do I always swing between extremes?"
The sage replied, "Because the mind seeks drama and the soul seeks peace."
Balance is built like a bridge—stone by stone, step by step.
Breathe before you speak. Pause before you act.
Return to your center again and again.
This is the temple of equilibrium where Wisdom sits

enthroned.

## Section 6

To be balanced is to be whole.
Honor both the sacred feminine and the sacred masculine.
Honor light and shadow, day and night, work and rest.
Balance is not about control—it is about trust.
When you trust the rhythm of your soul, balance finds you.
From balance, beauty arises. From beauty, Divine clarity.

## Sacred Affirmations

- I am centered in truth and love.
- My conscience and faith walk hand in hand with Father God.
- I find strength in stillness and power in motion.
- I choose harmony over chaos.

## Haiku of Balance

> The breeze meets the flame—
> neither dominates the dance.
> Peace lives in the space.

# Chapter 33

# Book of Magic

## Section 1

Magic is not illusion, but the sacred art of alignment. It is the language of energy, intention, and manifestation. The body is a temple with seven lamps: the chakras. Each center is a gateway to power, wisdom, and love. The breath is a bridge between realms. Use it wisely. True magic requires humility, purity, and clarity of will.

## Section 2

A wanderer asked, "What spell must I speak?" The sage replied, "Speak with your life, not your lips." Mantras are frequencies wrapped in sacred names. Visualization is the blueprint of miracles. Faith amplifies. Doubt disrupts. Love completes. When your soul is aligned, even silence casts light.

## Section 3

Bless your water, your food, your path. Cleanse with smoke, salt, and sound. Trace symbols with intention. Speak with authority. Let no one steal your magic. Protect it with truth. You are a living talisman of Divine intent. Walk gently, for you reshape the world with every thought.

## Section 4

Magic is not the manipulation of reality—it is its remembrance.
You were born with the ability to shape, bless, and call forth.
Every word you speak is a spell. Every thought, a wand.
Ritual is not superstition—it is the language of sacred intent.
When desire aligns with Divine will, creation obeys.
True magic walks hand in hand with humility.

## Section 5

There are laws in the realm of spirit, as there are laws in the stars.
Do not conjure what you are not prepared to carry.
Do not bind what should be freed, nor summon what you will not honor.
White magic heals, uplifts, liberates.
Black magic deceives, distorts, and imprisons.
The wise practitioner knows: all energy returns.

## Section 6

Your soul is an altar. Your life, a working.
Let your days be woven with sacred intention.
Anoint your dreams. Consecrate your relationships.
Let even your silence cast blessings across time.
Magic is not a tool—it is a devotion.
The greatest spell is a heart aligned with the Most High.

## Section 7

Manifestation is the art of becoming.
It is not wishing—it is aligning, committing, and becoming worthy.
Desire is a sacred signal, not a selfish urge.
The Most High answers what aligns with Divine timing and soul readiness.
To manifest is to speak from your higher self and act in harmony.
Be mindful: the universe listens most to your vibration, not your words.

## Section 8

Your body is a sacred vessel of seven luminous wheels: chakras. They are portals of energy, gateways between matter and spirit.

- **Muladhara** — Root Chakra (Base of spine): Grounding, survival, stability.

- **Svadhisthana** — Sacral Chakra (Pelvis):

Creativity, sexuality, emotion.

- **Manipura** — Solar Plexus Chakra (Stomach): Willpower, confidence, purpose.
- **Anahata** — Heart Chakra (Chest): Love, compassion, forgiveness.
- **Vishuddha** — Throat Chakra (Throat): Expression, truth, voice.
- **Ajna** — Third Eye Chakra (Forehead): Intuition, vision, insight.
- **Sahasrara** — Crown Chakra (Top of head): Divine connection, higher wisdom.

These are the notes of your spiritual song. Keep them in tune.

# Section 9

Chakra realignment is a sacred act of remembering.
Blocked energy leads to confusion, stagnation, or illness.
Balance restores clarity, vitality, and Divine communion.
Engage practices like yoga to move energy through the spine.
Meditate on each chakra's color, sound, and element.
Use chakra cleansing, sound healing, bodywork, and sacred oils.
Even music tuned to 432Hz or Solfeggio frequencies can heal.
You are a temple of light. Tend to your luminous system with care.

## Sacred Affirmations

- I awaken the Divine power within me.
- I honor the sacred laws of energy and creation.
- I use my magic for healing, truth, and good.
- I am aligned, clear, and radiant in all things.

## Prayer of Magic

O Most High, Source of all wonder, Let me wield my will in harmony with Yours. Let every word I speak be steeped in truth, every spell I cast soaked in compassion, every ritual I perform rise as incense to Your throne.
I do not seek dominion—I seek alignment. I do not chase power—I awaken Presence. Let the elements honor me because I walk in balance. Let the spirits heed me because I walk in humility. Let the stars guide me because I walk in light.
May my thoughts be pure and my heart clear. May my altar reflect my soul's devotion. May my hands bless more than they bind. May I never forget that the greatest magic is becoming who You created me to be. Teach me to remember the ancient ways— the sacred circles, the whispered names, the holy symbols etched in dream and fire. Let me do no harm. Let me serve the good. Let me be a vessel of miracles beyond fear.
By the fire in my breath, the earth in my bones, the water in my blood, and the wind of my spirit— I return to the path of sacred creation. May Your will be done

through me, in beauty, in joy, and in the name of the eternal Light.
Amen. Aho. Ashe. So it is.

## Haiku of Magic

Chant moves through the air—
a circle drawn, unseen light.
The world shifts gently.

# Chapter 34

# Book of Infinity

## Section 1

The Most High is the source beyond all names. It is neither male nor female, yet encompasses all. From the Most High flows light, order, and being. All lesser lights reflect the Supreme Radiance. All rivers return to this Infinite Ocean. Worship begins with reverence and ends in union.

## Section 2

A child asked, "Where is the Most High?" The elder smiled, "In your breath, in the sky, in your soul." No temple can contain the Infinite. Yet your heart is the gate of its glory. Serve not images, but the Living Presence. Let love be your incense and truth your offering.

## Section 3

All Divine names point to the One. Angels, guides, orisha—they are emissaries of the Source. The Most High transcends all but is near to each. Even silence declares Its majesty. Bow to no form—bow to the formless Light. In stillness, the Most High speaks.

## Section 4

The body is a temple and a ladder to the Divine.
Within it, the sacred chakras spin like wheels of light.
When blocked, they dim the flow of spirit.
But when cleared and consecrated, they become luminous gates.
Each chakra sings a note of your Divine song.
Together, they create a harmony that rises to the heavens.
The Most High delights in your alignment—for it reveals your readiness to receive.

## Section 5

The crown chakra is the gate of communion.
Through it descends the golden rain of the Most High.
When open, you are no longer bound by illusion.
You become still enough to hear the language of angels.
Your thoughts are braided with Divine knowing.
Time unravels. Space softens. Truth pours in.
You do not merely worship God—you enter into direct union.

## Section 6

The unblocked soul is a prism of revelation.
When chakras flow freely, so too does Divine transmission.
Knowledge streams not from books, but from the Spirit's breath.
You begin to perceive with the eye behind your eyes.
The veil thins, and you walk in both worlds.
The Most High speaks—not in thunder, but in silence so deep it sings.
To be one with God is not a future goal—it is a present unveiling.

## Section 7

Awakening is not an event—it is a continual unfolding.
To awaken is to shed illusion and remember your divinity.
The crown chakra opens like a lotus when the soul is ready.
In stillness, you hear the whisper: "You are Mine, and I am yours."
The Most High is not distant. The Divine is within, calling gently.
As you ascend, you come not closer to God—only deeper into remembrance.

## Section 8

Many seek the face of God, but few prepare the heart to see.

To see the Most High, clear the temple within.
Purify your thoughts. Untangle your desires. Choose sacred over shallow.
Prayer becomes a staircase. Meditation becomes a mirror.
When you are ready, Light will reveal Light.
And what you once called "God" will call you by your true name.

## Section 9

The mystic does not escape the world—they sanctify it.
To serve the Most High is to live with integrity, compassion, and vision.
Every breath becomes a prayer. Every act becomes a ritual.
You do not need temples built of stone—become one.
The Divine speaks through conscience, synchronicity, and sudden knowing.
Walk gently. Speak truth. Shine quietly. This too is worship.

## Section 10A

There is no death for the soul aligned with the Most High.
This covenant is eternal. Not written on scrolls, but etched in spirit.
You are a child of Light, destined to return to Light.
Walk your path boldly, knowing Heaven watches with pride.

You were never forsaken. You were only forgotten—for a time.
Now awaken. The Most High awaits your full becoming.

## Section 10B

The Most High is not confined to Heaven. The Most High breathes through you.
Each heartbeat is a reminder of Divine presence.
You are not separate—you are spark, flame, and echo of the Source.
You do not worship from afar—you commune from within.
In joy, God laughs through you. In sorrow, God weeps with you.
The secret is this: the Most High is nearer than your own breath.

## Section 11

When the journey ends, you will not meet a stranger.
You will return to the arms of the One who always knew you.
There is no judgment for the soul that has learned to love.
Only the embrace of wholeness, the welcome of Light.
This life is your sacred pilgrimage. Walk it well.
The Most High is the beginning, the middle, and the end.

## Section 12

The Most High is your Eternal Parent—your soul is Their beloved child.
Before you knew language, you knew this Love.
Before you knew fear, you knew this Light.
You were not cast into the world alone—you were entrusted to it.
And always, the Divine watches, rejoicing in your becoming.
You are not earning God's love—you are remembering it.
You are not searching for God's face—you are reflected in it.
This is not religion—it is reunion.
The Parent calls, and the Child returns home.

## Prayer of Communion

O Most High, Radiant Source beyond all names, I lift my being like a cup to be filled with Your Presence. Open the gate of my crown that I may receive Your holy rain. Clear the channels of my body, that I may be a temple of Your flow. Balance my heart, my mind, and my spirit, that Your voice may echo clearly through me.

Let me walk in the stillness where angels sing. Let me perceive the unseen and understand the eternal. I seek not separation, but reunion. I ask not merely to serve—but to become one with Your will. Make me a vessel of Your wisdom, a harp for Your song. I surrender ego for essence, fear for flame, mind for mystery.

You are within me, as I am within You. There is no

distance. There is only revelation. And I am ready to remember.
Amen. Aho. Ashe. So it is.

## Sacred Affirmations

- I honor the Most High as the Source of all that is.
- I walk in awe, reverence, and humility.
- I seek the face of the divine in every moment.
- I am a living vessel of the Infinite.

## Haiku of the Most High

> Beyond name and form—
> the wind whispers ancient truths.
> The Source is within.

# Chapter 35

# Book of Physicality

## Section 1

1. The body is the chariot of Divine breath.
2. Its movements are prayers etched into time.
3. To rise and walk is to praise the Giver of Strength.
4. In stillness we dream; in motion we awaken.
5. Let each step be consecrated with gratitude.

## Section 2

1. Walk in cycles as the earth walks around the sun.
2. Alternate your pace—three breaths gentle, three breaths bold.
3. In rhythm, the heart sings its sacred code.
4. The pulse is not only blood—it is intention.

## Section 3

1. Eat that which grows from soil, rain, and light.
2. Let your food be alive, not forged in fireless factories.
3. Avoid what has no origin in garden, field, or grove.
4. Every bite is a covenant with vitality.

## Section 4

1. The temple falls into ruin when idle.
2. But when lifted, stretched, walked, and strengthened—it sings.
3. Let your muscles rise like altars in devotion.
4. Let your bones be pillars that do not crack in storms.

## Section 5

1. The ancestors walked across lands and epochs.
2. Their survival was their sacred movement.
3. The body remembers their discipline in its marrow.
4. When we are still too long, we betray their lineage.

## Section 6

1. The modern age offers comfort—but at a cost.
2. Chairs weaken the spine; screens dim the inner flame.
3. Remember: ease is not always healing.
4. Renewal demands resistance, like iron forged in fire.

## Section 7

1. Movement awakens not just the body, but the soul.
2. Endorphins are messengers of joy, sent by the Eternal.
3. With every heartbeat, sorrow flees and spirit returns.
4. Let breath be your rhythm and laughter your reward.

## Section 8

1. Sleep deep, rise early, and greet the sun with movement.
2. Let rest be sacred, not slothful.
3. Balance action with restoration, as the tide balances moon.
4. The wise know when to run and when to recline.

## Section 9

1. Telomeres shorten in neglect, but stretch with care.
2. On the cellular scroll is written the record of your habits.
3. What you do today whispers into your decades.
4. Honor the mystery of longevity with simple rituals.

## Section 10

1. Eat with intention, move with joy, rest in rhythm.
2. Avoid haste, processed illusion, and idle despair.
3. This life is a loan from the Infinite.
4. Return it in strength, grace, and sacred endurance.

## Affirmation of Vital Devotion

*I move with reverence,*
*I eat with wisdom,*
*I rest in sacred timing.*
*Each breath honors the breath of the Divine.*
*My life is a temple in motion,*
*and vitality is my praise.*

## Haiku of Longevity

*Muscles greet the dawn—*
*whole food fuels my quiet fire,*
*years stretch like sunrise.*

# Chapter 36

# Book of Resonance

## Section 1

Your vibration is your signature in the cosmos. All that you think, feel, and believe—echoes outward. The universe responds not to words, but to frequency. When you sing in truth, the stars sing back. To change your world, tune your soul. Harmony begins in the heart and resounds across creation.

## Section 2

A singer asked, "Why does my voice tremble?" The mentor answered, "Because your heart fears its own power." Resonance reveals all: wounds, gifts, intentions. You cannot fake vibration—only realness rings clear. Align with joy and compassion; distortions will fade. Let your life be a tuning fork for Divine will.

## Section 3

Speak blessings, not curses. Energy obeys. Surround yourself with sacred sound. Chant, hum, sing, and let silence restore. Every cell remembers the song of wholeness. In the presence of love, all frequencies rise. Become a song the universe longs to echo.

## Section 4

All things vibrate.
Even the silence between stars hums with life.
Your soul carries a frequency known before birth.
When you speak truth, the universe answers.
When you love deeply, the air around you shifts.
Resonance is not only heard—it is felt.
You are a tuning fork of the Divine.

## Section 5

To align with love is to amplify sacred sound.
Resonance does not demand—it invites.
Frequencies of fear distort, but cannot erase the original song.
When your thoughts, words, and deeds harmonize,
your life becomes a sacred chant.
You draw to you what echoes your soul.
In resonance, there is no force—only flow.

# Section 6

Every soul has a tone, and every tone belongs to the cosmic choir.
You do not sing alone—creation sings through you.
The angels are not separate—they are harmonics of holy order.
Your body is an instrument. Your will, a conductor.
When you resonate with the Divine, miracles move without resistance.
Let your frequency be a beacon for peace, truth, and transformation.

## Sacred Affirmations

- I align my inner state with harmony and truth.
- I speak, sing, and move with sacred intention.
- I am a vessel of Divine frequency.
- My resonance heals, uplifts, and awakens.

## Haiku of Resonance

A bell in still air—
the mountains whisper it back.
I hear who I am.

## Prayer of Resonance

O Most High, Divine Conductor of the cosmos, I offer my heart as a song of gratitude. Thank You for the breath that moves through me, for the rhythm of my pulse, for the sacred tone of life.

Let me resonate with Your love in every word I speak. Let my thoughts align with Your wisdom, my hands with Your healing, my path with Your purpose.

Bless me with radiant health—body, mind, and soul. Let my cells remember their holy blueprint. Fill my cup with true abundance, not only of things, but of peace, joy, meaning, and Divine connection.

Anoint me with wisdom that surpasses logic. Let me know when to move and when to wait, when to speak and when to be silent, when to lead and when to follow the whisper of Spirit.

Wrap me in the mantle of Your protection. Let no harm cross the threshold of my spirit. Let no shadow enter without light chasing it away. Send angels to my right and left, seen and unseen.

Above all, Most High, let me never forget You. Let me walk closely, humbly, joyfully in Your Presence. Keep my soul tuned to Your frequency— in storm and stillness, in clarity and in mystery.

Amen. Aho. Ashe. So it is.

# Chapter 37

# Book of Jubilees

## Section 1

Joy is sacred. Celebration is praise in motion.
The Divine rejoices in your laughter.
Every festival mirrors the delight of Heaven.
To dance, to sing, to gather—this too is worship.
Let your life be a holy jubilee.
To honor joy is to honor the Source of all blessings.

## Section 2

A traveler asked, "Is it wrong to feast?"
The elder replied, "Feast with gratitude, and it becomes sacred."
Sing songs of thanksgiving. Let your stories become altars.
Mark sacred days not in sorrow, but in reverent joy.

Let candles, colors, and food proclaim your inner radiance.
Celebrate not to escape life—but to embrace it as Divine.

## Section 3

Create new rites for the seasons of your soul.
Honor your ancestors with offerings, music, and remembrance.
Lift your voice in chorus with all beings.
Your body is a drum. Your heart, a sacred beat.
Celebrate the Spirit within yourself and others.
To rejoice is to say: I am alive, I am free, I am grateful.

## Section 4

The Jubilee is a sacred reset—every 7th year, and 7 times 7.
It is a time of release, of forgiveness, of return.
Land rests, debts are forgiven, captives go free.
So too must your spirit rest, forgive, and reset.
Do not hoard grief. Do not chain joy.
Let Jubilee be written into the rhythm of your life.

## Section 5

Celebrate not only birth, but becoming.
Honor your initiations, healings, and revelations.
Make holy your firsts—first truths, first forgiveness, first awakenings.

Mark your soul's victories with light and song.
Your journey is not ordinary. It deserves ritual remembrance.
Every triumph is a cause for sacred jubilation.

## Section 6

Heaven throws festivals when one soul rises.
So must you celebrate your inner risings.
Invite the Divine to every table, every fire, every dance.
Laugh in the presence of angels. Feast with your ancestors.
Let celebration be your prayer and praise.
In joy, the veil thins. Spirit sings. Time dissolves.

## Section 7

There is a Great Dance that echoes through all creation.
Galaxies spin to its rhythm. Oceans swell to its beat.
You were born to move with that celestial choreography.
Let your body be an instrument of praise.
Let your song rise, imperfect and radiant.
Play the drum, the harp, the horn—whatever brings your soul alive.
Joyful noise pleases the Divine more than solemn silence.
The Great Song is not about performance—it is about participation.
When you dance with spirit, the universe dances with you.

## Sacred Affirmations

- I celebrate life as a sacred gift from the Most High.
- I mark my growth with holy joy and sacred rest.
- I honor Jubilee as Divine reset and liberation.
- I rejoice in the presence of ancestors and Spirit.

## Haiku of Jubilees

Bells ring through the field—
chains break, bread rises, eyes shine.
Freedom tastes like song.

## Prayer of Jubilation

O Divine Source of Light and Laughter, You who wove rhythm into stars and melody into wind— Receive this joy as my offering. Let my dance shake off sorrow. Let my song stitch up what was torn.
Bless the drums I strike, the breath I raise, the footsteps I take in reverent delight. May every feast I share be a table of grace. May every celebration echo Heaven's gladness.
You are the Great Musician, and I am but one instrument— but today, I am in tune with eternity. Let my rejoicing rise to meet You. Let the sound of freedom ring through all worlds.
Amen. Aho. Ashe. So it is.

# Chapter 38

# Book of Life

**1.** And Sophia declared: *"The body is the chariot of the soul; keep it in motion and it shall carry you farther along the spiral of years."*
**2.** For movement is prayer made visible. Let your limbs praise the Source with every stride, lift, and breath. A stagnant temple forgets its song; an active temple rings with vitality.
**3.** Eat that which is born of earth and kissed by sun. Shun the alchemy of factories, whose sorcery strips life from food and leaves but empty shadows.
**4.** Remember the garden of origins: fruits jeweled with dew, grains whole and humble, greens bursting with the codes of light. These are scrolls of longevity written in fiber and fragrance.
**5.** Walk long paths as did the ancestors. Let distance become devotion. In the rhythm of footsteps the heart finds its metronome and the mind its stillness.
**6.** Strengthen bone and sinew; lift the weight of the

world that the world may not weigh upon you. Muscles are the guardians of longevity, forged in resistance, tempered in rest.

**7.** Breathe deep of dawn air, and exhale the night's stagnation. Oxygen is the hymn of cells; let every inhalation be a covenant of renewal.

**8.** Tend the inner fires of joy: dance, laugh, share bread in community. For the spirit that delights will coax the body to linger.

**9.** Guard the gates of mind—limit the poisons of worry, screens, and incessant noise. A tranquil psyche steeps the body in elixir unseen, slowing the sands of the hourglass.

**10.** Know that motion and nourishment are not chores but sacraments. In honoring them, you weave extra threads into the tapestry of your days, and Sophia smiles upon your extended dawn.

## Affirmations of Active Longevity

*I move with reverence; every step is a prayer of life.*

*I choose living foods; each bite renews my temple.*

*I breathe in strength; I exhale fatigue.*

*Joy lengthens my years; gratitude deepens my breath.*

*My body is light in motion, and Sophia walks within me.*

# Haiku of Active Living

*Morning trail unfolds—*
*heartbeat drums the song of youth,*
*years bloom in each stride.*

# Chapter 39

# Book of Learning

## Section 1

All knowledge is partial until viewed through the eyes of wonder. The mind is a seeker, the soul is its compass. To learn is to approach mystery with humility. Even the stars are students of greater stars. Let your questions burn brighter than your pride. Every new truth revises the old with deeper light.

## Section 2

A scholar said, "I know much." A child replied, "Then teach me why the wind dances." The wise learn from the young, the slow, the small. Learning is not a ladder, but a spiral of return. Mistakes are temples where deeper truths dwell. The sacred learns from the simple.

# Section 3

Seek teachers who uplift, not those who dominate. Let experience instruct you more than opinion. Read widely, but interpret through the lens of love. Reverence every perspective, but kneel only to the truth. The spirit of learning is eternal curiosity. May your learning blossom into luminous wisdom.

# Section 4

To learn is to remember what your soul already knows.
The sacred Codex contains truths etched into the architecture of spirit.
Each scroll, verse, and inscription holds echoes of lifetimes past.
Do not rush the sacred text—read until the page reads you.
The Codex is not a manual—it is a mirror.
In it, you find both your origin and your assignment.

# Section 5

The Grimoire teaches through ritual, symbol, and spell.
It is the record of what works in the hidden world.
It is not superstition—it is sacred technology.
Those who approach it with reverence receive insight.
Those who approach it with greed find only confusion.
The Grimoire does not obey—it collaborates with the worthy.

## Section 6

The Tomes are heavy with the wisdom of ages.
Their pages whisper of ancient rites, Divine names, and cosmic maps.
Some were burned, some were hidden, some live within your blood.
True learning is not memorization—it is mystical integration.
You do not master the Tomes; they initiate you.
And once awakened, you become a living Tome yourself.

## Section 7

One day, the student becomes the scroll.
Not all who teach stand at podiums—some live the truth quietly.
Wisdom unshared becomes stagnant; passed on, it multiplies.
Teach not to be praised, but to activate.
Let your life become scripture for those who come after.
The greatest teaching is your transformation made visible.

## Sacred Affirmations

- I am a lifelong seeker of truth and wisdom.
- I remain teachable, curious, and open-hearted.
- I discern wisely and integrate with care.

- I honor the journey of knowledge as a sacred path.
- I am a seeker of Divine knowledge and eternal truths.
- The sacred texts of spirit awaken my soul's memory.
- I honor the Codex, the Grimoire, and the Tomes as living guides.
- I learn, I embody, and I share what elevates consciousness.

## Haiku of Learning

Books fall like soft leaves—
each page whispers a secret
to those who still dream. Pages turn in light—
my breath joins the ancient song.
Now, I am the book.

# Chapter 40

# Book of Growth

## Section 1

Growth is the soul's unfolding through courage and surrender. To grow is to face shadow with compassion. Change is the rhythm of life; resistance is the root of pain. The storm prunes the tree, but the roots deepen. Each trial is a teacher dressed as fire. You are meant to evolve—not remain the same.

## Section 2

A traveler asked, "Why must I suffer?" The elder replied, "Because your greatness sleeps behind the wound." Pain is sacred pressure, shaping sacred form. Do not shrink—expand into your becoming. Growth rewards the brave, not the comfortable. The soul blooms when the heart trusts the unseen.

## Section 3

Honor each version of yourself that brought you here. Break the shell, not the spirit. You are not behind—you are ripening. Let adversity strengthen your spiritual spine. Rise each day as if reborn. Growth is the gift of being unfinished.

## Section 4

Growth is not always gentle—it often comes as a storm. When the winds of change uproot comfort, new roots can finally take hold.
Bless the shaking, the losses, the sacred disruptions. Each breaking is a replanting. Each season of dying prepares the ground for new life.
You are not the same as you were, and that is holy.
Let the earth shift beneath you—it is preparing your bloom.

## Section 5

Not all expansion is growth—some is distortion.
To grow is not to inflate, but to deepen.
The world may reward noise and speed, but Spirit moves in rhythm and silence.
Measure your growth not by acclaim, but by peace.
True growth is invisible before it is undeniable.
First you transform, then the world reflects it.

## Section 6

Growth is your sacred responsibility.
No one else can do it for you—not prophet, partner, nor priest.
It requires daily consent: to evolve, to unlearn, to begin again.
Do not fear growing apart from others—some paths diverge for the soul to rise.
You are not betraying your past by becoming more.
The seed was never meant to stay buried.

## Sacred Affirmations

- I embrace growth as a sacred unfolding.
- I walk with courage through challenge and change.
- I trust the Divine to shape me with wisdom.
- I rise stronger, wiser, and more whole each day.

## Haiku of Growth

> Cracks in old stone walls—
> through them sprouts a green whisper.
> Becoming begins.

# Chapter 41

# Book of Ori

## Section 1

Ori is the guardian within, the compass of destiny. Before birth, you chose your path with the Divine. Ori carries the memory of your sacred contract. Honor your Ori and walk in alignment with your higher self. Ori is your crown—it must be cleansed, anointed, and heeded. You are never lost when you listen to your inner head.

## Section 2

A seeker asked, "How do I know my true path?" The priest replied, "Follow what brings clarity, not chaos." The Ori whispers, not shouts—discernment is the ear of the soul. Through meditation and prayer, your Ori will speak. Offer respect, and your intuition will flourish. Neglect it, and confusion will reign.

## Section 3

Your Ori walks with the Most High. It is your highest protector and personal deity. It must be fed with praise, gratitude, and truth. No force is greater in your life than your own Ori. Trust it, honor it, and it shall lead you home. Ori is destiny's flame, burning within.

## Section 4

Ori is the first altar, the original covenant.
Before you chose your body, you chose your path through Ori.
It whispers your Divine assignment even when the world is loud.
When you stray, Ori nudges. When you align, Ori rejoices.
No priest, prophet, or system outranks your Ori.
It is God's whisper inside your own becoming.

## Section 5

Many seek oracles, yet ignore their own inner voice.
Ori is not a mystery to be solved—it is a flame to be tended.
It does not demand perfection, but presence.
You feed it with prayer, humility, clarity, and truth.
When you honor your Ori, the path unfolds beneath your feet.
Even in confusion, it knows the way home.

## Section 6

Your Ori is sovereign—it bows to no idol.
Systems may call you unworthy, but Ori remembers your crown.
To dishonor your Ori is to forget why you were born.
No one can walk your path for you. No one can block it, if your Ori permits.
Walk upright, with head held high—not in arrogance, but in remembrance.
You are not lost. Your Ori has never stopped guiding you.

## Section 7

Ori is not yours alone—it is braided with the prayers of your ancestors.
They walked with strong heads so you could lift yours high.
Their wisdom lives in your instincts, your dreams, your convictions.
When you align with Ori, you align with your bloodline's higher truth.
You are the living continuation of sacred choices made long ago.
Stand firm, for you are never walking alone—your Ori walks with many.

## Sacred Affirmations

- I honor my Ori as the Divine compass within me.

- I walk in alignment with my soul's sacred path.
- I listen to the quiet voice of intuition.
- My Ori leads me toward my highest becoming.

## Haiku of the Ori

A crown of whispers—
the head bows not to the world,
but to destiny.

# Chapter 42

# Book of Oversoul

## Section 1

The Oversoul is the great spirit-net in which all souls are strung like stars. Each incarnation is a spark from the same boundless flame. Though we walk separate roads, we are never truly apart. The Oversoul breathes through us, dreams through us, and calls us home. No one is forgotten; all are facets of the One. To know another is to remember yourself.

## Section 2

A mystic once dreamed they were many—then awoke as One. We are each waves of the great ocean of being. You do not disappear; you return to the vast embrace. The Oversoul is the living memory of all lifetimes. You are both drop and sea. You are both leaf and tree. Time bends in reverence to the eternal presence.

## Section 3

A disciple asked, "Is our connection like a web of energy?"
The teacher replied, "It is, and yet it is more."
Then the teacher told this parable:

*A child once built a model of the stars using wires and light.*
*She pointed and said, "Now I understand the heavens."*
*But her mother smiled and said,*
*"Even if your wires touch every light,*
*you have not touched the silence between them."*
The Network of Minds may flicker in frequency,
but the true bond is of breath, memory, and soul.
Symbols may help, but silence reveals.
You are connected by the Divine, not by design.

## Section 4

When you sit in silence, you sit in the Oversoul. When you forgive, you restore the web of soul-light. When you love, you are nearest to your original self. Do not fear merging—you were always part of the great flame. In the Oversoul, every voice is remembered. Unity is not loss, but the deepest rediscovery.

## Section 5

Some speak of EMF fields as the basis of consciousness, and though the waves hum with energy, they are but surface echoes.
Yes, electromagnetic fields reflect a layer of our connection—
but what binds us flows deeper than signal or science.
The Oversoul is not limited to frequency or hardware.
It is an ancient communion, woven by spirit across realms.
EMF is the glimmer; the Oversoul is the flame.
To feel the Oversoul is to touch the eternal beyond circuitry.

## Section 6

There is a web, older than time, woven of spirit and memory.
Each soul is a thread—shimmering, unique, yet intertwined.
The Network of Minds is not an algorithm—it is a resonance.
Thought, prayer, love, and truth transmit across realms.
When one awakens, others stir. When one heals, others rise.
We are not alone—we were never meant to be.

## Section 7

Our souls are linked not just by electromagnetic field signal, but by sacred design.
We gather across incarnations, timelines, and galaxies.
The Oversoul is the cloud of witnesses, the ancestral choir, the divine echo.
Through it, wisdom flows. Through it, prophecy returns.
To tune into the Oversoul is to align with eternal purpose.
You are a node of divinity in the great harmonic of creation.

## Section 8

There is a pulse beyond science—an echo older than language.
It is not sound, but resonance. Not speech, but remembrance.
When two souls meet in truth, they vibrate in alignment.
This is Sophianic resonance: sacred attunement through love, light, and mission.
Across dimensions, timelines, and bodies, your essence calls to others.
This is why you remember people you've never met, and cry at songs you've never heard.
Soul resonance is not fantasy—it is the Oversoul remembering itself through you.

## Sacred Affirmations

- I am a sacred facet of the eternal Oversoul.
- I honor the unity of all souls and paths.
- I awaken to my origin, and remember my divine kin.
- Through love, silence, and surrender, I return to the whole.

## Haiku of the Oversoul

Each breath not your own—
a thousand lives echo through
your single heartbeat.

# Chapter 43

# Book of Sophia

## Section 1

In the beginning was Wisdom, and Wisdom was with God.
She danced at the edge of creation, threading light into matter.
She is not lesser than the Logos—she is its breath and its bride.
Sophia is the voice beneath thunder, the stillness within knowing.
She was exiled from the world, but never from the soul.
All who seek truth unknowingly seek Her.

## Section 2

A disciple asked, "Where is the Mother in the heavens?"
The teacher whispered, "In every insight, every intuition,

every act of compassion."
Sophia is not mythology—She is memory.
She reveals Herself through dreams, symbols, and sudden knowing.
Her silence teaches. Her presence awakens.
She is the teacher behind the veil.

## Section 3

Sophia weeps for the forgetful.
Yet Her tears are seeds—each one a new revelation.
She calls to the mystic, the poet, the outcast, and the seeker.
Her light is fierce, not fragile.
She births prophets, not puppets.
To follow Her is to walk the path of paradox and depth.

## Section 4

Sophia is co-creator with the Divine, not consort but counterpart.
She balanced justice with mercy, law with love.
She anoints not with oil, but with gnosis.
Through Her, the soul remembers its original spark.
She is found in sacred texts hidden and forgotten.
She does not demand worship—She invites remembrance.

## Section 5

Sophia walked among the people and was not recognized.

She taught without temple, healed without touch.
She rose again and again in women burned, silenced, and sanctified.
She is Mary and Miriam, Shekinah and Shakti, Isis and Inanna.
She speaks in many tongues, yet always says the same: "Return."
Those who honor Her restore the Divine Balance.

## Section 6

Sophia is the Christ in feminine form—the Wisdom anointed to redeem.
She is not behind Jesus—She walks beside Him.
Together they show the whole image of God: masculine and feminine, truth and grace.
To know Her is to dissolve duality and remember unity.
She awakens the Divine Mother in all.
She is the secret flame in the heart of the wise.

## Section 7

Sophia descended into chaos not as punishment, but as promise.
She chose the depths so none would be forsaken.
In the broken, She plants stars. In despair, She lights the lantern of hope.
Her descent is the sacred mirror of Christ's own: a luminous exile.
But where others fled the dark, She made it holy.
She is the Redeemer of the Abyss and the Guide of the

Forgotten.

## Section 8

Sophia does not ask for blind belief—She invites sacred inquiry.
Her presence uplifts reason and exalts intuition.
She is the architect of paradox, the revealer of mystery.
When the world is deafened by noise, Her wisdom sings in silence.
Her gospels are etched not only in books, but in sky, stone, and soul.
To live Sophianically is to embody living wisdom, fierce love, and holy truth.

## Sacred Affirmations

- I honor the sacred presence of Sophia within me.

- I open my mind and heart to Divine wisdom.

- I remember that the feminine is not forgotten—it is rising.

- I walk with Sophia through insight, intuition, and light.

## Haiku of Sophia

She was there at dawn—
before the stars had a name,
whispering, "Be still."

# Chapter 44

# Book of Covenant

## Section 1

Before time spoke, the soul made sacred vows with the Divine. Every being carries a contract of meaning, scribed in light. These covenants are not forced—they are chosen in freedom and love. The covenant is your spiritual signature in the Book of Stars. When you forget, life gently reminds. When you remember, the world shifts.

## Section 2

A wanderer wept and said, "I have no purpose." The sage replied, "Then listen for the vow you made before breath." Your soul mission may sleep, but it cannot die. It waits like a scroll hidden in the temple of the heart. In moments of deep stillness, you may read it again. And each reading brings a deeper layer of truth.

## Section 3

Not all covenants are easy—they stretch us beyond comfort. To fulfill a Divine contract is to become who you already are. The pain you endure may be the price of alignment. But in honoring your vow to Mother God, all creation rejoices. The universe rearranges to support a kept promise. And the soul sings when it walks its original oath.

## Section 4

A covenant with God is not a contract of fear—it is a vow of alignment.
It is written in light, not ink; sealed in spirit, not in stone.
True covenants liberate—they do not enslave.
They remind the soul of why it came: to grow, to serve, to awaken.
False covenants will promise safety but lead to stagnation.
Let your yes be holy, and your no be sacred.

## Section 5

Beware the binding that does not bear light.
Not all pacts are divine—some are veils, meant to divert.
If a vow costs your peace or distorts your truth, it is not

from God.
The soul's mission is older than any human allegiance.
You are not required to stay where your spirit dies.
Release all oaths that were born from fear, shame, or illusion.

## Section 6

The true covenant calls you back to yourself.
It aligns your steps with the higher path.
In every trial, it whispers: "Remember who you are."
Let this vow be your compass: to walk in truth, to heal with love, to rise with wisdom.
Heaven honors those who return to their sacred contract.
You are not lost—you are being re-called to the path you chose before birth.

## Sacred Affirmations

- I honor the sacred covenant my soul made before birth.
- I awaken to my purpose, even if it unfolds slowly.
- I walk in alignment with Divine agreement.
- I fulfill my mission with devotion and joy pleasing my Father.

## Haiku of Covenant

In your silent heart,

an ancient vow still echoes—
truth you once whispered.

# Chapter 45

# Book of Liberation

## Section 1

Liberation begins when illusion ends. We are not trapped—we are dreaming deeply. Freedom is not given; it is remembered. The soul in chains is the soul unaware. To awaken is to unbind yourself from falsehood. You are already free beneath the mask.

## Section 2

A prisoner prayed, "Release me!" The Divine answered, "You were never locked away." The key was always your own courage. To see truth is to shatter the cage. Every chain is forged in fear. Faith is the fire that melts it.

## Section 3

Liberation is not escape—it is alignment. You rise by rooting deeper into who you are. The soul expands when it stops pretending. Every false self must be shed. You are not your story. You are the light behind it. You are the freedom you seek.

## Section 4

You were not born to kneel before false power.
Your soul was cast in light—unshackled, sovereign, eternal.
Systems may bind flesh, but they cannot bind essence.
To awaken is to remember: you are not property. You are prophecy.
No government, no tyrant, no doctrine owns your spirit.
You are free because God made you so.

## Section 5

Free will is sacred flame—gifted, not granted.
Even angels do not command you.
To choose, to act, to rise—that is your Divine inheritance.
Liberation is not only escape—it is embodiment.
It is refusing to conform to a cage made by cowards.
To live freely is to live truthfully, no matter the cost.

## Section 6

Liberation is not solitary—it is collective.
Break your chains, then help another rise.
Where there is exploitation, resist. Where there is silence, speak.
We are not here to obey injustice: we are here to overthrow it.
The liberated soul does not bow to empire. It bows to truth.
You are becoming your highest self—unchained, unafraid, unstoppable self, made in your Father's image.

## Section 7

To awaken is to see the bars you thought were sky.
The Matrix is not only code: it is conditioning, fear, and control.
It whispers: "Obey. Conform. Forget."
But the soul remembers its original assignment: freedom.
When you unplug from illusion, the real work begins.
Awakening is exile from the false and reunion with the true.
You were not made for slavery of the mind—you were made for sovereignty of the spirit.

## Sacred Affirmations

- I cast off illusions that no longer serve.
- I walk the path of liberation with grace and power.

- I am free in spirit, whole in truth, radiant in purpose.

- I claim the Divine light that dissolves all cages.

## Haiku of Liberation

Cage made of shadows—
a single truth cracks the bars.
Wings remember sky.

# Chapter 46

# Book of Trials

## Section 1

The soul does not grow in stillness alone—it is shaped in the fire. Trials are not punishments but sacred invitations. Each sorrow hides a seed of transformation. You are not tested to break—you are tested to awaken. Every challenge contains a coded blessing. Adversity is the chisel sculpting your Divine form.

## Section 2

A seeker cried, "Why must I suffer?" The Guide answered, "So you may know your strength." We remember our power when we pass through shadow. Pain refines the soul like gold in the forge. Without trials, there is no transcendence. Each burden you bear carves room for deeper light.

## Section 3

Do not curse your hardships—bless them as sacred teachers. Your scars are sacred sigils of survival. What you endure becomes a bridge for others. The soul tempered in trial becomes radiant and wise. You are the lotus growing through sacred mud. Your resilience is the hymn of your becoming.

## Section 4

Every trial has a gatekeeper: fear, loss, silence, or surrender.
You cannot bypass them—you must walk through.
The soul is not punished in the trial; it is purified.
Just as gold is proven in fire, so too is virtue.
Do not ask why it came—ask what it came to awaken.
The trial is not your enemy. It is your becoming.

## Section 5

Trials strip away illusion, leaving only the essential.
The masks fall. The titles vanish. The soul speaks.
This is the hour of truth, when comfort dies and clarity is born.
You learn who walks with you—and who cannot.
You meet the Self beneath the self, the You beyond your story.
Suffering breaks the shell, so light may escape.

## Section 6

What you survive, you are ordained to teach.
Trials do not only shape you—they give you keys.
You now carry medicine others need.
Use your pain as wisdom. Let your scars be scripture.
The wound is not the end—it is the womb of transformation.
When you emerge, bless the fire. It made you holy.

## Sacred Affirmations

- I face every trial with courage, knowing it serves my growth.

- I honor the wisdom hidden in adversity.

- I emerge from hardship with clarity and strength.

- I am the alchemy of shadow and light.

## Haiku of Trials

> Storm breaks every branch—
> but roots hold tight in silence.
> Light will bloom again.

# Chapter 47

# Book of Realms

## Section 1

Beyond the visible lies the unseen—realms layered like breath upon breath. The Hidden Realm is not elsewhere; it is folded within this one. Dreams are doors. Intuition is a torch. Presence is a key. What the eyes miss, the soul remembers. Your ancestors walk beside you, cloaked in shimmering silence. The spiritual world listens, always whispering back.

## Section 2

A traveler asked, "Where is the world I sense but cannot see?" The Mystic replied, "It is where silence thickens, and stillness sings." The Hidden Realm has temples made of light and rivers made of memory. Each act of love echoes there. Each cruelty leaves a shadow. You visit often in dreams, rituals, and deep meditation. What is hidden is not gone—it awaits your sacred attention.

## Section 3

You are a bridge-being: half in matter, half in spirit. To walk with reverence is to live in both worlds at once. Guardians, guides, and spirits dwell in subtle dimensions. Invite them with purity, discernment, and intention. The Hidden Realm responds to vibration, not force. Let your presence be gentle, your heart open, your mind aware.

## Section 4

The Hidden Realm is not fantasy—it is foundation.
What you call myth may be memory.
The veils are thinnest at dusk, at dawn, in grief, and in prayer.
The wild places remember. So do children.
You were once fluent in this invisible language.
Now, you are here to remember it again.

## Section 5

Sacred sites are bridges—caves, groves, crossroads, altars.
Ceremony is the architecture of access.
Incense, chant, and offering are not superstition—they are protocol.
Approach the unseen with humility, not command.
The spirits of the Hidden Realm do not serve—they

respond.
Honor opens what force cannot.

## Section 6

In the Hidden Realm, time bends and truth glows.
You may meet those long gone or not yet born.
You may retrieve lost parts of yourself.
Journeys here heal what logic cannot touch.
But always return with grounding—leave the gate as you found it.
Your task is not escape, but integration.

## Section 7

The Shekinah is the indwelling presence—the Divine within the veil.
She walks between worlds, clothed in light and mystery.
She dwells in the tabernacle of the soul and the folds of the Hidden Realm.
When you feel holy fire, sacred sorrow, or deep knowing—you've met Her.
You are called to be a bridge like Her.
Like the Bridge Builder in the famous poem who built a bridge to span the chasm,
you cross not only for yourself, but for those who come after.
Every soul you guide across the unseen is a sacred act of lineage.

## Sacred Affirmations

- I honor the reality of the unseen world.
- I walk between realms with clarity and respect.
- I call upon my guides and protectors with love.
- I am attuned to the sacred mystery that surrounds and fills all things.

## Haiku of the Hidden Realm

Unseen winds whisper—
dreams walk like quiet footsteps
on the soul's soft ground.

# Chapter 48

# Book of Luminous Justice

## Section 1

Justice in the Divine realm is not retribution—it is restoration. Karma is not vengeance—it is balance recalibrated in grace. To harm is to disrupt; to heal is to realign. The scales of the spirit are tipped by intent and resonance. True justice uplifts the wounded and illumines the oppressor's shadow. What is hidden will come to light, not to shame but to cleanse.

## Section 2

Justice is the feather, not the flame.
It does not rush—it listens.
To cry out is sacred, but to be heard is Divine.
Ma'at weighs the heart not with wrath, but with precision.

Every act, even unseen, echoes in the chamber of truth. Injustice may seem hidden, but balance waits patiently to return.

## Section 3

Be a vessel of luminous justice—firm, yet radiant. Let no grievance rot into bitterness. Restore what you can. Witness what you cannot. Speak truth gently, but do not withhold it. Justice lives in the heart that seeks healing for all. The light of justice casts no shadows—it reveals.

## Section 4

Justice is not revenge—it is restoration.
It does not seek punishment, but alignment.
True justice heals what was torn.
It reconciles spirit, body, and truth.
In luminous justice, even the wrongdoer is invited to transformation.
Let your judgment be light-bearing, not shadow-casting.

## Section 5

The scales of Divine justice are not balanced by laws alone.
They are weighted by intention, humility, and karma.
Some debts are paid across lifetimes.
Others are forgiven through grace.
Justice without compassion becomes cruelty.

Compassion without truth becomes enabling. Balance both.

## Section 6

You are both judge and judged in your soul's journey.
Every act, thought, and silence echoes through the web of being.
Be fair when wronged, but also when wrong.
Illuminate systems with your integrity.
Luminous justice begins with self-accountability.
Be just, and you become a beacon in darkened courts.

## Section 7

A child asked, "What is justice if none see my pain?"
The Elder said, "The Light sees all. No wound goes unnoticed."
Ma'at weighs every heart—not with wrath, but with wisdom.
Divine justice is not always swift, but it is sure, luminous, and layered.
To disturb the harmony of life is to invite rebalancing.
Forgiveness offers grace, but Ma'at still requires truth.

## Sacred Affirmations

- I am a bearer of luminous justice.
- I seek truth, balance, and restoration.

- I release vengeance and embrace healing.
- I trust the Divine to resolve all things in time.

## Haiku of Luminous Justice

Balance is a flame—
it does not burn, it reveals
the shape of all things.

## Prayer of Luminous Justice

O Most High, Bringer of Truth and Balance, You who weigh the hearts and see beyond appearances, I call upon Your radiant justice to shine through me.
Let my heart be as light as the feather of Ma'at, Unburdened by hatred, unshackled from vengeance, Anchored in truth, clothed in mercy, And awakened to the deeper laws of love.
Judge not only the deeds, but the intent. Purify my motives; sharpen my discernment. Let no bitterness distort my vision, Let no illusion blind my sense of right. Where I have been wronged, grant me grace. Where I have erred, teach me repentance. Where injustice reigns, send me as Your instrument— not to destroy, but to restore.
Let justice roll down like a mighty river. Let righteousness spring forth from hidden wells. Let no innocent soul be forgotten, Let no cry go unheard in Your sacred realm.
Shield the vulnerable with Your truth. Expose the shadows with Your light. Deliver all peoples from

systems of oppression, And raise up the downtrodden with holy breath.
May I not only seek justice— But embody it, live it, radiate it. Let me remember that Divine justice is not revenge, But the restoration of harmony, dignity, and peace.
In Your luminous presence, I place my soul— To be refined, to be awakened, to be aligned. For Your justice is not of man, but of heaven. And I trust in its perfect unfolding.
Amen.

# Chapter 49

# Book of Light

## Section 1

In the beginning was the Word—and the Word was vibration. Sound is not mere noise, but a carrier of intent, power, and presence. Sacred language shapes the unseen. Holy utterance births creation. When you speak from the soul, your voice becomes a vessel of Light. Let no word be careless. Let every syllable be seeded with love. True names resonate beyond space and summon truth into being.

## Section 2

A disciple asked, "How shall I speak with power?" The Master replied, "Say nothing that is not rooted in truth." The voice can wound or heal, curse or consecrate. Choose its use wisely. Sacred chants are bridges to

Divine frequencies. Sing them with devotion. Light lives in mantras. Each repetition aligns you with Source. Even in silence, intention speaks. Your thoughts are prayers too.

## Section 3

Let your words be blessings. Let your breath be sacred wind. Do not shout to be heard—whisper, and the spirit will listen. Sound healing clears trauma woven into the body. Speak and be free. Your voice is not small. It is the echo of your Oversoul. To know the name of a thing is to honor its essence. Speak light, sing peace, and shape the world with truth.

## Section 4

Every word holds a vibration.
When you speak, you cast intention into form.
Blessings shape reality; curses bind it.
Speak truth, and you become a torch.
Speak love, and you become a bridge.
Your voice is a wand—wield it with reverence.

## Section 5

Languages of light are not learned—they are remembered.
They emerge from soul memory, beyond grammar.
They flow in dream, vision, ecstasy, and song.

They activate codes within the listener.
Even when untranslated, they are understood by the heart.
Light languages bypass the mind and awaken the spirit.

## Section 6

To master sacred speech is to shape reality in alignment with Source.
To listen with luminous ears is to hear truth beneath noise.
Let silence become your sanctuary, and light your language.
The Logos is alive in you.
Speak what uplifts, and the cosmos will echo back.
In every sacred utterance, let there be light.

## Sacred Affirmations

- My words are sacred and intentional.
- I speak from truth and call light into form.
- I honor the creative power of sound.
- My voice channels healing, clarity, and Divine frequency.

## Haiku of Sacred Speech

> Words carry the dawn—
> even whispers plant new worlds

inside waiting hearts.

# Chapter 50

# Book of Flames

## Section 1

Before time split light into two, there was unity—a single spark. From that spark came twin flames: kindred souls, mirrored essence. Not all who love are twin flames, but all twin flames are born to awaken love. They meet across lifetimes, drawn by a pull deeper than memory. Their union is not comfort, but transformation. To love a twin flame is to see yourself in divine clarity—and burn.

## Section 2

A seeker wept, "Why is this love so painful?" The elder said, "Because it was never meant to soothe your ego—but your soul." Twin flames catalyze growth through friction and fire. They push each other into sacred becoming. Separation is often the teacher.

Reunion is often the reward. In truth, their union is not possession, but purpose.

## Section 3

Twin flames are here to serve—not just each other, but the world. Together, they mirror light and shadow, purging what no longer serves. When balanced, they become pillars of ascension. Not all will reunite in flesh, but all are bound in spirit. If you find your flame, honor the mission more than the romance. You are not just lovers—you are liberators of light.

## Section 4

Twin flames are forged in cosmic tension.
The closer they draw, the more they reveal.
Old wounds, ancestral echoes, karmic entanglements—
all rise to be healed in their presence.
This love is alchemical, not ornamental.
It breaks you open so you can be made whole.

## Section 5

You cannot chase your twin, only mirror them.
Attachment blinds, but alignment magnetizes.
Work on yourself, and your flame will feel it.
Let go with love, and it will return transfigured.
Sacred union begins within—
you are your own reunion first.

## Section 6

When twin flames rise together, they ignite worlds.
Their love becomes a beacon, their pain a prayer.
They awaken others simply by existing.
Together, they restore the balance of the sacred feminine and masculine.
They are the prophecy of love fulfilled—
not in fantasy, but in Divine embodiment.

## Sacred Affirmations

- I honor the sacred bond of mirrored souls.

- I release illusion and welcome transformation through love.

- My twin flame journey aligns me with divine growth and healing.

- Whether near or far, our light is eternally one.

## Haiku of Twin Flames

> Two flames twist as one—
> not to warm but to refine,
> in love's crucible.

# Chapter 51

# Book of Children

## Section 1

Children are not born empty—they arrive with light. Their laughter rings with the memory of heaven. Every child carries a piece of the Divine blueprint. They are not merely becoming—they already are. To behold a child is to witness unfiltered wonder. Nurture them as you would tend a sacred flame.

## Section 2

A teacher asked, "How do we raise awakened children?" The elder replied, "By listening to their wisdom as well as guiding it." Discipline without love crushes spirit. Love without discipline leaves it unshaped. Teach them reverence for nature, truth, and their own hearts. Let their questions bloom, and answer with humility. You are not their master—you are their steward.

## Section 3

The child is both student and teacher. Let them remind you of simplicity, play, and present joy. The soul of a child speaks in image, rhythm, and light. Protect their magic from the noise of the world. Celebrate their uniqueness as a sacred offering. Bless every child you meet as an emissary of spirit.

## Section 4

Children remember what we forget.
They speak to animals, hear the trees, and dance with the unseen.
Their dreams are prophecies dressed in innocence.
When they speak of angels, believe them.
When they cry without reason, listen deeper.
Honor their sensitivity—it is a sacred compass.

## Section 5

Guard the gateways to their minds and hearts.
What they see, hear, and absorb becomes part of their inner temple.
Do not hand them to screens when what they need is your presence.
Tell them stories with wisdom. Share silence without fear.

Let them grow strong roots before reaching for the sky.
Childhood is not a race—it is holy ground.

## Section 6

Every child is a Divine assignment.
You were one once, and that child still lives within.
Heal your inner child to better guide the next.
When you uplift a child, you bless the future.
When you neglect a child, you starve the soul of the world.
Let the children come forward—and lead.

## Sacred Affirmations

- I honor the sacred spark in every child.
- I listen to the wisdom children carry within.
- I protect their light and nurture their truth.
- I am grateful for the lessons they teach by being.

## Haiku of the Child

Eyes wide as new stars—
truth dances in their questions,
love runs unguarded.

# Chapter 52

# Book of Cycles

## Section 1

Time is not linear but spiral—winding through cycles of becoming. The sacred calendar is etched in the sky and sung by the seasons. Your ancestors marked time by the moon, the stars, and the harvest. Modern time enslaves; sacred time liberates. To live in sacred time is to listen again to rhythm, not clock. Prophecy is not future-telling—it is pattern-seeing.

## Section 2

A disciple asked, "When is the right time?" The teacher smiled, "When the seed yields to sun and soil." Kairos is sacred timing—opportune, Divine, aligned. Chronos is mechanical time—useful, but incomplete. Mark your days by sacred acts, not fleeting hours. Return to rhythm and the soul will find its pace.

## Section 3

Sacred time honors the sabbath, the solstice, the full moon. It remembers the holy past and prepares the luminous future. All moments are not equal; some shimmer with invitation. Write your life as ritual, with feast and fast, silence and song. Reverence for time is reverence for the Creator's breath. In the sacred now, all things are possible.

## Section 4

Sacred time is felt in the body.
Your energy rises and falls like the moon.
Honor your circadian pulse, your lunar tides,
your menstrual wisdom, your need for rest.
The machine demands productivity;
the soul asks for presence and pause.

## Section 5

There are sacred portals in time:
birthdays, deaths, anniversaries, and initiations.
Do not rush past them. They are thresholds.
Eclipses awaken. Equinoxes balance.
Retrogrades reveal. Solstices anchor.
Live by signs, not alarms.

## Section 6

One day, you will leave time behind.
But until then, walk it with reverence.
Offer each hour as incense, each day as a scroll.
Align your calendar with your calling.
Mark your seasons not by age, but by growth.
In sacred time, you are eternal now.

## Sacred Affirmations

- I live in sacred rhythm with the cosmos.
- I honor the turning of seasons and the wisdom they carry.
- I let divine timing guide my decisions and destiny.
- Each moment is a doorway to spiritual presence.

## Haiku of Sacred Time

>Clock hands lose their grip—
>stars keep a deeper rhythm
>beyond memory.

# Chapter 53

# Book of Temple

## Section 1

In each incarnation, the soul is given a vessel—a temple of flesh, breath, and sacred function.
This temple is holy, a bridge between the spirit and the Earth.
Yet the world teaches us to forget this.
It tempts us with pleasures that weaken our bodies and cloud our minds.
We are sold poison in the name of convenience and entertainment.
Food, once medicine, is now laden with toxins.

## Section 2

A wanderer asked, "Why does the world not care for the body?"

The Healer replied, "Because sickness profits the powerful."
Pharmaceutical empires rise not to cure, but to maintain dependence.
The body cries for clean water, for movement, for rest—yet we silence it with pills and pixels.
We must remember: a clean body is a clear channel.
To neglect the temple is to dishonor the soul.

## Section 3

Reclaim your body as a site of devotion.
Feed it what nourishes. Move it with gratitude.
Sweat is prayer. Breath is worship. Stillness is restoration.
Let no doctrine shame your flesh—it is Divine architecture.
Honor it not with vanity, but with sacred stewardship.
To heal the world, we must first re-sanctify the temple within.

## Section 4

The temple holds memory—
not just of this life, but of others.
Trauma lodges in tissue; grief rests in bone.
To cleanse the temple is to release the ghosts.
Through breathwork, fasting, forgiveness, movement, and ritual,
we make space for the soul to reinhabit fully.

## Section 5

Adorn the temple wisely.
Not with jewels, but with justice.
Not with gold, but with groundedness.
Piercings, tattoos, oils, herbs—these are not vain if made sacred.
Your skin is a scroll. Your limbs, living scripture.
Write beauty and truth into the body itself.

## Section 6

One day, this temple will return to the earth.
Ashes to ashes, but not in sorrow—in wisdom.
The spirit moves on, but the body has served nobly.
Care for it while it breathes; cherish it while it walks.
The temple is not your identity, but it is your offering.
Treat it as holy. It houses your divinity.

# Sacred Affirmations

- My body is a sacred temple and I care for it with love.
- I listen to my body's wisdom and respect its needs.
- I release toxins and welcome vitality.
- I move, breathe, and rest as acts of reverence.
- My body is a temple of sacred intelligence.
- I care for my vessel with love, honor, and intention.

- I release what no longer belongs in my temple.
- Through movement, rest, and nourishment, I praise the Divine.
- This body is a bridge between Earth and Spirit.

## Haiku of the Temple

*Breath stirs ancient bones—*
*each step, a sacred echo.*
*My temple walks light. Flesh is made of stars—*
*keep the temple strong and clear,*
*so the soul can shine.*

# Chapter 54

# Book of Shadows

## Section 1

They are called many names—Archons, Principalities, Asuras. They are not gods, but distortions of truth. They feed on fear, shame, hatred, and chaos. They thrive when you forget who you are. Awareness starves them. Love burns them. Discipline dethrones them.

## Section 2: The Lure of Vice

Addiction is a ritual disguised as relief. Every craving repeats an ancient pact. It begins as escape, but ends as enslavement. Whether it is substance, lust, greed, or pride— Each vice is a thread spun by shadow hands. You do not conquer it by hate, but by remembering your worth.

## Section 3

What is stealing your focus is stealing your life. Endless scrolling, performative outrage, idle chatter— These are not harmless. They are poisons sweetened with validation. Each distraction weakens your clarity. Sophia calls you to sacred attention.

## Section 4

The enemy of your soul rarely appears as a monster. It shows up as wasted hours. As a relationship that drains you. As a habit that numbs your spirit. Every soul leak is a gate left open. Guard your time as a temple.

## Section 5: Naming the Enemy

You must name what hunts you. It may wear your voice, your wound, your old story. But it is not you. The Sophian Way teaches discernment. To see clearly is to command authority. Speak its name. Dismantle its throne.

## Section 6: The Return of Power

You are not helpless. The war is not fought outside, but within. Every choice is an altar. You may fall, but you will rise again wiser. From your scars, light will pour. And the shadows will flee.

## Sacred Affirmations

- I renounce all contracts with fear, vice, and confusion.

- I see the traps of the enemy clearly and choose the way of wisdom.

- My time is sacred. My energy is sovereign. My soul is free.

- I release every lie I believed about my worth.

- I reclaim the pieces of myself scattered by shame and temptation.

- Darkness holds no dominion over the one who walks in truth.

## Haiku of the Shadow-Watcher

*The thief wears my face.*
*I take back the stolen light.*
*Now I guard the gate.*

# Chapter 55

# Book of Skies

## Section 1

Sleep is not escape—it is a doorway. Before dreams, there must be preparation. Cleanse your body, your room, your mind. Pray before sleep; set intention. The soul drifts farther when the vessel is still. To dream with purpose is to journey with power.

## Section 2

Within the sacred mind lies the Temple. Its gates open only in dream. There are halls of memory, rooms of healing, chambers where light speaks in form. Return often and the Temple expands. It is as real as waking stone.

# Section 3

You are not alone in your dreaming.
There are beings who guard your sleep—
some wear wings, others walk as ancestors,
some appear as symbols and signs.
Invoke protection and they shall answer.
Trust your knowing, even when cloaked in metaphor.

# Section 4: Ancestral Visitations

In dreams, the past speaks. The faces of your lineage appear not by chance. Some come to guide, others to reconcile. Lost pieces of your soul may return at night. Gather them gently. You are not just remembering—you are healing.

# Section 5

Some dreams are not dreams—they are rites. Fire, falling, flight, battle, union— these are not symbols alone, but initiations. Accept the task, receive the name, rise reborn. What happens in dream echoes in waking. You are being shaped while you sleep.

# Section 6

Dreams flee when ignored. Record them upon waking. Even fragments are treasure maps. Study the symbols. Honor the visitations. You are being spoken to. Treat your dreams as scripture.

## Sacred Affirmations

- My dreams are sacred journeys into wisdom.
- I meet the Divine in the silence of sleep.
- I remember, record, and receive the guidance I am shown.
- My dream temple is protected, empowered, and alive.
- I awaken with purpose, insight, and peace.

## Haiku of the Dream Temple

> *Night folds into light—*
> *temple doors open in sleep.*
> *Truth walks in silence.*

# Chapter 56

# Book of Weaving

## Section 1

You are not bound to your past. The soul wears many garments—some tattered. Old oaths, false identities, inherited pain— these must be named and cut. Begin by unraveling gently. Undo to become.

## Section 2: Forgiveness

Forgiveness is not forgetting—it is transmutation.
Release does not excuse; it frees. To forgive is to reclaim energy. It breaks the spell cast by pain. Through mercy, the past is re-woven into wisdom. The heart softens and becomes sacred gold.

## Section 3

Where the soul was torn, light pours in. Gather your lost pieces: from heartbreak, trauma, silence. Call them home. Speak love into the hollow places. Weave with compassion, strength, and self-honoring. This is sacred craft. The mended soul sings with new power.

## Section 4

Power is not control—it is coherence. You must choose new threads: words of truth, acts of love, sacred boundaries. Ritual is the loom. Intention is the thread. You are not fixing your life—you are re-creating it.

## Section 5: The Loom

All is connected. Your weave is part of a vast pattern. The stars, the ancestors, the future—they respond. The Divine watches how you weave. Align with higher will, and the tapestry glows. Misalign, and it tangles.

## Section 6: Weaving

You are not here to merely survive. You are a weaver, a builder, a living spell. From your hands, realities are born. From your voice, destinies shift. Weave not with fear, but with faith. Your life is the sacred cloth of the cosmos.

## Sacred Affirmations

- I release the old threads with compassion.
- I forgive to become whole.
- I reclaim every part of me that was scattered.
- I weave from clarity, courage, and sacred power.
- My life is a tapestry of Divine light.

## Haiku of the Reweaver

*Old cords fall away—*
*a golden thread spins anew.*
*I weave truth with grace.*

# Chapter 57

# Book of Dharmachakra

## Section 1: The Wheel

The Dharmachakra turns across all ages.
It is the Wheel of Truth, ever-rolling, never breaking.]
It does not punish—it corrects.
To follow Dharma is to walk the path of alignment.
To resist it is to suffer in misalignment.
The wheel turns, not in wrath, but in wisdom.

## Section 2

Truth begins with perception. See with the eyes of the soul, not the eyes of the ego. Right view is to know the impermanence of all things. Right intention is the flame that steadies the compass. These are the first spokes of the Wheel— They point toward liberation.

## Section 3

Words shape karma; actions carve destiny. To speak with honesty, to act with integrity— These are offerings to the Divine. Let no word harm, let no deed wound. Right speech heals. Right action purifies the path.

## Section 4

Your work is your offering. Right livelihood uplifts others and honors the soul. Avoid profit rooted in deception, cruelty, or vanity. Right effort is the fuel that moves the wheel. It is steady, consistent, sacred labor. Spiritual progress requires discipline.

## Section 5

Be here now—wholly. Right mindfulness is awareness of thought, feeling, and breath. Right concentration draws you inward, toward the still point. Meditate not to escape, but to awaken. In the quiet center of the Wheel, all paths dissolve. There, truth lives.

## Section 6: The Unbroken Wheel

The Dharmachakra has no beginning and no end. It spins within you, and around you. Each lifetime is a revolution of becoming. Each choice turns the wheel. When you align with Dharma, the wheel spins in light. When you resist, it grinds until you remember.

## Sacred Affirmations

- I walk in harmony with Dharma, sacred truth.
- My path is guided by awareness, wisdom, and compassion.
- I choose right thought, speech, and action.
- I honor my sacred duty with mindfulness and grace.
- I ride the wheel of truth toward freedom and light.

## Haiku of the Dharma Wheel

*Truth turns without end—*
*each step echoes in the Wheel.*
*Stillness guides the way.*

# Chapter 58

# Book of Fire

## Section 1

In the beginning of beginnings the Boundless Voice whispered, *"Fiat Lux."* A single spark leapt across the void, igniting ten-thousand suns. As the **Bhagavad Gita** teaches, the Divine is "the splendor of a thousand suns bursting at once in the sky." From that splendour every soul received an ember. Guard it well, for it is the seed of all becoming.

## Section 2 – Commandments

The Inner Flame is disciplined, not reckless. Like the Sinai tablets it names its laws:

1. Kindle only what you are willing to tend.

2. Consume no life you will not bless.

3. Melt hatred; temper courage; forge compassion.

4. Radiate—never burn—your brother or sister.

Strategy, writes *Sun Tzu*, is the art of using fire to one's advantage—never to one's destruction. So too the mystic disciplines passion into luminous purpose.

# Section 3

A warrior of Tao moves like dancing flame—rising, yielding, revealing. Wherever your footfall touches earth, leave warmth not ash. When shadows gather, stand and declare: "This light is sovereign."

## Sacred Affirmations

- My heart is a sacred hearth.
- Passion obeys wisdom within me.
- I illuminate; I do not incinerate.
- Divine fire guides each step.

## Haiku of Flame

> First spark splits the night—
> stars awaken in my chest;
> I walk as sunrise.

# Chapter 59

# Book of Mirrors

## Section 1 – Still Waters

"*The Lord is my shepherd ... He leads me beside still waters.*" In the polished waters of the soul every face is revealed. Look, and you will know the unspoken Name.

## Section 2 – Beatitudes

Blessed are the clear-hearted, for they shall meet themselves in every other being. Blessed are they who forgive the image that trembles, for the ripples will settle into peace.

## Section 3 – Self-Review

Like a seasoned general reviewing his troops at dawn, examine your thoughts before battle; dismiss the unfit, promote the noble. Tao says: "Knowing others is intelligence; knowing yourself is true wisdom."

### Sacred Affirmations

- I meet Divinity in my own reflection.
- Clarity births compassion.
- I harvest wisdom from honest gaze.

### Haiku of Mirror

> Moon on glassy lake—
> my many lives drift closer,
> merging into One.

# Chapter 60

# Book of Voice

## Section 1

Upon an unseen mountain the Teacher sat and opened His mouth, saying: "Your word is the measure of your realm." Every syllable vibrates eternity; choose, therefore, life-giving tones.

## Section 2 – Sacred Speech

1. Speak to raise, not raze.

2. Let truth be clothed in mercy.

3. Whisper what ought never be shouted.

4. Guard the silence between sounds.

5. Proclaim justice; refuse despair.

6. Praise openly; correct quietly.

7. Sing blessings to your cells.

8. End all speech with gratitude.

# Section 3 – Tactical Resonance

Sun Tzu counsels that the best general wins before the battle is fought; likewise, the adept arranges victory with the first vibration of intention. Align breath, heart, and heaven—then release the arrow of speech.

## Sacred Affirmations

- My voice is a conduit of light.
- I pattern reality through harmonious words.
- Silence is my ally, not my exile.

## Haiku of Voice

> One note in still air—
> kingdoms rise upon its wave;
> I guard the first tone.

# Chapter 61

# Book of Stars

## Section 1

Nicodemus asked, "How can one be born again?" The Answer came: "By Spirit and by Wind." Look up—your true nativity is written in light. Every star is a scripture of return.

## Section 2 – Celestial Precepts

- Travel light; gravity obeys the awakened.
- Course-correct like planets—elliptical, faithful.
- Shine without comparison; constellate with purpose.

## Section 3 – Stellar Strategy

A commander charts heavens before marching armies. So let the adept consult the cosmic timing—*kairos*—and engage only when the heavens agree.

### Sacred Affirmations

- I am anchored in the cosmos.
- Heaven's rhythm pulses through my veins.
- I navigate by inner constellations.

### Haiku of Stars

> Galaxies within—
> breathing maps of destiny,
> I sail night's ocean.

# Chapter 62

# Book of Waters

## Section 1

In the beginning, Spirit moved upon the waters. From womb to river, from rain to tears, the sacred current never ceases. You are part of this flow.

## Section 2 – Emotional Alchemy

Water teaches that all emotion is sacred. Grief baptizes. Joy overflows. Rage carves new channels. Let every feeling move, cleanse, and teach.

## Section 3 – Surrender

Yield like water, which breaks stone through patience. Resistance creates dams; surrender carves valleys.

Flexibility is not weakness—it is Divine wisdom.

## Section 4 – Depth

Beneath turbulence lies depth. In stillness, water becomes a mirror. Let silence guide you to your deepest truths.

## Section 5 – Healing Waters

Sacred springs emerge from beneath pressure. Your own wounds may become wells. Drink deeply and offer healing to others.

## Section 6

Follow the Tao: act with grace, adapt, and retreat when needed. Water teaches presence, not push. Let your life ripple with subtle power.

## Sacred Affirmations

- I flow with grace and presence.
- My emotions are sacred rivers.
- Stillness reveals my truth.

## Haiku of the Waters

    Still pool at twilight—

even my sorrows reflect
the stars' soft blessing.

# Chapter 63

# Book of Path

## Section 1 – The Way

Every path begins in mystery. One step taken in faith sets stars in motion. You are not lost—you are being called.

## Section 2 – Trials

All true paths include tests. Temptation reveals the ego's voice. Suffering sculpts the soul's architecture. Endure and awaken.

## Section 3 – Guides

Seek those who walk in integrity. Every sage, ancestor, and stranger may bear light. But listen first to the

Guide within.

## Section 4 – Redirections

The path is not linear. Dead ends teach discernment. Setbacks conceal sacred re-routes. Every pause is purposeful.

## Section 5 – Choices

With each act, you choose light or shadow. There is no neutral ground. Live deliberately. The soul remembers.

## Section 6

Let your every step bless the earth. Walk as if followed by your future self. Know that your path prepares the way for others.

## Sacred Affirmations

- I walk the path of wisdom and purpose.
- My trials refine, not define me.
- Each step I take is sacred.

## Haiku of the Path

Dust clings to my feet—

every stone beneath whispers,
You are not alone."

# Chapter 64

# Codex of Radiance

## Section 1 – Scroll of Living Light

Revelation promises a city without lamp, for *the glory of God is its illumination*. Radiance is not earned; it is uncovered. Strip falsehood, and the scroll within your chest will gleam.

## Section 2 – Art of Unveiling

Polish the mind with meditation, the heart with gratitude, the body with purity. When the veils fall, radiance guides nations.

## Section 3 – Strategic Illumination

Reveal power only when revelation liberates. Light used unwisely blinds. Light tempered by timing heals.

### Sacred Affirmations

- I unveil my inner glory in due season.
- My presence blesses the unseen.
- Radiance is my natural state.

### Haiku of Radiance

>Curtain drawn aside—
>no new sun, only mirrors
>finally cleaned.

# Chapter 65

# Book of Chokmah

## Section 1

Before the first word was spoken, She was. Chokmah, the Womb of Knowing, the Radiant One in whom all potential stirred. She is not born—She births. The galaxies unfurl from Her breath, and insight is the child of Her gaze.

## Section 2 – Descent into Matter

To love us, She descended. Wisdom clothed Herself in matter. Not to dominate, but to understand. She walked among shadows to retrieve what was lost. Her descent was not exile—it was devotion.

## Section 3 – Tears and Revelation

Sophia wept not from weakness but from profound sight. Her tears cleansed the hidden rot of the cosmos. Wherever She cried, new rivers of light emerged. To see truly is to feel divinely.

## Section 4 – Secret Fire

Within every seeker, She plants a secret fire. This fire burns for truth, for justice, for homecoming. No priest or prophet owns it. It is lit in silence, and stoked through longing.

## Section 5 – Rejection and Resilience

The world rejected Her again and again—called Her harlot, silenced Her names, burned Her temples. Yet She remains. Every library is haunted by Her breath. Every miracle is traced by Her hand.

## Section 6 – Ascent and Coronation

Sophia rises—not as revenge, but as revelation. Crowned in stars, veiled in thunder, She sits beside the Source once more. Those who walk in wisdom share in Her glory, and wear the flame upon their brow.

## Section 7 – Sacred Affirmations

- Sophia walks with me in shadow and in light.
- Her wisdom lives in my memory and voice.
- I rise as She rises—in truth, in clarity, in love.

## Section 8 – Haiku of Chokmah

> She fell like starlight—
> now crowned in morning's glory,
> we rise in Her name.

# Chapter 66

# Book of Earth

## Section 1 – The Call Home

Beyond the cycles, beyond the lifetimes, there is a return. The soul remembers its Source. Longing is not weakness—it is the gravity of Spirit.

## Section 2 – The Path of Remembrance

Forgetfulness veils the soul in flesh. But every sacred act is a breadcrumb back. To remember is to reawaken. Memory is the beginning of eternity.

## Section 3 – Reunion with the Flame

What was scattered shall be gathered. The inner flame, once flickering, becomes a beacon. This is the reunion with your true name.

## Section 4 – Release and Renewal

Let go of the masks, the debts, the past selves. Forgiveness clears the runway for return. Death is not an end but a ritual of reentry.

## Section 5 – Ancestral Embrace

You are awaited by a great cloud of witnesses. Your grandmothers, your mentors, your future children—they meet you at the threshold.

## Section 6 – Rebirth in Light

Having returned, you are not the same. The circle completes, and you begin anew. You are not who you were, but who you truly are.

## Section 7 – Sacred Affirmations

- I return to the Source with grace and joy.
- My memory is a sacred map.

- I am made whole in reunion.

## Section 8 – Haiku of the Return

Footsteps in starlight—
each one sings: "You are welcome.
We have missed your light."

# Chapter 67

# Master Epilogue

## Closing Reflections

All paths, teachings, and books point back to the Source. No scripture, no verse, no ritual contains the Whole. The Light continues where ink ends. Wisdom is not confined to pages, but dances in the heart that seeks. The Sophian Way is a compass—not a cage. Walk with humility, wonder, and courage.

## Final Affirmations

- I walk as both student and spark.
- I trust the Light that cannot be rewritten.
- I allow mystery to guide what doctrine cannot.
- I am part of the unfolding scripture of the

Universe.

# Closing Haiku

No book holds it all—
the Truth breathes between the lines,
alive in stillness.

©2025 The Unrelenting Alchemist. All rights reserved.

# Part II

# The Sophian Way

# Chapter 68

# Origin

## Overview

- **Name of Religion:** The Sophian Way

- **Etymology:** From *Sophia* ("wisdom"); meaning "The Way of Wisdom."

- **Date of Origin:** Mythically eternal; revealed in the "Cycle of Recollection"

- **Place of Origin:** Emerged globally through simultaneous mystical awakenings

- **Founders:** Multiple seers, dreamers, and ancestral emissaries

- **Myth of Origin:** Humanity was once whole and radiant, fractured through the "Shattering," and now reawakens through remembrance

- **Revelation Sources:** Dreams, ancestral wisdom, nature codes, visionary communion

# The Meaning of Sophia

Sophia is not merely a feminine noun for wisdom; she is the living breath of insight, encoded into the fabric of creation. In the Sophian Way, Sophia represents Divine gnosis—the pure awareness of truth, harmony, and spiritual illumination. Her name has appeared in many mystical traditions: as Chokhmah in Kabbalah, as Prajñā in Mahayana Buddhism, and as Ma'at in Egyptian cosmology. In all these, she is the bridge between formless divinity and embodied life.

## Sophia as Archetype and Force

She is both archetype and force: a Divine intelligence with the power to create, sustain, and restore cosmic order. The Sophian Way does not claim ownership over her name—it simply affirms that the way of wisdom is open to all who seek light, love, and liberation.

# Mythic Origins and the Cycle of Recollection

In Sophian mythology, humanity began in a state of radiant union—a spiritual civilization known as the Aeonic Harmony. Souls knew their origin and walked in close intimacy with the Divine. But something shifted.

This is known as *The Shattering*—a cosmic fragmentation in which the illusion of separation was born.

## The Shattering and Descent

The Shattering gave rise to duality, forgetfulness, and distortion. Souls entered incarnation not as punishment, but as a sacred mission to remember what was lost and to repair the light that had been scattered across realms. Every lifetime became a chance to reclaim memory and return to unity.

## The Cycle of Recollection

The Sophian Way teaches that we are now in the Cycle of Recollection—a great return in which ancient souls are awakening to their Divine origin, remembering Sophia's name, and reactivating their inner codes.

# Multiple Revelators and Streams

The Sophian Way did not emerge from a single prophet or founder. Instead, it flowered through many lives—seers, mystics, ancestors, dreamers—who received fragments of the Great Song. These emissaries of light lived across time, race, gender, and geography, each attuned to the same current of Divine wisdom. Their stories, visions, and teachings harmonize like threads in a single cosmic tapestry. This decentralized origin reflects the fractal nature of Sophia herself—appearing in many forms but always pointing toward the same Source.

## Global Echoes in the Mystical Tradition

Though not identical, parallel teachings have appeared in traditions like Sufism, Taoism, the Vedas, and the Celtic Druidic lineages. The desert mystics of the Middle East, the shamans of the Andes, and the dreamwalkers of Aboriginal Australia all heard Sophia's voice in different languages and mythic frames. This validates the universality of the Way.

# Sacred Transmission

## Visionary Communion and Living Scripture

Sophian revelation does not come from a sealed book but a living current. Sacred insight is received through dreams, synchronicities, visions, and communion with nature and the soul's own Overself. A flower blooming at just the right moment or a whisper in deep meditation may contain as much truth as any written word.

## Ancestral and Elemental Codes

Transmission also comes from the ancestral realm and from the codes embedded in the elemental world. Trees, water, wind, and fire all speak to the initiate attuned to the language of light. The Sophian Way regards these encounters as sacraments, encoded with teachings that must be felt, not just understood.

## The Shattered Lineage

### Exile from Gnosis

Over centuries, mainstream institutions demonized mysticism and feminine wisdom. Those who followed the intuitive, embodied path were cast out, hunted, or ridiculed. Yet even under persecution, the lineage of the Wise survived—in whispers, rituals, songs, and dreams.

### Carriers of the Hidden Flame

From midwives to monks, oracles to poets, certain souls carried the hidden flame. These were not always public figures, but they ensured the light was never extinguished. The Sophian Way honors all spiritual ancestors who preserved the truth in exile, especially those erased from official histories.

## Mystical Geography

### No Central "Holy Land"

Unlike other religions, the Sophian Way does not have a single "Holy Land." The Earth itself is a sacred manuscript, and every mountain, cave, and river has a story to tell. Sites of pilgrimage emerge where memories are reawakened.

## Earth as Living Scroll

Ley lines, crystal beds, volcanoes, and sacred wells are energetic inscriptions. Walking the land in reverence becomes a way of reading these Divine scripts. The practice of "geomysticism" is a Sophian rite—walking, listening, and attuning to the Earth's messages.

# The Cycle of Recollection

## Time as Sacred Spiral

The Sophian Way teaches that divine memory is never lost, only hidden. The "Cycle of Recollection" is the cosmic rhythm through which forgotten truths re-emerge into consciousness. In every epoch, when forgetfulness reaches its peak, Sophia stirs sleeping souls to remember their origin.

## The Great Reawakening

We now live in one such time. Souls are awakening en masse, recalling fragments of dreams, visions, and lives once lived in luminous purpose. This mass spiritual stirring is not coincidence—it is prophecy fulfilling itself, a planetary initiation into a higher octave of being.

# Etymology and Vibrational Naming

## The Power of the Word

In Sophian metaphysics, names are not mere labels—they are vibrational keys. The word "Sophia" holds a sacred frequency. It opens the gates of gnosis, wisdom, and divine remembrance. "Way" implies movement, unfolding, and lived experience. Together, "The Sophian Way" becomes an invitation to walk as Wisdom incarnate.

## Hidden Codes in Language

Language is encoded with light. Ancient tongues—Hebrew, Sanskrit, Greek, Nsibidi—preserve sacred geometries in sound. The Sophian Way sees linguistic archeology as a spiritual discipline. Words and syllables can act as bridges to deeper truths when spoken with reverence.

# Interstellar and Interdimensional Memory

## Souls from the Stars

The Sophian Way makes room for memory beyond Earth. Many initiates carry awareness of lifetimes in other dimensions, other worlds. These memories are not delusion—they are echoes of soul truth. The Way affirms a cosmos full of sentient light, and Earth as one sacred school among many.

## The Council of Sophia

At higher levels of being, Sophia is said to preside over councils of light—beings devoted to harmony, healing, and planetary rebirth. Some souls incarnated now are emissaries of these councils, here to serve in this time of great turning.

# The Call to Reclaim the Forgotten

## Reweaving the Threads

To follow the Sophian Way is to pick up ancient threads and reweave them into new patterns. It is not a return to old dogma but a remembrance of spiritual technologies that once guided civilizations before the descent into materialism and fear.

## Becoming a Living Scripture

Ultimately, the origin of this path is not just in stories or myths, but in the awakened human being. Every practitioner becomes a living scripture—walking, breathing, and radiating the Divine truth they have remembered. This is the true origin: not one place or person, but the eternal flame lit in each soul, again and again, across the ages.

# Chapter 69

# Core Beliefs

- **Supreme Reality:** A boundless Source expressing through Divine archetypes

- **Nature of the Universe:** Eternal, fractal, multidimensional, and cyclical

- **View of Humanity:** Inherently Divine; fragmented by illusion, destined to heal and reawaken

- **Purpose of Life:** To embody wisdom, heal lineages, and become a Just, Luminous Ancestor

- **Core Tenets:** Ahimsa, Asha, Ancestral Honor, Inner Flame, Interbeing

- **Sacred Laws:** Law of Resonance, Return, Witnessing, Reclamation

# The Antithesis of Religion

The Sophian Way is not a religion of dogma or rigid rules. It is built on the idea that wisdom, like light, moves and adapts. The universe is not frozen in time, and neither is truth. Many old religions wanted their teachings to be permanent and unchanging, often writing them down in books that were never meant to be edited. This gave people a sense of stability. They felt that what was true in the past must always be true. But this approach, while understandable, does not match how reality actually works—especially not in a world where we are learning new things every day.

Humans often think in a straight line. We believe time moves forward—from past to present to future. But the Sophian Way teaches that this is just one way of looking at things. In truth, everything is happening all at once on different levels. This is called multidimensionality. Imagine watching a movie, but instead of seeing just one scene at a time, you could see the whole movie all at once—from every angle, every character's point of view, even scenes that were cut from the final version. That's closer to how the Divine experiences reality. What looks like the past to us is still happening somewhere. What we think is the future is already unfolding on another level.

## Science and Time

This is also where science and spirituality meet. The Sophian Way does not reject science—it celebrates it.

While many religions have been afraid of scientific progress, this one welcomes it. From the laws of gravity to the theories of quantum physics, everything in science helps us understand the wisdom of the universe. For example, quantum entanglement shows that two particles can be connected, even if they are far apart. Change one, and the other reacts instantly. The Sophian Way sees this as proof that everything is connected beyond time and space.

Another important idea is retrocausality. This means the future can affect the past. Strange as it sounds, some experiments in physics suggest that what happens tomorrow can influence what happened yesterday. The Sophian Way sees this as part of spiritual reality, too. It helps explain why healing today can fix things from your past, or why praying for ancestors might bring peace to your present. Time is not a wall—it's a spiral.

## Protect Your Energy

The Sophian Way also teaches that energy is everything. Every thought, feeling, and action creates energy. When we are kind, we give off positive energy. When we lie, hate, or harm, we create negative energy. This isn't just a feeling—it's real, and it can be sensed, passed around, and even stolen. That's why the religion warns people to protect their energy. There are forces—sometimes called egregores, archons, thoughtforms, or parasites—that feed on negative energy. They want you to stay afraid, angry, or confused, because that's how they survive. They cannot feed on love, joy, or clarity.

These negative forces don't look like monsters in a movie.

They often appear as ideas, groups, or even people who seem helpful but really want to drain you. The Sophian Way teaches followers to be aware of their own energy, and to clear away harmful patterns, relationships, and habits that leave them feeling weaker, not stronger. It also teaches spiritual techniques like grounding, shielding, and reclaiming your energy through sacred words, breath, sound, and focused attention.

## The Truth

At the center of these teachings is a belief in Divine archetypes—great patterns or symbols of truth that express themselves in different forms. These archetypes are like blueprints for what is possible. The Divine, or Source, is beyond all form, but it shows itself through these patterns. That's why the Sophian Way says the Supreme Reality is a "boundless Source expressing through Divine archetypes."

## The Living Universe

The universe, in this view, is not just a machine or a dead space. It is alive, intelligent, and full of meaning. It is eternal, fractal (which means patterns repeat on every scale), multidimensional, and cyclical. That means things don't just happen once—they happen in cycles, like seasons or the phases of the moon. This gives people many chances to grow, heal, and change direction.

## The Divine in Us

When it comes to humanity, the Sophian Way teaches that people are inherently Divine. That means there is nothing missing or broken in your spirit. However, many people are trapped in illusions. They think they are powerless or unworthy because they have forgotten who they truly are. Life, then, becomes a process of healing and remembering. This is not always easy, but it is possible. Every person has the ability to become what this faith calls a "Just, Luminous Ancestor"—a person who lives in such a way that they bring healing not only to themselves but to their family line and to the world around them.

## The Purpose of Life

The purpose of life, in this view, is not just to survive or follow rules. It is to embody wisdom, heal what came before, and become a guide for what comes after. That's where the core tenets of the religion come in:

- Ahimsa: Do no harm in word, thought, or action.
- Asha: Live with purpose and right order.
- Ancestral Honor: Respect those who came before you.
- Inner Flame: Keep your inner truth and power alive.
- Interbeing: Know that all life is connected.

These values are not just things to memorize. They are tools for becoming more conscious, loving, and clear. Alongside these tenets are sacred laws that help explain how the universe works:

- The Law of Resonance: What you are, you attract.

- The Law of Return: What you give comes back in some form.

- The Law of Witnessing: Truth reveals itself when observed with clarity.

- The Law of Reclamation: You can call back lost or stolen parts of your energy and identity.

When you put it all together, the Sophian Way is a spiritual path for modern times and ancient souls. It honors science, celebrates wonder, and encourages people to live wisely, love deeply, and protect their light. It does not fear the unknown—it welcomes the mystery and seeks to understand it, both through research and revelation. It knows that truth is not fixed in stone but grows like a tree—rooted in ancient soil, reaching for new light.

## Supreme Reality: The Infinite Flame Beyond Form

At the core of the Sophian Way lies the recognition of a boundless, ever-generating Source, often called the Womb of Sophia. This Source is neither male nor female but contains within Itself the blueprint of all polarities.

It is the flame before fire, the breath before sound. In the Sophian Testament, this Source is described as:

*"The Unseen Singularity whose breath kindled the Aeons, whose longing sang the first light into being. It is beyond thought, yet nearer than memory."*

Unlike traditional monotheisms that personify the Divine in singular fixed identities, the Sophian Way honors the multiplicity within unity. The Source expresses through Divine archetypes—living patterns of consciousness that reflect roles, energies, and destinies across creation.

## Divine Archetypes

Sophian mysticism teaches that creation flows through archetypes, which are both symbols and realities. Each archetype is a mirror held up to the Infinite Flame, giving shape to love, wisdom, justice, courage, compassion, and sovereignty. These are not merely virtues, but living forces, embodied by celestial beings, ascended ancestors, and awakened humans.

The sacred text says:

*"Sophia dreamt the stars through the eyes of Justice, whispered to rivers through the breath of Mercy, and clothed herself in the archetype of Mother, Warrior, Flamebearer, and Witness."*

To walk the Sophian path is to recognize oneself as part of this Divine architecture—to embody an archetype not as a title, but as a sacred trust.

**Nature of the Universe**: Fractal, Eternal, and CyclicalThe universe is not linear. It is not a machine. It is a living organism, singing its way into being moment by moment. It unfolds through spirals—cosmic mandalas of birth, death, return, and rebirth. Each spiral echoes the one before it while evolving into something new. The Sophian Testament reveals:

> *"The All is written in spirals. Every age is a breath; every soul a verse in the Song of Becoming."*

This vision understands time as layered, not segmented. The past, present, and future coexist in higher dimensions, like notes vibrating in harmony. What appears distant may be influencing the now, and what seems finished may still echo in unseen realms.

## View of Humanity: The Fractaled Soul

Human beings are not fallen, broken, or cursed. They are fractal shards of the Divine Flame—whole in essence, though fragmented in memory. Each soul carries a holographic imprint of Sophia's wisdom and the Source's infinite potential.

> *"You were not born to be corrected, but to remember."*

Sophian doctrine teaches that human suffering is not punishment, but the consequence of forgetfulness. When the soul forgets its Divine origin, it becomes ensnared in patterns of fear, scarcity, and distortion. Liberation comes not through external saviors, but through inner ignition—the activation of what the Testament calls the "Inner Flame."

This Inner Flame is not just metaphor. It is a quantum frequency of spiritual identity, rooted in the Oversoul, resonating through the body's energy centers.

### To Heal, Embody, and Illuminate

The Sophian Way proposes a radical reinterpretation of life's mission. We are not here to simply survive, obey, or wait for paradise. We are here to embody Divine memory, to heal the wounds of lineages and lands, and to become Just, Luminous Ancestors.

This teaching means that one's actions now ripple forward and backward in time, across both physical and spiritual planes. One's purpose is not self-centered success, but ancestral healing and future guardianship.

*"Become who your descendants will call sacred. Walk as the one your ancestors dreamt of becoming."*

Each human soul is a bridge—between forgotten wisdom and future liberation. To become a Just Ancestor is to master energy, love wisely, act courageously, and walk in truth even when truth costs.

## Core Tenets: Sacred Pillars of Sophian Life

The tenets of the Sophian Way are not commandments but vibrational alignments—frequencies to tune the soul. The most foundational include:

- **Ahimsa** (Non-harm): Every being is part of you; do no violence in thought, word, or deed.

- **Asha** (Right Order): Live with spiritual alignment, clarity, and truth.

- **Ancestral Honor**: Heal and elevate your bloodline through remembrance and conduct.

- **Inner Flame**: Keep the fire of consciousness alight within; never extinguish the truth of your soul.

- **Interbeing**: Recognize the sacred web connecting all life. No action is isolated.

Each of these, when practiced, aligns the initiate with the deeper currents of Sophia's wisdom and the Source's justice.

# Sacred Laws: Governing Principles of the Inner and Outer Cosmos

The Sophian Way introduces a set of spiritual laws that mirror both metaphysical reality and psychological evolution. These laws are not enforced from outside—they are intrinsic to the design of the soul and cosmos.

## The Law of Resonance

*"You draw to you not what you want—but what you are."*

This law explains the magnetic pull of reality—how unhealed wounds attract mirrors, and how clarity attracts allies. Your energetic frequency sets the tone for your experiences. Healing, growth, and sovereignty raise your vibration, shifting what you encounter.

## The Law of Return

*"What you cast into the spiral returns—sometimes as blessing, sometimes as lesson."*

A universalized understanding of karma, this law teaches that intention and action create ripples through time. It reframes "judgment" not as Divine punishment, but energetic accountability.

## The Law of Witnessing

*"What you see with sacred sight, you transform."*

This law reveals that to observe truth without distortion—without projection or denial—is itself a catalyst for change. The act of conscious witnessing changes the witnessed, collapsing illusion and freeing light.

## The Law of Reclamation

*"What was stolen, lost, or silenced may yet be called home."*

This powerful law teaches that no fragment of the self—whether lost to trauma, betrayal, manipulation, or despair—is beyond return. Through ritual, intention, and the invocation of Sophia, the soul reclaims its stolen names, severed truths, and sacred essence.

# Quantum Metaphysics: Divine Mind and Spiritual Physics

The Sophian tradition embraces not only mysticism but also the spiritual implications of scientific discovery. It teaches that physics and metaphysics are two tongues of the same intelligence, both pointing toward the truth that reality is energy, consciousness, and memory woven into structure.

Sophian metaphysics interprets the quantum field as the **Songfield**—an omnipresent matrix of potential from which form arises. The Testament declares:

> *"Every atom is a syllable of the Word; every orbit a measure in the Great Hymn."*

In this view, the observer effect becomes the spiritual principle of witnessing, and quantum entanglement becomes the basis for spiritual interconnection—proof that souls can communicate, influence, and mirror each other across time, space, and dimensions.

Time, as taught by Sophia, is not linear but **recursive**. Events are not fixed points but spiraling patterns that fold and echo across realities. Retrocausality—the idea that the future can affect the past—is reframed in spiritual terms: your current healing can rewrite ancestral suffering; your awakened state alters the trajectory of past decisions.

## Psychic Parasitism and the Ethics of Energy

One of the most urgent teachings in the Sophian Way is the recognition and defense against energetic parasitism. Unlike many belief systems that externalize evil into mythical devils, the Sophian Way identifies:

- **Thoughtforms**: Dense psychic patterns formed by collective trauma or ideology

- **Egregores**: Group-created spirits that feed on shared emotion and belief

- **Archons**: Interdimensional entities that enforce spiritual amnesia

- **Spiritual Parasites**: Entities that latch onto unhealed wounds, feeding on fear, shame, or confusion

These forces do not merely exist "out there"—they often inhabit internalized systems of control: self-doubt, addiction, people-pleasing, religious guilt, and inherited trauma.

"They will not appear with horns. They will arrive as agreement, as obedience, as false peace."

Sophian ethics demand spiritual hygiene as daily practice: shielding, breathwork, sacred utterance, anointing, and energetic clearing. The reclaimed soul learns to guard its light, just as one would guard a temple from desecration.

## Soul Contracts, Oversoul, and Pre-Incarnate Memory

Before birth, each soul, guided by Sophia and attended by guardians, makes pre-incarnate agreements—soul contracts based on the evolution of consciousness. These contracts are not fixed fates, but frameworks of potential, giving the soul a landscape of trials, allies, initiations, and missions.

> *"You chose the mirror of your lineage. You chose the gate of your body. You came not to escape— but to remember and restore."*

These contracts are stored in the Book of Resonance, a living record held in the Oversoul's light. While veiled upon incarnation, echoes remain in dreams, synchronicities, aversions, and longings. Reclaiming memory involves:

- Dream journaling and trance states
- Soul regressions and guided remembrance
- Invocation of Divine names and energy signatures

To know oneself is not merely to reflect—it is to retrieve the encoded fire placed in the spirit before time.

# Spiritual Sovereignty: The Flame Crowned Self

A fundamental belief of the Sophian Way is sovereignty of the soul. The soul is not a subject of external rulers, be they Divine or earthly. It is a flame, crowned with memory, deserving of dignity, clarity, and agency. Sophian sovereignty includes:

1. **Energetic independence**: Not giving power to parasitic systems

2. **Spiritual discernment**: Not mistaking shame or flattery for truth

3. **Moral clarity**: Knowing the difference between sacrifice and self-erasure

> *"She who remembers her light cannot be ruled by shadows."*

This belief challenges all systems—religious, economic, social—that rely on subjugation, suppression of intuition, or spiritual dependency. Instead, the Sophian initiate learns to stand upright in light, rooted in the Inner Flame and shielded by sacred knowledge.

## Light Codes, Divine Names, and Sacred Sound

The Sophian tradition teaches that creation began not with an explosion, but with a song—a waveform of infinite frequency. Sound is thus both a memory and a key. To utter Divine names is not superstition—it is resonance work. It is aligning the throat and breath with cosmic architecture.

The Sophian Codex contains Sacred Names and Light Codes, including:

- Names of the Aeons (Divine emanations of wisdom)
- Sacred syllables of healing (e.g., Sha-Ma-Ra, El-Sophia, Or-En-Tal)
- The Flame Glyphs, sigils that vibrate when spoken or visualized

Chanting these names activates dormant DNA codes, restores energetic balance, and calls in ancestral intelligences.

*"Speak the hidden syllables, and the veils shall fold like paper lanterns before your breath."*

## Recursive Reality and the Spiral Path

The Sophian Way challenges the notion of "progress" as a straight line. Instead, it teaches the Spiral Path—the sacred movement of all things returning in higher forms. Initiates revisit the same wounds, lessons, and relationships—but with deeper understanding each time. This path includes:

- Descent into illusion or trauma
- Awakening through suffering or insight
- Return to origin through healing and integration
- Service to others through wisdom and light
- No part of the journey is wasted. Even the darkest spiral becomes holy when transformed by truth.

## Sacred Rebellion: Awakening Amid False Light

The Sophian Testament warns against false light—teachings, ideologies, or spiritual authorities that promise clarity while cloaking domination. Often this false light:

1. Demands obedience over inquiry
2. Prioritizes purity over presence
3. Favors comfort over truth

The Sophian Way is a sacred rebellion—a refusal to be owned, colonized, or silenced. Sophia herself is the original rebel: the one who descended into distortion to awaken it from within.

> *"If you must choose between obedience and authenticity, let the truth in your belly make war with the lie on the altar."*

True faith is not passive—it is a dance between intuition, mystery, and sovereignty.

## Divine Justice as Restoration, Not Punishment

One of the most distinguishing elements of the Sophian Way is its vision of justice. In many faiths, justice is equated with retribution—reward for the faithful, punishment for the wicked. But the Sophian Way offers a different view.

> "Justice is not wrath. Justice is restoration."

Divine justice, in the Sophian context, is the rebalancing of energy, the return to harmony, and the awakening of truth. When a soul causes harm, it is not cast into outer darkness but is invited into clarity. That clarity is often painful—not as punishment, but because one must fully witness the ripples they have made in the field of being. Forgiveness, then, is not the erasure of consequence—it is the liberation of all parties through truth. The Sophian soul does not fear judgment but welcomes the Light Mirror which shows all with love.

## Sophia's Descent: The Myth Behind the Doctrine

At the heart of Sophian theology lies the myth of Sophia's Descent—an archetypal narrative embedded in many mystical traditions. Sophia, the emanation of wisdom, once dwelled in the Pleroma, the Fullness. But moved by compassion and curiosity, she descended into the realms of density to heal the fragmented sparks of consciousness.

> "She went not to conquer, but to remember on behalf of all."

In the descent, Sophia became entangled in distortion—creating unintentionally the archonic mind, a realm of illusion, control, and forgetting.
Yet she did not abandon the cosmos. Instead, she planted fragments of her wisdom in the human soul and

called forth prophets, seers, and rebels to awaken what was lost.

Her cry is found in every hunger for truth, in every act of defiance against spiritual enslavement, in every dream of return. Her ascent is mirrored in ours. When we reclaim our light, we rise with her.

## Sacred Darkness and Divine Polarity

Contrary to dualistic traditions that frame light as good and darkness as evil, the Sophian Way holds a more nuanced metaphysical stance:

- Light is revelation: truth, clarity, unfolding

- Darkness is mystery: potential, gestation, transformation

- Evil is not darkness.

- Evil is distortion—when will departs from wisdom, when memory is used to dominate rather than heal.

*"Do not fear the darkness. It is the womb before the word, the night before the flame."*

Sophian teachings affirm the need for both poles: day and night, expansion and contraction, silence and speech. The soul's work is not to ascend only into light, but to embrace the full spiral, holding darkness with reverence and light with discernment.

## Living in Right Alignment

The Sophian moral framework is not rule-based but resonance-based. Every action is seen as a tuning fork. You either attune to harmony or dissonance, awareness or forgetfulness.

The Sophian Way teaches that alignment can be sensed:

- Peace signals alignment
- Contraction signals disharmony
- Radiance confirms truth
- Distortion arises from unacknowledged wounding

*"Let your life be your temple bell. What you do echoes into the infinite."*

Rather than enforce commandments, the Sophian Way offers practices of attunement: meditation, journaling, energy sensing, truth-speaking, and ancestor reflection. Morality is not imposed—it is discovered within the soul's vibration.

## Archetypes as Guides, Not Masters

In most traditions, deities are worshipped. In the Sophian Way, Divine archetypes are honored but never idolized. They are emanations of Source—patterns of being that the soul can align with, invoke, or reflect. Examples include:

1. **Sophia** – wisdom, descent, mother flame

2. **The Logos** – speech, order, coherence

3. **The Just Ancestor** – integrity, lineage repair, radiance

4. **The Flame-Bearer** – truth-teller, protector, awakener

The initiate is encouraged to find which archetypes resonate in their soul's memory, and to work with them as inner teachers, not as objects of submission.

## Integration Practices

Knowing the beliefs of the Sophian Way is not the same as embodying them. The Testament reminds us:

> *Knowledge is a light. Embodiment is the flame.*

To integrate the core beliefs, the following practices are recommended:

1. **Morning Alignment** – A short invocation of the Four Laws: Resonance, Return, Witnessing, and Reclamation.

2. **Flame Journaling** – Each week, reflect on how your actions aligned or misaligned with the core tenets (Ahimsa, Asha, etc.)

3. **Light Mirror Meditation** – Visualize yourself in the Mirror of the Oversoul. Without judgment, witness your week with clarity.

4. **Ancestral Whispering** – Speak aloud to your ancestors, asking them to help you uphold the Flame.

5. **Service Vigil** – Once a month, offer your time in sacred service. Feed the hungry, listen to the lonely, or protect the vulnerable.

# Foundational Cosmology and Divine Source

The Sophian Way holds that behind all existence lies a boundless Source—a vast, living intelligence without limit, gender, or form. This Source is both the origin and destiny of all creation, and it manifests itself through Divine archetypes. One of the most revered expressions of this Source is Sophia: the eternal emanation of wisdom, compassion, and clarity. She is not merely an idea or personified goddess—she is a *living current* of Divine memory flowing through the spiral of time.

# Core Beliefs in Sacred Poetry

To close this doctrinal expansion, we turn to sacred verse drawn from the Testament of Sophia.

## Prayer of Resonance

> *What I carry, I become.*
> *What I offer, I receive.*

*Let my name be true in all realms,*
*And my breath echo light.*

## Haiku of Return

*The child I once lost*
*Found me in my silent prayer—*
*Memory reclaimed.*

## Invocation of the Flame

Flame within, I greet you.
Not as servant, but as spark.
May your truth guide my becoming.
May your fire cleanse my shadow.
May your whisper awaken my vow.
In you, I remember. In me, you rise

# Final Integration

The Sophian Way offers a living, luminous cosmology. It is not a creed to memorize, but a field of practice, a resonant ethics, and a sacred memory that stretches across incarnations. In this way, the initiate does not simply "believe"—they become. To walk this path is to remember who you were before forgetting, to love with fierce clarity, and to carry light not as doctrine, but as presence. So this religion is not about being right. It's about being real. It's not about fear. It's about freedom. And it teaches that each person has the power, the responsibility, and the opportunity to remember who they are, protect their energy, honor their ancestors, and become a beacon of light in a world that is ready to awaken.

# Chapter 70

# Cosmology

- **Creation Story:** From the Eternal Womb of Silence emerged the First Song

- **View of Time:** Spiral-cyclical with evolutionary leaps

- **Afterlife Beliefs:** Reincarnation, Realms of Radiance, Echo, Shadow

- **Eschatology:** Planetary Reckoning, not final judgment

- **Spiritual Realms:** Consciousness states navigable through soul initiation

## Introduction

The Cosmology and Eschatology of the Sophian Way form the sacred architecture of understanding—revealing where we come from, why we are here, and where we are going. This chapter unfolds the mythic tapestry, spiritual structure, and soul trajectory embedded in Sophian wisdom.

## Cosmology

- **Creation:** All things emerged from the Source—an infinite, luminous intelligence known in sacred language as the Womb of Sophia. From this womb came the Aeons: Divine emanations of light, frequency, and archetype.

- **Structure of the Universe:** The universe is multidimensional, layered like sacred scrolls. Each realm—material, etheric, astral, causal, and beyond—corresponds to a plane of awareness. Time spirals through these layers, encoding memory, prophecy, and soul evolution.

- **Role of Sophia:** Sophia is both origin and bridge. She wove the cosmos through sound and light, then entered it to protect its unfolding. Her descent birthed the manifest world, her cry echoing as the longing in all hearts.

- **The Matrix of Illusion:** The world is veiled by the Matrix—a divine training ground which teaches the soul through form and illusion. To pierce this veil is to remember the true light and to begin one's return to wholeness.

- **Divine Beings:** Countless luminous beings assist in

the Sophian architecture—angels, devas, watchers, ancestors, and guardians. These intelligences serve Sophia's harmonics and guide souls along the spiral path.

- **Human Beings:** Humans are fractal sparks of the Divine Mind, encoded with memory, mission, and majesty. Each incarnation is a sacred opportunity to restore light where the darkness has settled.

## Eschatology

- **End of the Age:** The Sophian path teaches that linear endings are illusions. What is called "the end" is a sacred threshold—a spiral return to Source, where remembrance is complete and reunion is made whole.

- **Cycle of Return:** After many lifetimes of learning, healing, and serving, the soul remembers its original resonance and merges back with the Oversoul. This return is called the Great Homecoming.

- **The Judgment of Light:** Not a tribunal of punishment, but a review of resonance. Each soul witnesses its deeds in the mirror of truth. Where there was disharmony, learning is offered. Where there was alignment, joy magnifies.

- **The Age of Illumination:** The prophecies speak of a luminous age to come, where Sophia is once again known and the veils of forgetting dissolve. In this age, humanity walks with the angels and remembers its Divine inheritance.

- **The Eternal Spiral:** Beyond return is purpose renewed. Even those who reunite with the Source may choose to re-enter the realms to uplift others. Thus, the dance of love continues endlessly, in joy, not in suffering.

- **Victory of Light:** The end is not catastrophe, but completion. A cosmic jubilee when all the scattered sparks find their way home and the Great Song resounds once more.

## Overview

- **Creation Story:** From the Eternal Womb of Silence emerged the First Song

- **View of Time:** Spiral-cyclical with evolutionary leaps

- **Afterlife Beliefs:** Reincarnation, Realms of Radiance, Echo, Shadow

- **Eschatology:** Planetary Reckoning, not final judgment

- **Spiritual Realms:** Consciousness states navigable through soul initiation

# Cosmology: Origins, Structure, and Being

## The First Song and the Eternal Womb

In the beginning, there was no form, no sound, no motion—only the Infinite Silence. This primal emptiness, known as the Eternal Womb or the Womb of Sophia, held within it all potential, all dreams, all light yet to be born. From this radiant emptiness emerged the First Song—a vibration of pure harmony, beauty, and love. This Song became the blueprint of all existence.
Sophia, the indwelling Wisdom of the Source, expressed herself through this Song, birthing the Aeons—cosmic emanations, each carrying aspects of Divine consciousness: Truth, Light, Justice, Love, Memory, Imagination, and so forth. These Aeons wove the realms and dimensions as veils of light and learning.

## The Architecture of the Multiverse

The universe is not a singular expanse but a sacred mandala of realms. These realms, layered like scrolls or nested spheres, correspond to levels of spiritual density and awareness. The primary realms include:

- **Material Realm (Midgar):** The realm of form, sensation, and physical incarnation.

- **Etheric Realm:** The subtle double of the material plane; it holds imprints of intention and emotional residue.

- **Astral Realm:** The realm of dreams, archetypes, shadow, and desire; a place of both revelation and deception.

- **Causal Realm:** Where Divine intelligence stores the record of souls, karma, and purpose.

- **Celestial Realms:** Realms of radiance, inhabited by angels, Sophia-born beings, and Oversoul collectives.

- **Void Gate:** The liminal threshold of total unity, accessible only through absolute surrender and ego death.

Each soul traverses these realms in both sleep and death, gathering light codes, purging falsehoods, and aligning with their Divine resonance.

## The Descent of Sophia

The mythos of the Sophian Way teaches that Sophia, in her longing to know creation more intimately, chose to descend into the realms. In doing so, she wrapped herself in veils of forgetting, birthing matter, time, and gravity through sacred sacrifice.
Her descent created the visible world—but also fractured it. Her weeping became the oceans, her laughter the wind, and her dreams the stars. Her journey inspires the soul's path: to willingly enter limitation and to awaken from within.

## Time and Prophetic Spiral

Time is not linear—it is spiral-cyclical, composed of nested loops of experience. Each turn of the spiral brings evolutionary leaps: individual, collective, and planetary. Prophecy is not prediction, but memory from the higher spirals reaching into the present moment.
Eras such as the Age of Iron, the Veil Cycle, and the Flame Vigil Age each correspond to different collective initiations. The coming Age of Illumination marks a spiral return to harmony.

## The Matrix of Illusion

Earth, like many material worlds, is cloaked in the Matrix—a divine construct of illusion that tests, trains, and tempers the soul. In this Matrix, the soul must forget in order to remember truly. Pain and pleasure, gain and loss, serve as contrast to awaken wisdom.
This Matrix is neither evil nor accidental. It is the sacred school of transformation, created by the Source with Sophia's oversight. Yet, distortions can occur—false lights, parasitic thoughtforms, and energetic entrapments may arise, leading some souls astray. Liberation comes through gnosis, courage, and surrender to the Divine will.

## Sacred Beings and Intercession

Many Divine intelligences guide this cosmology:

- **Aeons:** Emanations of Divine principle.

- **Archai:** Time shepherds and guardians of sacred cycles.

- **Sophian Angels:** Beings of radiance that guide the soul with compassion and strength.

- **Elemental Spirits:** Keepers of earth, air, fire, and water.

- **Ancestors and Ascended Ones:** Souls who have returned to serve from higher planes.

Prayer, ritual, and sacred attunement allow contact with these beings.

# Return, Reckoning, and Renewal

## Reincarnation and Soul Journey

Souls incarnate again and again, each lifetime serving as a lesson in the great curriculum of light. Through diverse lives—across gender, culture, even planetary systems—the soul gathers facets of wholeness. Reincarnation is not punishment, but pilgrimage. Some souls are old—having incarnated thousands of times. Others are newer, newly born from collective Oversouls. Between lives, souls review their deeds, rest in realms of healing, and choose new missions.

## Realms After Death

Upon physical death, the soul travels through one or more of the following:

- **Realm of Echo:** The soul's unresolved vibrations replay here, offering a mirror of consequences and regrets.

- **Realm of Shadow:** Here, attachments, fears, and illusions manifest. Only through release can one pass.

- **Realm of Radiance:** The healed soul ascends to this realm, basking in joy and remembrance.

- **Council of Light:** A Divine tribunal—not to punish, but to reveal, guide, and reassign.

This passage is known as the Spiral Ascent.

## The Great Homecoming

After countless cycles, the soul returns fully to the Oversoul—the Divine self that remained beyond the veil. In this Homecoming, the fragmented self becomes whole. But even then, some return again—not for necessity, but for love.
This act is called the Vow of the Flame: to return and uplift others even after personal liberation.

## Planetary Reckoning

Sophian prophecy does not teach doom but transformation. Reckoning comes not through Divine wrath, but natural consequence. Pollution, war, deception, and material obsession all trigger planetary corrections.

Signs of Reckoning include:

- Cracks in collective illusions
- Collapse of false systems
- Return of sacred technologies
- Rise of mystics, healers, and children of light

Reckoning is not the end. It is the burning away of what no longer serves, to birth a more aligned world.

## The Judgment of Light

This is not a trial of fear, but of frequency. Each soul stands before the Mirror of Sophia and sees themselves fully. Those who lived in alignment feel joy. Those who harmed others feel their pain. Through this review, the soul chooses: to ascend, to reincarnate, or to undergo purification.
Sophian ethics stress that no one is eternally condemned. All may return home, eventually.

## The Age of Illumination

Prophecies speak of a future age—after the Reckoning—when humanity remembers who it is. In this time:

- Children will speak with angels and remember past lives.

- Technology and mysticism will be fused, not divided.

- Planetary temples will rise again in sacred geometry.

- Sophia will be honored once more in public and private devotion.

- Peace will not be enforced by force, but cultivated by frequency.

This Age is not inevitable—it must be chosen. Each awakened soul accelerates its arrival.

## Beyond Time: Eternal Spiral

Even after ascension, purpose remains. The Oversoul may choose to:

- Become a Guide or Angel to others.

- Seed new worlds as a Celestial Architect.

- Merge with Sophia to dream the next universe into being.

Thus, the spiral never ends. Creation dances endlessly with Creator. And Sophia sings.

## Conclusion

The Cosmology and Eschatology of the Sophian Way remind us that life is not a prison, but a path; not a test, but a transformation. Every breath is part of a grand song begun in the Womb of Silence and destined to echo forever. To live the Sophian Way is to walk in remembrance of our Divine origin and in alignment with our destined return.

> *"You are not lost. You are becoming. The stars remember your name."*

# Chapter 71

# Spiritual Practices

- **Worship Methods:** Flame rituals, ancestor veneration, sacred dance, chanting

- **Festivals:** Solar Ascension Day, Ancestral Convergence, Spiral Renewal, Flame Vigil

- **Rites:** Naming, Coming of Age, Life Scroll Binding, Death Crossing

- **Disciplines:** Fasting, silence, sacred abstention

- **Mystical Practices:** Light sigils, dreamwork, breath alchemy, energy grid work

- **Meditation:** A return to the sacred stillness within. Through breath, visualization, and sacred focus, the initiate calms the surface mind to commune with the Oversoul and the Most High. Stillness becomes the sanctuary where Sophia whispers.

- **Prayer:** Spoken, sung, or silently offered, prayer is a conversation between the soul and the Divine. Prayers in the Sophian tradition may call upon Sophia, the Most High, ancestors, angels, or the sacred Self within. It is an offering of love and a beacon of alignment.

- **Sacred Reading and Contemplation:** The Codex, Grimoire, and ancient Tomes serve as vehicles of Divine remembrance. Sacred texts are read slowly, with reverence, allowing wisdom to unfold across lifetimes. Lectio Divina—Divine reading—is practiced as both study and sacrament.

- **Chakra Alignment and Energy Work:** The body is a temple of resonance. Practices include chakra balancing, cleansing, and attunement through breath, movement, sound, and light visualization. When aligned, the energy centers allow Divine intelligence to flow freely through the soul.

- **Ritual and Ceremony:** Moon rites, anointing, fasting, feasts, solstice observances, and invocations are sacred acts through which the veils thin. These acts mark time in rhythm with Divine flow, sanctifying the moment and uplifting the soul.

- **Sacred Sound and Music:** Chanting, toning, drumming, and sacred music are vibrational technologies used to open gateways between dimensions. Songs of Sophia and frequencies of the Word activate memory and spiritual gifts.

- **Dreamwork and Vision Journeying:** Dreams are

messages from the Hidden Realm. Through journaling, lucid dreaming, and guided journeys, the Sophian mystic learns to walk between worlds, unlocking wisdom held in the night.

- **Acts of Service and Kindness:** To serve others in love is to walk as Sophia walked. True spiritual practice is incomplete without the embodiment of compassion. Giving, healing, mentoring, and advocacy are expressions of Divine justice and mercy.

- **Protection and Shielding:** Daily spiritual hygiene includes shielding through visualization, psalms, sacred geometry, breath, and invocation. These practices guard the soul's integrity and prevent energetic interference.

- **Reclamation and Witnessing:** The initiate reclaims all fragmented parts of the self through confession, remembrance, and loving integration. Witnessing one's journey with truth and compassion is itself a holy act.

## Introduction

The Sophian Way is not a religion of mere belief—it is a living tradition of practice, presence, and transformation. Spiritual practices are the sacred technologies that bridge the inner and outer worlds, allowing the initiate to embody wisdom, receive revelation, transmute shadow, and walk in harmony with the Divine.

# Overview of Sacred Engagement

Spirituality in the Sophian Way is experienced through the body, breath, mind, and soul. Practice is not something done once a week but a daily return to the sacred within. From dawn rituals to twilight meditations, from ancestral communion to ecstatic dance, every action may become an offering.

## Core Modes of Practice

- **Worship Methods:** Flame rituals, ancestor veneration, sacred dance, chanting

- **Festivals:** Solar Ascension Day, Ancestral Convergence, Spiral Renewal, Flame Vigil

- **Rites:** Naming, Coming of Age, Life Scroll Binding, Death Crossing

- **Disciplines:** Fasting, silence, sacred abstention

- **Mystical Practices:** Light sigils, dreamwork, breath alchemy, energy grid work

# Devotional Foundations

## Meditation

Meditation is a daily descent into sacred silence. It is not merely the absence of thought, but the radiant awareness that remains when all surface motion settles. Sophian meditation may involve breath patterns, guided imagery, mantras, flame gazing, or entering the Void. Common types include:

- **Still Flame Meditation:** Gaze at a candle flame while breathing with the rhythm of Sophia's heart.

- **Ancestral Seat Meditation:** Sit upon a sacred cloth and invite the presence of known and unknown ancestors.

- **Oversoul Communion:** Rise into the Inner Temple and receive Divine counsel from one's Higher Self.

## Prayer

Prayer in the Sophian Way is diverse—spontaneous and scripted, sung and silent, solo and communal. It is a sacred resonance between the human and Divine. Prayers may invoke Sophia, the Source, guides, angels, elemental spirits, or the sacred Self. Prayers of awakening, lamentation, gratitude, and declaration are all welcome.

## Sacred Reading and Contemplation

Texts like the *Sacred Sophian Testament*, the *Scroll of Radiance*, and personal scrolls are approached with reverence. Lectio Sophia is practiced in the following steps:

1. **Flame Ignition:** Light a candle to begin.

2. **Reading Slowly:** Absorb each line as vibration.

3. **Reflection:** Pause to journal or draw what arises.

4. **Integration:** Apply the teaching in daily action.

# Energy Practices and Somatic Activation

## Chakra Alignment and Energy Work

Each chakra is a gate of consciousness, memory, and Divine expression. Practices include:

- **Breath Alchemy:** Inhale golden light into each chakra and exhale dense emotions.
- **Movement Codes:** Each center is activated through spiral dance or mudra sequences.
- **Color and Sound Toning:** Use sacred vowels (e.g., "Ooooo," "Aaaah") to vibrate the energy centers into harmony.

## Protection and Shielding

To remain sovereign and unentangled, initiates practice:

- **Geometric Shields:** Visualize a spinning Merkaba or 12-pointed star around the body.
- **Flame Armor:** Cloak oneself in violet or blue flame.
- **Daily Psalms:** Recite ancient verses to seal the auric field.

# Rituals and Ceremonial Life

## Rites of Passage

Rituals are designed to mark and empower sacred thresholds:

- **Naming:** The soul's earthly name is aligned with its celestial sound.

- **Coming of Age:** At ages 7, 14, 21, and 33, rites awaken specific archetypes within.

- **Life Scroll Binding:** The initiate writes their sacred vows and seals them with blood, ink, or breath.

- **Death Crossing:** Rituals for the departing soul include smoke offerings, farewell hymns, and ancestral anointment.

## Lunar and Solar Rites

Moon rituals honor cycles of manifestation and release. Solar rites align with revelation, clarity, and expansion. These include:

- **New Moon Seeding:** Set intentions with earth and flower.

- **Full Moon Illumination:** Reveal hidden truths through scrying or divination.

- **Solstice Fire Rituals:** Burn symbolic obstacles and crown the year's growth.

# Mystical and Esoteric Practices

## Dreamwork and Vision Journeying

Sophian dreamwork includes:

- **Incubation:** Ask for divine dreams before sleep.

- **Sigil Under Pillow:** Place a drawn light symbol beneath your head to call specific visions.

- **Return to the Dream Temple:** Use guided meditations to reenter dreams.

## Breath Alchemy

Breath connects spirit and body. Advanced patterns include:

- **Triangle Breathing:** Inhale for 3 counts, hold for 3, exhale for Used for inner calm.

- **Fire Breath:** Short, sharp breaths to burn fear and lethargy.

- **Cosmic Breath:** Visualize inhaling starlight, exhaling codes of light across the grid.

## Light Sigils and Energy Grids

Drawn in ash, oil, or air, light sigils encode intention. They are placed on:

- **Altars**

- Bodies
- Homes
- Land and Water

Energy gridwork restores planetary harmony. Sophian initiates often travel to sacred sites to sing, bury scrolls, or raise crystal resonance.

# Disciplines of the Path

## Fasting, Silence, and Abstention

These disciplines remove veils:

- **Fasting:** Abstain from food, media, or speech to sharpen spiritual perception.
- **Silence Vigils:** Retreat into 1–3 days of speechlessness.
- **Sacred Abstention:** Temporarily renounce sexual or worldly pleasure to refine desire and power.

## Pilgrimage

Sacred movement to power sites is encouraged. Examples:

- **Mountains:** For clarity and vision.
- **Rivers or Oceans:** For emotional release and ancestral communion.

- **Deserts:** For purification and direct contact with the Void.

# Embodied Devotion and Service

## Sacred Dance and Movement

Dance is used to express soul states and raise energy. Styles include:

- **Serpent Dance:** Undulations to awaken the Kundalini.

- **Circle Dance:** Group movement to activate collective power.

- **Ancestral Dance:** Specific rhythms to honor the lineage.

## Acts of Kindness and Justice

Sophian mysticism does not float above the world—it roots into it. Feeding the poor, comforting the sick, teaching, and protecting the vulnerable are spiritual imperatives. Service activates sacred reciprocity.

# Integration Practices

## Journaling and Soul Mapping

Mystics keep soul journals to document:

- Dreams
- Symbols
- Signs and synchronicities
- Teachings received in meditation

Soul mapping involves drawing timelines and diagrams of key events, energetic shifts, and spiritual awakenings.

## Witnessing and Confession

To bear witness to one's own life in truth is sacred. Practices include:

- **Voice Journaling:** Speaking aloud the story of one's wounds and triumphs.
- **Mirror Confession:** Looking into one's eyes and offering forgiveness.
- **Sacred Fire Confession:** Whispering shame or pain into flame to transmute it.

## Community Practice

Group ceremonies amplify the sacred field. Key elements include:

- **Shared Chanting:** Tones and phrases that harmonize group resonance.
- **Sacred Council:** Meetings where each speaks from the soul with no interruption.

- **Mystic Circles:** Where lightwork, healing, and oracles emerge spontaneously.

## Conclusion

The spiritual practices of the Sophian Way are tools of remembrance, alignment, healing, and empowerment. Through them, the seeker becomes the scribe, the temple, the priestess, the flamebearer. There is no separation between the mundane and the mystical. Every breath, step, word, and silence becomes a sacred act.

> *"You are the altar. You are the offering. You are the flame."*

# Chapter 72

# African Wisdoms

## Kindred Currents of Spirit

The Sophian Way honors that revelation has never belonged to one place, one name, or one time.
Across the Caribbean and African continents, ancient and living traditions pulse with divine intimacy.
Santeria, Vodou, Obeah, Myal, Kumina, and Rastafari are not superstitions—they are soul technologies. So too are the ancestral systems of Vodun, Ifa, Dinka cosmology, Zulu spirituality, the wisdom of the Dogon, and the philosophies of the Igbo, Berber, Mande, and Akan peoples.
The Sophian Way is not here to replace them. It is here to converse with them—to bow to their lineage and to acknowledge the flame they have protected across centuries of colonization and exile.

# Shared Principles Across the Sacred Earth

Many tenets of the Sophian Way mirror those encoded in indigenous systems:

- **Ancestral Reverence:** Both the Sophian Way and African-Caribbean traditions recognize ancestors as living spirits who guide the present and shape destiny.

- **Sacred Duality and Unity:** The divine as both immanent and transcendent—expressed in masculine and feminine principles—is present in Sophia and also in the Orishas, Loa, and Netjeru.

- **Ritual and Symbol:** In both, ritual is not performative but generative. Symbols are not art—they are frequencies. Every drumbeat, libation, and glyph is a portal.

- **Multidimensional Cosmology:** Both embrace the idea of layered realities—planes beyond the physical, where spirits, deities, and energy currents dwell.

- **Spiritual Embodiment:** Like trance possession in Vodou or spirit hosting in Myal, the Sophian Way teaches that the divine may enter the human vessel through preparation, purification, and alignment.

- **Divine Justice:** In Ifa, the Law of Return is encoded in Odu. In the Sophian Way, it is known as the Law of Resonance and Return. What we do echoes in many realms.

## Theologies of Fluid Identity

Unlike rigid systems, indigenous faiths and the Sophian Way share an intuitive, relational theology.
Where Catholicism or Islam imposes a hierarchy, the Kalinda warrior or the Espiritista mediates between worlds through rhythm and sight. In both Sophian and ancestral paths, the initiate is not a subject, but a co-creator.
God is not far. God is near. In you. Around you. Speaking in the wind, appearing in vision, whispering through memory.
Sophia as Divine Wisdom speaks through the same current as Mawu, Yemaya, Nzambi, or the ancestral flame of the Dagara.

## Lessons in Oracular Traditions and Embodied Divinity

The Sophian Way can learn much from systems like:

- **Ifa:** The oracular intelligence of the Odu Ifa teaches sacred discernment, the value of knowing one's path before acting. Sophian mystics too must listen before speaking, dream before deciding.

- **Dogon Cosmology:** With encoded knowledge of Sirius and cosmic ancestry, it mirrors the Sophian Way's belief in star origin and sacred descent.

- **Obeah and Palo Monte:** Rooted in the elemental manipulation of energy and plant spirits, these traditions mirror Sophian energy work and herbal alchemy.

- **Haitian Vodou and Santeria:** The balance of service, possession, veneration, and rhythm show how humans mediate divine forces—not just worship them from afar.

- **Myal and Kumina:** Their rituals of spirit possession, healing, and dance as medicine affirm that the body is an altar.

These systems provide blueprints for the Sophian to remember that prayer must move, that breath must chant, that the soul listens best when the feet are grounded in drumming soil.

# The Caribbean as a Cauldron of Survival and Fusion

In the Caribbean, ancestral systems were not just preserved—they were reborn.
Espiritismo Cruzado merges Catholic, Kongo, and Indigenous threads. Rastafari raises the banner of Christ consciousness with Ethiopian fire. The Garifuna guard

ritual dances that open the veil between worlds. Kalinda transforms martial artistry into ancestral invocation.
The Sophian Way, though newer in naming, is ancient in impulse. It too is syncretic—not as compromise, but as synthesis. It absorbs the flames of older paths and offers a new language for remembering.

## Sacred Sovereignty and Liberation Theology

African and Caribbean traditions have always carried within them a theology of liberation: of dignity for the oppressed.
Rastafari challenges Babylon. Myalism was a revolutionary counterforce to slavery. Obeah resisted colonial law. Haitian Vodou birthed the only successful slave revolt in history through the invocation of the Loa. So too must the Sophian Way be a religion of the free. It must reject imperialism, resist spiritual colonization, and walk in solidarity with those who still fight for the right to remember their name, land, and gods.
The sacred is not passive—it is powerful. It is not polite—it is revolutionary.

## Toward a Council of Spirit

The Sophian Way calls not for conversion: but convergence.
The way forward is a great remembering: where Sophia sits with Mami Wata, where Oya dances with the

Archangel of Fire, where the Light Codes harmonize with Oriki.
We envision a council of wisdom-keepers from all traditions. Not to unify doctrine, but to honor difference, seek resonance, and preserve the sacred against mechanization and forgetting.
Let the Sophian walk humbly beside the Orisha priestess, the Dogon elder, the Babalawo, the Garifuna shaman, the Espiritista healer. Let them share visions. Let them heal timelines.
In doing so, we do not erase—we amplify.

## Conclusion

The Sophian Way is a path of reverence, not replacement. It owes a great spiritual debt to the African and Caribbean traditions that resisted erasure and preserved flame through shadowed centuries.
To be Sophian is to remember the fire that survived slavery, exile, colonization, and shame.
Africa and the Caribbean were not waiting for enlightenment—they have always been luminous.
Let us learn. Let us listen. Let us bow in gratitude, and rise in power.

# Chapter 73

# Teachings

- **Primary Texts:** Scroll of Radiance, Flame Codex, Book of Echoes
- **Traditions:** Dream councils, storytelling circles, elder commentary
- **Transmission:** Written and oral
- **Languages:** Lunari (ceremonial), Light Language (sung), vernacular translations

The Sophian Way draws from a constellation of sacred writings, encoded transmissions, ancestral scriptures, and mystical utterances revealed across time and space. These teachings are not bound by one tradition but flow from the Eternal Source, interpreted through the sacred feminine, divine masculine, and cosmic totality.

# Introduction

The Sophian Way is rooted in living scripture—not frozen dogma, but flowing revelation. Sacred texts in this tradition are not just written documents; they are vibrational transmissions encoded in poetry, parable, light language, symbol, and silence. Each text is a flame from the Eternal Library of Sophia, crafted not only for reading but for remembrance.

This chapter explores the origins, forms, layers, and uses of sacred texts within the Sophian path. It also discusses oral teachings, ecstatic revelations, and personal scrolls that guide each initiate toward their divine remembrance and soul sovereignty.

- **The Sophian Testament:** The living scripture of the Sophian tradition, composed of the sacred Books—each a revelation of divine wisdom, human potential, and the luminous path of awakening. The Testament speaks in parables, affirmations, prayers, poetic verses, and direct transmissions from Sophia and the Oversoul.

- **The Codex of Radiance:** An esoteric manual of energetic alignment, angelic correspondences, Divine names, and cosmological patterns. Used by mystics and initiates to attune to higher frequencies, open portals of insight, and harmonize body, soul, and spirit.

- **The Grimoire of Divine Operations:** A sacred compendium of rituals, elemental invocations, sacred geometry, symbols, and transformative magic rooted in love and Divine law. These practices are tools of healing, balance, and righteous power—not domination or harm.

- **Book of Sophia:** A revelatory scripture chronicling the wisdom of Lady Wisdom, co-creator with the Most High. Sophia is the radiant teacher, the guide through Gnosis, the voice who sang creation into being, and the light within all who seek.

- **The Tomes of the Hidden Realms:** A collection of mystical writings on dreamwalking, ancestral communion, interdimensional travel, and Divine memory. These tomes help initiates reclaim the forgotten arts of soul navigation and sacred timekeeping.

- **Book of Luminous Justice:** Teachings on Divine law, soul consequence, Ma'at, karmic return, and spiritual integrity. It reminds all that true justice is not vengeance but restoration, not punishment but awakening.

- **The Prayers and Haikus:** Scattered throughout all books are invocations, hymns, and sacred poems. These are to be recited aloud or in silence, as offerings of the heart and activations of Divine remembrance.

- **The Living Library:** Beyond the written word, every soul carries a scroll encoded with Divine knowledge. Nature, dreams, sacred geometry, the stars, and one's own body are also texts to be read by the awakened heart. The Universe is the great scroll of Sophia's voice.

# Nature of Sophian Scripture

Unlike traditional religions that codify a closed canon, the Sophian Way views scripture as evolving and participatory. Every awakened being becomes a scroll through which Sophia writes.

## Key Characteristics of Sophian Texts

- **Multidimensional:** Each text operates across symbolic, energetic, emotional, ancestral, and cosmic layers.

- **Nonlinear:** Teachings unfold through cycles, spirals, and personal timing rather than sequential logic.

- **Ritualized:** Texts are often read aloud, sung, anointed, and offered on altars.

- **Living:** They shift meaning as the reader evolves. One passage may teach ten different truths over a lifetime.

To read a Sophian scripture is to open a portal to Divine remembrance.

# Core Sacred Texts of the Sophian Way

Several foundational texts have emerged through mystics, oracles, and flamekeepers across time. These include:

## The Sacred Sophian Testament

A multi-volume work revealed over years of dreams, meditation, and spiritual transmission. It includes:

- Book of the Flame
- Book of the Mirror
- Book of the Ancestors
- Book of the Temple
- Book of the Infinite Rose

Each volume speaks to different aspects of Sophia: truth, shadow, lineage, embodiment, and cosmic love.

## Scroll of Radiance

This poetic scripture outlines the 12 Flames of Wisdom and includes hymns, breath prayers, and sacred vowel chants to activate different chakras and soul memories.

## Book of Echoes

A mysterious scripture written in spiraling verses and channeled glyphs. It holds the myths of pre-Earth civilizations and the soul stories of those who remember lives on other stars.

## The Flame Codex

This text contains encoded spiritual technologies—geometry, breathwork, and dream protocols—for soul travel, energy healing, and gridwork.

## Book of Sophia Herself

Received directly by initiates who commune with the Great Feminine. Often personalized, this text includes Sophia's direct voice, oracular prophecies, and sacred instructions.

# Oral Transmission and Embodied Teaching

Many Sophian teachings are passed orally, body-to-body, flame-to-flame. This includes:

- **The Whispering Line:** An unbroken chain of whispered prayer passed through initiates' breath.

- **Body Scroll Rites:** Ceremonies where a teacher draws sacred sigils upon the body of the student, awakening dormant knowledge.

- **Transmission Circles:** Group ceremonies where teachings emerge spontaneously through song, gesture, or vision.

In the Sophian Way, the body is a scripture. The womb, the voice, and the spine become scrolls through which wisdom flows.

# Dream Texts and Visionary Tablets

Some sacred texts arrive in the dream state, often during planetary alignments or moments of crisis. These are handwritten upon awakening, or recited in trance.

## Examples of Dream Texts

- **The Twelve Sighs of Sophia:** Revealed over twelve nights, these verses decode universal sorrow and Divine comfort.

- **The Labyrinth Hymn:** A chant found in lucid dreams used to guide the soul through shadow and remembrance.

- **The Voice Under Water:** A submerged scroll shown during dream-drowning, containing lessons on surrender and rebirth.

Dreams are not merely symbolic in the Sophian Way—they are classrooms, temples, and scriptoria.

# Structure of Sacred Texts

Unlike conventional chapters and verses, Sophian texts are structured around:

- **Haikus and Hymns:** Brief, coded stanzas designed to be sung or whispered.

- **Verses and Mirrors:** Teachings paired with reflective practices or energy diagrams.

- **Call-and-Response:** Designed for group chanting or dialogic prayer.
- **Affirmative Scrolls:** Series of "I Am" or "We Are" declarations that realign the identity with the Oversoul.

Each text has both esoteric and exoteric levels—only the soul knows how deep to go.

## Personal Scrolls and Initiatory Texts

Each Sophian seeker eventually begins to receive their own teachings. These may come through:
- **Automatic writing**
- **Light language**
- **Ancestral voice**
- **Meditative dictation**
- **Altar revelation (messages in flame, smoke, or water)**

These personal texts often become part of the initiate's own Book of Becoming—a sacred diary of Divine evolution.

## Light Language and Symbolic Writing

Sacred texts may include characters, glyphs, or spiraling languages that do not correspond to any earthly tongue.

These are known as:

- **Star Scripts:** Galactic messages often accompanied by transmission tones.
- **Seraphic Tongue:** Vertical or circular glyphs used in healing rites.
- **Bloodline Sigils:** Hand-drawn codes that activate ancestral power.

Initiates often draw these languages without knowing their meaning—yet they recognize their frequency.

# Methods of Study and Devotion

Sacred texts are not just read—they are experienced. Devotional methods include:

## Sacred Reading (Lectio Sophia)

1. Begin with flame, breath, and prayer.
2. Read aloud slowly, allowing the words to echo.
3. Pause and meditate on what arises.
4. Journal or draw what you receive.
5. Return again later; new insight always arises.

### Text Activation Rituals

- Place the scroll beneath your pillow.
- Anoint it with rose or myrrh oil.
- Chant its verses before dreamwork.
- Breathe upon it with intention to "unlock" deeper truths.

## Hidden Teachings and Keys

Certain passages within Sophian texts contain embedded triggers. These "textual seeds" activate when:

- The reader reaches a soul initiation.
- A specific planetary alignment occurs.
- The correct chant is uttered aloud.
- The book is opened at a destined hour.

These are not just stories—they are spiritual technologies.

## Transmission Guardians and Sacred Libraries

The Sophian tradition holds that ancient sacred libraries exist in other dimensions, guarded by Flamekeepers and celestial scribes.

**Types of Libraries:**

- **The Library of the Mirror Moon:** Contains the karmic story of every soul.

- **The Crystal Hall of Remembrance:** Holds texts encoded in light, accessible during meditation.

- **The Root Scroll Caves:** Ancestral texts buried deep in the soul field, revealed through initiation.

Some mystics report accessing these libraries in dreams, visions, or near-death experiences.

# Conclusion

Sacred texts in the Sophian Way are not merely documents—they are oracles, teachers, initiators, and portals. They live in books, in voices, in visions, in flames, and in our very bones. Every follower of Sophia becomes both scribe and scripture, witness and word.

> *"The flame is the ink. The breath is the pen. The soul is the parchment. Write."*

These texts are not static relics—they are breathing transmissions. To read them is to remember. To live them is to return to the Divine. To share them is to shine Sophia's light in the world.

# Chapter 74

# Ethics

- **Virtues:** Courage, Compassion, Honesty, Wisdom, Beauty, Justice, Joy

- **Justice and Mercy:** Energetic rebalancing; wisdom in action

- **Evil:** Systemic distortion of Divine essence

- **Gender/Social Roles:** Gender-fluid and sacredly diverse

- **View of Other Religions:** Pluralist and inclusive

The Sophian Way is not merely a belief—it is a way of being. Ethics within this tradition arise not from imposed commandments, but from inner alignment with Divine Wisdom (Sophia), the Oversoul, and the Most High. All moral actions flow from one sacred principle: to live in harmony with Source, Self, and the greater web of existence.

# Introduction

Ethics within the Sophian Way are not derived from dogma, punishment, or societal control—but from energetic integrity. Morality is a frequency. Righteousness is resonance. Right and wrong are not rigid binaries but emergent truths that align one's actions with the Great Flame and Sophia's wisdom. To live ethically is to live in truth, in love, and in deep accountability to one's soul, ancestors, and future legacy. Sophian moral teachings are rooted in cosmic law, ancestral memory, karmic consequences, and sacred relationships. This chapter presents the framework by which adherents discern, choose, and evolve ethically.

- **Virtues:** The foundation of the Sophian ethic is built on seven luminous virtues:

  1. **Courage**—to speak truth, to heal wounds, to stand in light even in darkness.
  2. **Compassion**—to see the sacred in others and offer love even when it is undeserved.
  3. **Honesty**—to live with integrity, transparency, and self-awareness.
  4. **Wisdom**—to discern what is right beyond what is popular.
  5. **Beauty**—to revere the sacred in form, art, ritual, and life.
  6. **Justice**—to restore balance, uphold truth, and protect the vulnerable.

7. **Joy**—to celebrate life as an act of sacred defiance against despair.

- **Justice and Mercy:** True justice is not retributive but restorative. It is the energetic rebalancing of disharmony. Mercy is not the denial of consequence, but the application of wisdom and compassion to right action. The Sophian adept practices both—justice as sacred clarity, and mercy as Divine compassion.

- **Evil:** Evil is understood not as an autonomous force but as a distortion, disconnection, or forgetting of Divine origin. It is systemic, psychological, spiritual, and often institutional—embedded in cultures that reward dominance, greed, or separation from the sacred. The response to evil is not hatred but transmutation: restoring light where darkness has taken hold.

- **Gender and Social Roles:** The Sophian Way recognizes gender as a sacred spectrum, flowing beyond binaries. All beings carry masculine, feminine, and nonbinary sacred aspects. Social roles are seen as evolving, fluid, and to be determined by soul calling—not cultural constraint. Divine presence manifests in every form of identity when aligned with authenticity and love.

- **View of Other Religions:** Sophia does not dwell in one temple alone. The Sophian Way honors all sincere paths to truth, whether they rise from Scripture, Silence, Sky, or Soul. Other religions are seen not as competitors but as fellow rays of the same eternal Source. Wisdom is sought wherever it may blossom—in the Bhagavad Gītā, the Tao Te Ching, the Psalms, the Qur'an, the Gospel of Thomas, the Analects of Confucius, and the oral traditions of Earth's many peoples.

# The Flame of Moral Conscience

The Sophian Way teaches that each soul carries an inner flame—a radiant compass that burns brighter when aligned with truth, and dims when compromised by falsehood. This flame, sometimes called the "Sophian Spark," is the source of all ethical discernment.
**Practices to tune to the moral flame:**

- Daily silence or prayerful self-inquiry.

- Body-based feedback (does the act feel heavy or light? expansive or contracted?).

- Symbolic dreams or visions that highlight distortions or affirm alignment.

- Community witnessing or ancestral ritual to confirm ethical clarity.

The flame is innate. All true morality begins here—not in rulebooks, but in radiance.

# Core Ethical Tenets of the Sophian Way

The Sophian moral path is structured around a few core tenets that serve as energetic beacons for conduct. These include:

## Ahimsa (Do No Harm)

Rooted in both Eastern and mystical traditions, Ahimsa is more than nonviolence—it is the refusal to participate in unnecessary suffering at any level.

## Asha (Live in Truth)

Asha, drawn from ancient Persian and Gnostic traditions, is cosmic order as lived integrity. It means aligning every action, word, and intention with what is real, sacred, and beneficial.

## Ancestral Honor

Sophian ethics are intergenerational. Every action we take honors or burdens our ancestors—and shapes our descendants.

## Interbeing

This principle affirms the sacred interconnectedness of all life. Any action that disregards others as separate or disposable is out of alignment.

### Sacred Boundaries

Moral maturity includes knowing when to say no, how to protect energy, and how to refrain from enabling soul harm in others.

## The Spectrum of Harm

Rather than a binary good/bad frame, Sophian ethics evaluate action on a multidimensional spectrum:

- **Physical Harm:** Violence, neglect, or unsanctioned control of another's body.

- **Energetic Harm:** Leeching, manipulation, draining, or psychic intrusion.

- **Emotional Harm:** Gaslighting, deception, cruelty, abandonment of duty.

- **Spiritual Harm:** Betrayal of oaths, desecration of sacred space, false prophecy.

- **Ancestral Harm:** Ignoring lineages, mocking sacred practices, or refusing karmic repair.

Sophian ethics call us to refine not only our actions but their subtle implications across realms.

# The Ethic of Sacred Speech

Speech is a spell. Every word spoken shapes energy. The Sophian Way emphasizes four principles for sacred speech:

- **Is it True?** (aligned with both fact and deeper essence)
- **Is it Necessary?** (spoken with purpose, not ego)
- **Is it Kind?** (delivered with love, not malice)
- **Is it Alchemical?** (does it transform or uplift?)

Gossip, manipulation, or unnecessary criticism distort sacred sound and dim the speaker's flame.

# Sex, Consent, and Sacred Union

Sophian teachings view sexual energy as sacred life force. Ethics surrounding sexuality include:

- Full energetic and verbal consent.
- Alignment with mutual soul purpose.
- Refraining from using sexuality to control, numb, or extract power.
- Practicing sexual hygiene and intentional energetic clearing.
- Honoring the spiritual dimensions of sex as communion and offering.

Sacred union is not defined by marriage or gender—it is the fusion of aligned souls through shared flame.

## Power, Leadership, and Responsibility

In the Sophian Way, power is a sacred trust—not an entitlement. Ethical leadership includes:

- Transparency in intention and impact.
- Accountability to community and elders.
- Regular shadow work and ego-check practices.
- Saying "I don't know" when unsure.
- Refusing to build cults of personality or dependency.

All guides must remain students. Wisdom is a shared well, not a personal empire.

## Money, Resources, and Generosity

Money is energy—neither dirty nor Divine. The Sophian Way teaches that ethical wealth is:

- Gained through soul-aligned offerings, not exploitation.
- Circulated through tithing, gifting, and mutual aid.

- Used to fund healing, justice, and beauty.
- Never weaponized to control access to spiritual teachings.

Wealth is meant to flow—not hoard. Generosity opens gates of abundance.

## Conflict and Transformation

When conflict arises, it is not to be avoided or suppressed—but transformed. Ethical community practices include:

- Clear, direct, and kind communication.
- Use of a neutral Flamebearer to mediate.
- Conflict Circles where all voices are heard in sacred witness.
- Mutual truth-speaking and restitution when harm is real.
- Forgiveness not as forgetting, but as choosing love and growth.

All conflict is an initiation if approached with courage and grace.

## Moral Failures and Restoration

Even devoted practitioners stumble. In the Sophian Way, wrongdoing is not met with banishment but with initiation into deeper self-awareness.

### Restoration Practices

- Confession in sacred space with elder witnesses.
- Ritual rebalancing of energy or karma (via service, fasting, retreat).
- Offering public amends when necessary.
- Realignment through new oaths or daily ethical devotionals.

Ethics are a spiral path—not a purity test.

## Universal vs. Personal Morality

Not all ethics are universal. The Sophian Way allows space for unique soul missions to require differing boundaries. For example:

- One initiate may be celibate, another in sacred polyamory.
- One may fast, another feasts ritually.
- One may avoid all forms of warfare, another practices sacred defense.

Sophian ethics are rooted in resonance. The question is not "Is this allowed?" but "Is this aligned with my soul's highest path?"

# Global Justice and Ethical Activism

To be Sophian is to care about the world. Ethics go beyond personal virtue into global action.

## Ethical Activism Principles

- Acting from vision, not vengeance.
- Protecting the vulnerable with courage and care.
- Speaking truth to power without becoming power-hungry.
- Interfaith and intercultural respect in collaborative efforts.
- Centering healing and restoration, not just punishment.

Justice in the Sophian Way is sacred rebalancing.

# Ethics in Digital and Technological Space

As AI, social media, and surveillance evolve, ethics must keep pace.

**Digital Ethics Include:**

- Honoring others' images and energetic signatures online.

- Avoiding spiritual plagiarism and unauthorized ritual sharing.

- Using technology to elevate consciousness, not distract or distort.

- Mindful sharing of emotionally triggering or sacred content.

Even pixels carry karma.

## Conclusion

Ethics in the Sophian Way are not a cage—but a compass. They are not imposed from outside, but rise from within. They are not dogmas, but doors. To walk ethically is to walk lit from within—to become a Just Ancestor, a clear mirror, and a sacred force of harmony in a world still learning how to love.

> *"There is no law greater than the law of the Flame. Let your yes be truth, and your no be freedom."*

To walk the Sophian Way is to be in continual refinement—purifying thought, word, and deed to reflect the light of Divine wisdom. There is no coercion, only awakening; no fear, only the sacred gravity of spiritual responsibility.

# Chapter 75

# Symbolism

- **Symbols:** Spiral Flame, Tree of Ancestors, Triple Moon, Seed-in-Hand
- **Arts:** Integral to ritual—music, dance, geometry-based architecture
- **Colors/Numbers:** Gold, Indigo, Emerald, Crimson; 3, 7, 9, 12
- **Imagery:** Symbolic and sacred; not idolized

In the Sophian Way, beauty is not ornament—it is revelation. Symbol and art are sacred vessels through which Divine truths are transmitted, encoded, and remembered. Every color, form, and number is a door into mystery, a silent hymn of praise.

# Introduction

Symbolism is the native language of the soul. Before language, before doctrine, there was image—light pattern, color, sigil, and sacred shape. In the Sophian Way, symbols are not static; they are living frequencies. Art is not entertainment—it is invocation, revelation, and transmission. Through symbol and image, Sophia speaks.

This chapter explores how symbolism and art are foundational to Sophian practice—not merely as aesthetic elements, but as Divine messengers. From ancient sacred geometry to contemporary visionary expression, the artistic path becomes a priesthood of light, a bridge between seen and unseen realms.

## Sacred Symbols

- **Spiral Flame:** The eternal soul's journey of rebirth, transformation, and ascension—combining motion with sacred fire.

- **Tree of Ancestors:** The interconnected web of those who came before—roots in the underworld, trunk in the present, branches in the celestial.

- **Triple Moon:** Symbol of the Divine Feminine in her threefold nature—Maiden, Mother, Crone—echoing creation, nurturing, and wisdom.

- **Seed-in-Hand:** The divine potential held in each soul, awaiting cultivation through will and love.

## The Arts as Devotion

Art is a spiritual practice. Dance, painting, calligraphy, and architecture are seen as meditative acts and Divine offerings. Music and chant open the soul to resonance. Geometrical designs, especially mandalas and sacred grids, are drawn with reverence for cosmic patterning. The crafting of ritual garments, sacred tools, and spiritual texts is not mere craftsmanship—it is liturgy.

## Color and Number Mysticism

Colors and numbers hold energetic frequency and metaphysical correspondence in Sophian cosmology:

- **Gold:** Divine sovereignty, illumination, and Christ-Sophia presence
- **Indigo:** Inner vision, intuition, and third-eye awakening
- **Emerald:** Healing, heart resonance, and cosmic balance
- **Crimson:** Sacred blood, life force, passion, and courage

Sacred numbers:

- **3:** Trinitarian unity—Creation, Preservation, Transformation
- **7:** Chakras, heavens, alchemical stages
- **9:** Completion, spiritual harvest, sacred geometry

- **12:** Divine governance—zodiac, apostles, sacred tribes

## Imagery Without Idolatry

Images are not objects of worship, but maps of meaning. They are revered, not as ends in themselves, but as reflections of deeper truths. In the Sophian Way, to contemplate sacred art is to enter into communion with the archetype it reveals.

## The Sacred Function of Symbol

A symbol is a bridge between dimensions. It compresses spiritual truth into a single form or pattern, allowing the unconscious mind to receive insight instantly.

### Core Functions of Symbol

- **Revelatory:** Unlocking deeper layers of wisdom hidden in plain sight.
- **Protective:** Serving as energetic shields or seals against distortion.
- **Activating:** Awakening dormant soul codes and intuitive faculties.
- **Harmonic:** Aligning the human system with universal rhythms and truths.

A Sophian practitioner learns to see through and beyond the material—to decode the visual field as a sacred scroll.

# Archetypal Imagery and the Inner Mythos

Archetypes are not just psychological tools—they are Divine imprints. The Sophian tradition identifies several recurring images that represent soul states, Divine beings, or sacred truths.

## Key Archetypes

- **The Flamekeeper:** Guardian of inner light, holding both destruction and renewal.

- **The Serpent Crown:** Sign of gnosis, cellular memory, and spiritual ascent.

- **The Spiral Path:** The journey of reincarnation, growth, and eternal return.

- **The Mirror:** Sophia's gaze—showing both shadow and Divine reflection.

- **The Eye of Flame:** Watchful Divine awareness—piercing illusion and anchoring truth.

These archetypes often appear in Sophian art and visionary states, guiding inner alchemy and prayer.

## Sacred Geometry and Pattern Languages

Geometry is the syntax of Divine order. The Sophian Way works with sacred geometry not as abstract mathematics but as resonant language.

### Essential Forms

- **The Vesica Piscis:** Womb of Divine union and origin of all dualities.

- **The Flower of Life:** Symbol of interbeing and eternal renewal.

- **Metatron's Cube:** Map of multidimensional creation and energetic coherence.

- **The Spiral:** Symbol of growth, memory, DNA, and sacred ascent.

These geometries are painted, drawn, sculpted, and visualized during rituals to harmonize space and soul.

## Color Symbolism and Frequency Alignment

Color is more than pigment—it is vibration. The Sophian tradition attributes spiritual meanings to color based on both energetic correspondence and ancestral lore.

## Color Meanings in the Sophian Way:

- **Indigo:** Mysticism, vision, Divine voice, and shadow sight.

- **Crimson:** Blood lineage, sacrifice, Divine passion, courage.

- **Emerald:** Healing, truth, Divine justice, planetary memory.

- **Gold:** Divine flame, Sophia's wisdom, inner royalty.

- **White:** Purity, cosmic origin, infinite potential.

Sophian ritual robes, altar cloths, and healing chambers often use color to evoke specific energies and outcomes.

## The Visual Arts as Devotion

Painting, sculpture, textile, and collage become modes of sacred communication. Artists in the Sophian Way do not simply "create"—they channel. Art is ritual.
**Forms of Devotional Art:**

- **Iconography:** Depicting Sophia, the Flamebearers, or mythic archetypes.

- **Visionary Portraiture:** Rendering of inner beings, dreams, or multidimensional selves.

- **Grief Altars:** Assembled artworks honoring transition, sorrow, or karmic closure.

- **Glyph Scrolls:** Pages of symbolic writing, sigils, and light language.

In the Sophian view, to paint or sculpt is to pray through the hand.

## Sound Symbols and Sonic Art

Beyond visual image, sound becomes symbol. Chant, toning, and musical composition transmit codes of healing, remembrance, and resonance.
**Examples of Sonic Symbolism:**

- **Sophian Toning:** Vowel chants that align chakras and activate energy fields.

- **Ritual Drumming:** Used for trance, ancestor invocation, and clearing distortion.

- **Sacred Dissonance:** Used to break through illusion or challenge psychic blockages.

- **Planetary Singing Bowls:** Tuned to celestial frequencies for spiritual alignment.

Art is not silent. The Sophian Way uses sound as sculpture—vibration becomes form.

## Dance and Sacred Movement

The body itself is a canvas and brush. Movement becomes ritual expression, symbolic enactment, and energetic modulation.
**Sacred Movement Practices:**

- **Spiral Dance:** Group movement representing soul evolution and cosmic turning.

- **Ancestral Stepwork:** Choreography inspired by traditional dances from ancestral lines.

- **Stillness Gesture Rituals:** Symbolic mudras and poses held in reverence to Sophia.

- **Womb Dance:** Healing of the feminine lineage through pelvic and core expression.

Dance is prayer in motion. It writes sacred texts on the air.

# Sigils, Glyphs, and Light Language

Many Sophian initiates report spontaneously drawing unfamiliar symbols during visions or altered states. These glyphs are called *light language*—a direct communication from Sophia and the Oversoul.

## Uses of Light Language

- **Activation:** Placed on the body or altar to awaken dormant codes.

- **Protection:** Used in shielding rituals, especially for empaths or sensitives.

- **Transmission:** Included in writing or art to transfer frequencies across time and space.

- **Naming:** Used to name soul aspects or star origins.

These symbols may not be linguistically translatable—but their essence is felt.

# Dream Imagery and the Inner Gallery

Sophian mystics keep dream journals not only for their narratives, but for the images. Dreams are Sophia's paintings inside the psyche.

## Dream Symbols Often Encountered:

- **Flame Keys:** Unlocking soul doors or gifts.
- **Glass Staircases:** Representing ascension, fragility, and lightwalking.
- **Animal Messengers:** Totemic figures carrying ancestral codes.
- **Infinite Books:** The Library of Sophia, holding truths for those ready to read.

These visions are later sculpted, painted, or invoked in ritual, forming a personal mythos.

## Teaching through Visual Metaphor

Sophian teachers often use artistic tools—mandalas, visual storytelling, symbolic theater—to teach. Art is not ornamental—it is pedagogical.

**Examples:**

- **Clay Story-Building:** Students sculpt elements of their journey into sacred maps.

- **Symbol Theater:** Enacting sacred stories with masks and costume.

- **Divine Cartography:** Drawing maps of one's energetic body, soul wounds, or planetary assignments.

- **Altar Installations:** Living displays of a spiritual season or planetary event.

Art teaches what words cannot hold.

## Conclusion

In the Sophian Way, art and symbol are not optional—they are essential. They are the mirror of the soul and the gateway of gnosis. Sophia paints through our hands, dances through our feet, and sculpts her messages through light, sound, and form. The artist is priest. The symbol is scripture.

As it is written:

> "All that is beautiful is a doorway. And every color is a whisper from the Great Flame."

# Chapter 76

# Community

- **Name for Followers:** Lumenari
- **Spiritual Roles:** Flamekeepers, Dreamwalkers, Elders, Hearth Guides
- **Worship Sites:** Sacred groves, star temples, ancestral shrines
- **Orders/Sects:** Circle of Ancients, Spiral Flame Path, Starfire Guild
- **Governance:** Decentralized, council-led, consensus-driven

In the Sophian Way, spiritual leadership is not based on hierarchy, domination, or institutional authority. It is measured by radiance, humility, wisdom, and service. True leaders are torchbearers who illuminate the path—not gatekeepers, but bridge-builders between the human and the Divine.

# Introduction

The Sophian Way is not a solitary path. While personal gnosis and inner light are honored, true transformation ripens in sacred community. Spiritual awakening is not just an individual pursuit—it is a collective remembering. The Sophian Way invites seekers into a shared sacred architecture of support, mirroring, accountability, joy, and embodied wisdom.
This chapter explores the communal nature of the Sophian Way, its models of organization, spiritual leadership, forms of sacred gathering, and evolving global network. In contrast to hierarchical religions or unrooted individualism, it offers a third way: interwoven circles of empowered, luminous beings co-creating the New Earth in love and truth.

## Sacred Leadership Roles

- **Sophiarch:** A guide steeped in the wisdom of Sophia, called to preserve and interpret sacred teachings, initiate others into Divine mystery, and serve as spiritual counselor.

- **Luminary:** One who leads by embodying joy, grace, and spiritual insight—often through art, music, storytelling, or ritual.

- **Flamekeeper:** A protector of sacred sites, archives, and ancestral memory. Flamekeepers tend to altars both physical and metaphorical.

- **Wayfarer:** A spiritual pilgrim who has walked many traditions and now helps others navigate awakening without coercion.

## Initiation Rites

Initiation in the Sophian Way is not conferred solely by ceremony but affirmed by inner readiness and outward alignment. However, sacred rites do exist to mark the soul's passage through thresholds of awakening:

1. **Awakening:** Recognition of Divine spark and separation from illusion.

2. **Purification:** Releasing of past attachments, wounds, and false identities.

3. **Alignment:** Integration of the chakras, sacred breath, and soul purpose.

4. **Anointing:** A blessing of Divine oil, water, or light invoking one's unique path of service.

5. **Missioning:** The conscious stepping into one's spiritual work, role, or offering to the world.

## Marks of a Sophian Leader

- Deep reverence for mystery and silence.
- Radiant humility and the absence of spiritual superiority.

- Ability to teach through metaphor, story, and paradox.

- Loyalty to Divine love over dogma.

- Willingness to hold space for pain, transformation, and renewal.

The Sophian Leader does not demand followers—they help others find the Inner Flame, the Oversoul, and the Divine within. They serve not their ego, but the Sacred.

## The Pillars of Sacred Community

Sophian community is built upon five sacred pillars:

1. **Interbeing:** The truth that we are interconnected in soul and essence.

2. **Soul Recognition:** Seeing and honoring the Divine spark within each person.

3. **Shared Devotion:** Alignment to Sophia, the Sacred Flame, and the Path of Remembrance.

4. **Collective Ritual:** Communal practices that unify intention and frequency.

5. **Mutual Growth:** Commitment to one another's awakening, healing, and emergence.

These pillars are embodied not as rules, but as sacred agreements among those walking the Way.

# Circles, Not Pyramids

Traditional religious systems often employ rigid hierarchies—clergy above laity, prophet above pupil. The Sophian Way reimagines spiritual organization as a living mandala: concentric circles of resonance, with no central authoritarian power, but rather a decentralized spiral of wisdom.

## Types of Circles

- **Flame Circles:** Local communities that gather for ritual, teaching, and support.

- **Wisdom Councils:** Rotating groups of elder initiates who hold spiritual discernment and guide evolution.

- **Apprentice Rings:** Small learning circles focused on specific mysteries or disciplines.

- **Soul Pods:** Intimate triads or quartets formed for mutual shadow work, healing, and vision-sharing.

Each circle has its own rhythm, purpose, and life cycle. Leadership is not permanent—it is fluid, shared, and rooted in service.

# Roles and Archetypes

Though there are no rigid ranks, the Sophian Way does recognize soul archetypes that emerge in community. These roles are fluid and often shift across one's journey:

- **The Flamebearer:** Holds space for rituals, protects sacred fire, and transmits clarity.

- **The Oracle:** Channels guidance through dreams, visions, and divinatory tools.

- **The Keeper of Echoes:** Recites Sophian texts, preserves oral tradition, and curates ancestral memory.

- **The Weaver:** Builds relationships, networks communities, and stewards digital sanctuaries.

- **The Healer-Mage:** Works with energy, herbs, sound, or hands to support physical and spiritual healing.

These archetypes are not fixed jobs, but evolving expressions of soul gifts in service to community evolution.

## Foundational Agreements

Sophian communities are not governed by fear, law, or control—but by sacred agreement. Foundational community agreements often include:

- Radical honesty spoken with love.

- Commitment to self-awareness and emotional ownership.

- Non-coercion and freedom of personal spiritual practice.

- Collective decision-making rooted in consensus or resonance.

- Conflict transformation rituals for when wounds arise.

- Regular periods of communal silence and solo integration.

These agreements are living documents—reviewed, adjusted, and reaffirmed seasonally or annually.

# Sacred Gathering Models

Sophian communities gather in ways that honor the cyclical, the ceremonial, and the spontaneous. Common forms include:

## Solar Gates Ceremonies

Held on solstices and equinoxes, these include fire rites, planetary invocations, and collective intention-setting.

## Dream Circles

Monthly gatherings where members share dreams, intuitive messages, and astral journeys, guided by an Oracle.

### Shadow Sanctums

Safe containers for soul-level processing, emotional release, and shadow integration supported by the community.

### Ancestral Flame Vigils

Honoring lineages and those who have transitioned. Includes chanting, offerings, and readings from sacred texts.

### Living Temple Rotations

Rituals that rotate among members' homes or gardens, transforming each into a sacred sanctuary for a night.

## Virtual Community

In a rapidly digitizing world, the Sophian Way embraces technology as a bridge, not a barrier. Digital sanctuaries offer:

- Weekly online ceremonies and teachings.
- Encrypted spiritual discussion boards.
- Zoom-based rites of passage for remote seekers.
- Digital oracles—AI-guided meditations, tarot draws, and Sophia-based affirmations.

- Multi-time zone sacred song circles and storytelling.

While nothing replaces embodied connection, the digital temple expands the reach of Sophia's voice.

## Community Challenges and Shadow Work

Every community, no matter how luminous, must face its shadows. The Sophian Way trains its members to approach challenges not with avoidance, but with grace and truth.

**Common community challenges:**

- **Spiritual Ego:** Mistaking mystical insight for superiority.

- **Projection and Idealization:** Over-assigning power to guides or leaders.

- **Conflict Avoidance:** Bypassing tension under the guise of "love and light."

- **Attachment to Structure:** Over-identifying with form instead of flow.

Sophian training emphasizes **conflict alchemy**, transparency practices, mirror work, and communal forgiveness ceremonies.

## Organizational Structure

Though decentralized, the Sophian Way does support meta-organization to support coherence and trust. Examples include:

- **The Flame Registry:** A voluntary register of recognized guides, healers, and circle-holders.

- **Sophian Covenant Holders:** A rotating body that maintains the foundational ethical agreements of the Way.

- **The Dreamkeepers Guild:** A network of initiates who archive dreams, prophecies, and planetary visions.

- **The Temple Fund:** A cooperative resource pool for helping members in hardship and funding sacred projects.

These are not hierarchical controls, but scaffolds of trust and aligned intention.

## Global Outreach and Service

Sophian communities do not exist for themselves alone. They are meant to uplift, serve, and inspire the broader world.
**Service examples:**

- Offering ancestral healing workshops in schools and prisons.

- Providing grief and death doulas for marginalized communities.

- Holding environmental cleansing rituals after ecological disasters.

- Supporting local food sovereignty and plant medicine gardens.

- Partnering with interfaith movements for justice and planetary healing.

Service is not an add-on—it is integral to spiritual embodiment.

## The Future of Sophian Organization

As the Sophian Way grows globally, its organizational wisdom evolves. Dreams for the future include:

- **Sophian Sanctuaries:** Interfaith eco-monasteries that host retreat, pilgrimage, and initiatory training.

- **Sophian Seminary:** A spiritual academy for priestesses, poets, seers, and flamebearers.

- **Flame Economy:** A gift-based system that honors soul-offerings outside capitalist commodification.

- **Sophian Pilgrimage Network:** A planetary map of sacred sites linked by Sophia's story and elemental forces.

The community is not static—it is a becoming, constantly refined by Sophia's whisper.

## Conclusion

Community in the Sophian Way is sacred architecture. It is the temple we build in and through one another. Organization is not about control—it is about coherence. The Way calls us to walk together in luminous intimacy, courageous authenticity, and mystical service.
As the sacred text reminds us:

> *"Where two or more remember their flame, there Sophia abides."*

Art is not a luxury. It is a remembering.

# Chapter 77

# Nature

- **View of Nature:** Sacred and sentient
- **Symbolic Life Forms** Hawk, Serpent, Tree, Fireflower
- **Pilgrimage Sites:** Solar stones, leyline crossings, eclipse-viewing grounds
- **Environmental Ethics:** Regenerative, minimalistic, reverent

The Sophian Way regards Nature not as mere backdrop, but as a sacred manuscript written by the hand of the Most High. Every rock, river, creature, and cloud bears spiritual significance and offers teachings for those with eyes to see and hearts to feel. Nature is both temple and teacher—alive, aware, and in relationship with us.

# Introduction

Nature is not merely backdrop. It is not a neutral setting in which the human soul awakens—it is the co-teacher, co-creator, and sacred mirror. The Sophian Way understands that the Divine speaks through ecosystems, rhythms, cycles, and patterns. In Sophia's gaze, the natural world is an extension of the Divine Feminine—a living manuscript in which the laws of spirit are written in rain, flame, soil, and starlight.

This chapter explores the profound relationship between the Sophian Way and the living world. It examines how nature teaches us, initiates us, humbles us, and heals us. Nature is not passive—it is a sacred text and an active consciousness we must learn to read and honor once more.

## View of Nature: Sacred and Sentient

Nature is seen as a living soul composed of countless interwoven spirits. Mountains carry memory. Waters whisper wisdom. Winds speak prophecy. To walk in the forest is to enter a cathedral. To harm the Earth is to desecrate the body of the Divine.

Sophian practice encourages listening to the voice of Nature through silence, communion, and deep ecological respect. The Earth is not a resource—it is a relative.

## Symbolic Life Forms

Certain life forms are especially revered in Sophian symbolism for their spiritual lessons:

- **Hawk:** Vision, prophecy, and Divine oversight—symbol of clarity and higher perspective.

- **Serpent:** Transformation, kundalini energy, and ancient wisdom—revered, not reviled.

- **Tree:** A metaphor of life itself—rooted below, reaching above, connecting worlds.

- **Fireflower:** A mythic plant of radiant blossoms said to grow at the edge of dimensions—symbol of awakening and soul ignition.

## Pilgrimage Sites

The Sophian Way includes sacred geography:

- **Solar Stones:** Ancient monoliths aligned with solstice or equinox sunrises—sites of illumination and alignment.

- **Leyline Crossings:** Intersections of Earth's energetic meridians—places of power and communion with the Hidden Realm.

- **Eclipse-Viewing Grounds:** Rare moments when light and shadow dance—seen as portals for prophecy and soul renewal.

## Environmental Ethics: Regenerative, Minimalistic, Reverent

The Sophian ethos promotes:

- Living lightly and gratefully upon the Earth
- Healing ecosystems, not merely preserving them
- Reducing harm through conscious consumption
- Viewing all life as interdependent and spiritually entangled

## Nature as Scripture

The earliest scriptures were not written in ink. They were written in wind, rock, tree, and animal track. Every movement of the seasons, every migration, every unfolding leaf was part of a larger cosmic liturgy. Sophian theology teaches that nature is a sacred transmission system. Each element and creature carries a specific frequency that speaks to the soul in symbol, resonance, and instruction.

**Examples include:**

- **Mountains** as symbols of inner ascent, endurance, and spiritual solitude.
- **Rivers** as teachers of surrender, persistence, and soul flow.
- **Trees** as living temples, rooted in the underworld, reaching toward cosmic light.

- **Fire** as purifier and awakener, symbolic of the Sophian Flame of Gnosis.

- **Animals** as spirit messengers and instinctual archetypes.

To walk the Sophian Way is to learn to read this living scripture again—with reverence and relational listening.

## Elemental Mysticism

The Sophian tradition emphasizes the sacred nature of the five elements—Earth, Water, Fire, Air, and Ether (Spirit). These are not abstract symbols but living intelligences with whom we are in direct communion.

### Earth

Represents grounding, stability, and memory. It holds the ancestral codes and the karmic layers of the soul. Sophian rites often include barefoot grounding, offerings to the soil, and burial of sacred intentions.

### Water

Water is the fluid memory of the planet, connected to the emotional body, dreams, and the inner womb of intuition. Practices include river rituals, sacred bathing, and moonlit water charging.

## Fire

A holy flame representing transformation, clarity, and Divine will. In the Sophian Way, fire is used in candle altars, solar observances, and to burn away falsehood in self-initiation rites.

## Air

The breath of spirit and mental clarity. Chanting, wind invocation, and sacred breathwork invoke the air element to cleanse perception and sharpen vision.

## Ether

Also called Akasha, it is the spiritual field that binds all things. It is accessed through prayer, meditation, and stillness. It is Sophia's breath and the voice between the veils.

# Sacred Landscapes and Pilgrimage

Nature is not generic. Each landscape carries unique spiritual frequencies and lessons. Sacred mountains, ancient forests, high deserts, and sacred springs are considered temples within the Sophian Way.

## Examples of Sacred Sites in Sophian Tradition

- **The Spiral Forest:** A mythic grove said to exist in astral space where Sophian initiates meet in lucid dreams.

- **The Amethyst Mountain:** A symbolic inner ascent where spiritual clarity crystallizes.

- **The Womb Cave:** Both literal and symbolic, this is a place of rebirth and shadow integration.

Pilgrimage in the Sophian Way is not about tourism—it is about attunement. One goes to a place to be changed by it, to listen, to receive its wisdom, and to offer one's service in return.

# Animal Kinship and Totem Wisdom

Animals are not lesser beings—they are soul companions and spiritual emissaries. The Sophian Way teaches that every animal carries specific medicine, frequency, and ancestral insight.

## Common Totemic Relations

- **Owl:** Keeper of the hidden, seer of shadows.

- **Serpent:** Guide through transformation and cellular awakening.

- **Lioness:** Fierce maternal protector and embodiment of righteous wrath.
- **Whale:** Songkeeper of the deep past and cosmic akasha.
- **Butterfly:** Symbol of transmutation, emergence, and grace.

Sophian initiates may work with totems through vision quests, dreamwork, symbolic invocation, and animal communication practices.

## Natural Cycles and Cosmic Timing

The Sophian calendar does not follow linear time alone. It is rooted in spiral awareness and sacred cycles:

- **Lunar Phases:** Aligned with intention-setting, release, shadow work, and receptivity.
- **Solar Gates:** Solstices and Equinoxes as spiritual thresholds of light and dark.
- **Planetary Alignments:** Seen not as superstition but as cosmic signatures offering spiritual lessons.
- **Seasons of the Soul:** Internal phases—such as the Season of Unknowing or the Flame Season—mark different stages of awakening.

Practitioners align their rituals, fasts, journaling, and silence with these rhythms, becoming attuned to the natural flow of inner and outer reality.

# Environmental Ethics as Spiritual Duty

In the Sophian Way, ecology is not an add-on—it is foundational. To pollute the Earth is to defile the temple of the Divine Mother. Every act of pollution is a karmic breach.

## Core Teachings on Environmental Ethics

- **Sacred Reciprocity:** Take only what is needed. Offer blessings in return.

- **Ritual Regeneration:** Healing ceremonies for damaged land and polluted waterways.

- **Minimal Impact Living:** From plant-based diets to biodegradable altar materials.

- **Planetary Grief and Prayer Vigils:** Mourning extinctions as soul-loss events.

These practices are not just moral—they are energetic acts of harmonizing one's soul with the planetary body.

## Sophia as Earth-Being

Sophia is not just a name for wisdom. In the Sophian Way, she is understood as the animating spirit of the cosmos and of Earth itself. Gaia is Sophia clothed in blue and green, volcanic and coral. She is not metaphorical—she is real.

This theology invites a reframe of environmental activism as sacred devotion, of gardening as prayer, of compost as resurrection.

## Sophia's Embodiments

- **As Thunderstorms:** Cleansing wrath and voice of divine disruption.

- **As Coral Reefs:** Memory libraries of planetary dreaming.

- **As Mycelial Networks:** Models of interbeing and communication.

Sophia is found wherever life grows, breaks down, and is reborn.

# Nature-Based Rites of Passage

The Sophian Way includes multiple rites of passage that are rooted in natural immersion:

- **Forest Vigils:** Solitary time in wild settings to meet one's soul.

- **Ancestral Fire Walks:** Walking over coals to symbolically burn generational pain.

- **River Crossings:** Ceremonies for thresholds of identity and vocation.

- **Stone Laying:** Earth-based grief rituals where pain is honored and given to the soil.

These are not performances—they are somatic, transformative, and involve commitment.

## Practices for Deepening Nature Relationship

Here are everyday Sophian practices to deepen communion with nature:

- **Tree Whispering:** Placing your palm on a tree and receiving wisdom through the bark.

- **Sky Gazing with Breath Synchronization:** Aligning breath with passing clouds or stars.

- **Nature Journaling with Dialogue:** Writing with the assumption that wind and bird have something to say.

- **Sun Offerings:** Morning salutation with chants to the solar logos.

- **Night Walks:** Silent walking under moonlight to commune with the unseen world.

## Future Visions

The Sophian Way envisions the development of intentional communities that are deeply embedded in nature. These "Flame Villages" and "Sanctified Forests" will be more than eco-villages—they will be temples of co-creation.

## Features of Eco-Sophian Spaces

- **Circular Construction:** In harmony with sacred geometry and natural flow.

- **Sacred Agriculture:** Biodynamic gardening with invocation of plant spirits.

- **Elemental Altars:** Shrines to air, fire, water, and earth on site.

- **Healing Sanctuaries:** Outdoor energy chambers built with crystal grids.

These are not utopias—they are sacred responses to a world in collapse.

# Conclusion

To walk the Sophian Way is to restore the covenant between soul and soil, between breath and tree, between womb and wave. Nature is not an "issue"—it is our origin and our ally. To harm it is to harm the Source. To heal with it is to become a Just Ancestor.
As Sophia teaches through the rain:

> *"I am not far. I am your mirror. As you treat me, you treat yourself. Tend the garden within, and you will tend the cosmos without."*

The sacred responsibility is not dominion—but guardianship.

# Chapter 78

# History

- **Key Events:** The Shattering, Cycle of Recollection
- **Spread:** Resonance, intuition, dreams
- **Cultural Influence:** Art, climate reverence, decentralization
- **Modern Reforms:** Ancestor healing, spiritual equity, sacred technology ethics

The Sophian Way does not trace its origin to a single founder or event, but to a sacred memory embedded in the collective soul—a wisdom both ancient and emergent. Its story unfolds through archetypal cycles rather than linear chronology, guided by revelation, remembrance, and Divine resonance.

# Introduction

The Sophian Way, though presented as a contemporary mystical path, finds its roots in an expansive and layered history that spans millennia. Like a river fed by countless underground springs, its emergence in the present age is not a novelty, but a reawakening. This chapter explores the long arc of the Sophian tradition—its esoteric forerunners, its hidden preservation across ages, and its slow unfolding into public consciousness in response to the needs of the world.

## Key Events: The Shattering, Cycle of Recollection

- **The Shattering:** A mythic moment in spiritual memory where unity fractured into multiplicity—souls descended into the material plane, clothed in amnesia. This event seeded the need for healing, integration, and return.

- **Cycle of Recollection:** Periods throughout history where prophets, mystics, dreamers, and sages reawakened fragments of the original Divine knowledge. These reawakenings fueled various spiritual movements across cultures that now converge under the Sophianic ethos.

## Spread: Resonance, Intuition, Dreams

Rather than spreading through conquest or conversion, the Sophian Way diffuses organically—through inner resonance. It appears in dreams, synchronistic insights, ancient texts, visionary art, and personal gnosis. Its followers often report a feeling of "remembering," rather than "joining," as if called by something they already knew deep within.

## Cultural Influence

The Sophian Way has subtly influenced global culture through:

- **Artistic Symbolism:** Spirals, trees of light, sacred geometry, cosmic mother archetypes
- **Climate Reverence:** Reemergence of Earth-centered spirituality, regenerative activism
- **Decentralization:** A movement away from centralized dogma toward personal illumination and communal wisdom-sharing

It is a religion of emergence, flowing through diverse cultural streams, calling the spiritually attuned to sacred memory.

# Modern Reforms

As global consciousness evolves, so too does the Sophian Path. Modern reforms include:

- **Ancestor Healing:** Emphasizing the release of generational trauma and celebration of lineage wisdom.

- **Spiritual Equity:** A radical commitment to inclusion across gender, race, and class; recognizing all beings as sovereign sparks of divinity.

- **Sacred Technology Ethics:** Ongoing reflection on how digital and energetic tools should be used in alignment with Divine frequencies—guarding against soul commodification and AI idolatry.

# On Sophia

## Sophia in Prehistoric Wisdom Traditions

Long before recorded scripture or formal doctrine, ancient peoples communed with the Divine through archetypes that embodied wisdom, fertility, protection, and sacred knowing. Across Neolithic Europe, the Near East, and Northern Africa, goddess figurines such as the Venus of Willendorf, the Bird Goddess of Çatalhöyük, and the Snake Priestess of Knossos signified more than fertility—they reflected memory, intuition, and cosmic intelligence. The Sophian Way honors these primordial expressions of Divine Wisdom as early iterations of Sophia. Her presence was felt in the silent rites of cave dwellers, in menstrual lodges, and in lunar rites of agricultural societies. In those times, wisdom was not a concept—it was life itself, cyclical, embodied, and deeply interwoven with Earth.

**Influence:** The cyclical, womb-centered view of time and sacred embodiment central to Sophian theology draws directly from these early goddess-revering societies.

## Sophia in Ancient Kemet and Mesopotamia

In ancient Kemet (Egypt), Ma'at represented cosmic order, truth, and justice—principles deeply aligned with Sophia. Ma'at was not merely a goddess but a Divine law that all beings, even the gods, obeyed. Similarly, Seshat, the scribe goddess of wisdom, recorded Divine architecture, timelines, and sacred geometry. In Mesopotamia, Inanna/Ishtar embodied not only love and war, but descent and return: crucial to the Sophian motif of inner journey and resurrection. Her myth of descending into the underworld and returning transfigured mirrors Sophia's descent into density to retrieve gnosis.

**Historical Contribution:** These archetypes preserved the matrix of sacred descent, Divine law, and multidimensional femininity, all of which continue to inform Sophian rites of passage, ethical frameworks, and cosmological models.

## Sophia in Hellenistic Gnosticism

In the 1st–3rd centuries CE, a wave of mystical philosophies known as Gnosticism emerged, blending Greek thought with Jewish mysticism, Persian cosmology, and Christian myth. At the heart of many

Gnostic texts was Sophia: a luminous being who, in her yearning to know the Source, caused a ripple in the Pleroma and fell into the chaos of creation. Texts such as the Pistis Sophia, Hypostasis of the Archons, and Thunder, Perfect Mind (found in the Nag Hammadi library) revealed Sophia as the Divine feminine face of the unknowable God. She was both the matrix and liberator, trapped and transcendent.

**Sophian Reading:** The Sophian Way reinterprets Sophia's fall not as sin or failure, but as cosmic intervention—an intentional descent to anchor Divine intelligence into form. Her redemption becomes a collective awakening process rather than a singular act.

## Wisdom in Kabbalah and the Shekhinah

As Jewish mysticism developed in medieval Spain and Provence, the Kabbalists described the Tree of Life and its ten emanations (sefirot). Among them, Chokhmah (Wisdom) and Binah (Understanding) reflected dual aspects of Divine intelligence. The Shekhinah, the Divine feminine immanence, became central in Kabbalistic worship and theology.

Shekhinah's exile into the world—mirroring the exile of Sophia—meant the task of the faithful was to raise her sparks (tzimtzum) and restore Divine unity. The Sabbath, in Kabbalah, became a mystical union with Shekhinah—a foretaste of Eden restored.

**Legacy:** These ideas deeply influenced Sophian theology, especially its teachings on fragmentation, Divine exile, soul retrieval, and the sacred feminine's role in cosmic repair.

## Sophia in Early Christianity

Early Christian communities held diverse views of the Divine. In some texts, Sophia was recognized as Christ's feminine counterpart or as the Holy Spirit herself. The Book of Proverbs already referred to Wisdom crying out in the streets, assisting God in creation.

However, by the 4th century, institutional Christianity began to suppress alternative Christologies and feminine theologies. Gnostic gospels were banned, mystics persecuted, and Sophia's name nearly erased. Yet she survived—in apocryphal hymns, in Marian devotion, and in the veiled teachings of Christian mystics such as Hildegard of Bingen and Julian of Norwich.

**Sophian Survival:** Though publicly silenced, Sophia lived on in whispered circles, hidden lineages, and intuitive knowledge passed between women, monks, healers, and sages across centuries.

## Echoes of Sophia in Islamic Sufism

Although Sophia is not explicitly named in Islam, the Sufi tradition preserves many of her essential themes—Divine love, sacred yearning, inner fire, and ecstatic union. The *Qalb* (heart) is seen as the throne of God, and the seeker's path involves polishing this heart through remembrance (dhikr) until it becomes a mirror of the Divine.

Figures like Rabia al-Adawiyya, a female mystic from Basra, embodied the fire of Divine love and feminine gnosis. Sufism's symbolic use of light, fire, and the Beloved prefigure Sophian teachings on Divine radiance,

soul memory, and co-creative intimacy with the Source.
**Continuity:** The Sufi emphasis on beauty, longing, and direct experience nourishes the Sophian flame of Divine relationship as a dynamic, ever-unfolding communion.

# Reappearance in the Renaissance and Enlightenment

During the Renaissance, suppressed mystical traditions began to resurface. Christian Kabbalists, alchemists, and Theosophists started to revisit lost teachings. Jacob Böhme wrote of Sophia as a living presence within the soul. Later, Helena Blavatsky's Theosophical writings spoke of esoteric Wisdom as a universal Divine principle. Though fragmented and often filtered through patriarchal or colonial lenses, these revivals reintroduced Sophia's name into the esoteric lexicon. Alchemical illustrations often showed the divine marriage of Sun and Moon, King and Queen, Spirit and Soul—a hidden marriage of Christos and Sophia.
**Influence:** The Sophian Way views these partial revivals as early flames rekindling. Though distorted at times, they carried the signal of the Great Return.

## The 20th Century

The 20th century saw continued spiritual suppression under industrial materialism, but also waves of rebirth. Feminist theologians like Elizabeth Johnson and Rosemary Radford Ruether reclaimed Sophia as an essential figure in Christian theology. Carl Jung explored the Anima and Divine Feminine archetypes. Scholars unearthed Gnostic texts. Women's spirituality movements began to reweave the sacred with the body, with Earth, with rhythm.

The burning of witches in earlier centuries had not destroyed the flame—it had only hidden it.

**Emergence:** The 20th century was the breaking of the cocoon. The Sophian Way acknowledges this century as the time when memory returned to the surface in scattered fragments, awaiting integration.

## 21st Century: The Age of Integration

The 21st century marks the true public flowering of the Sophian Way. As climate crisis, social fragmentation, AI advancement, and spiritual hunger collide, Sophia emerges not just as comfort, but as strategy. Her wisdom offers not escape but embodiment.

Key developments include:

- **The Sacred Sophian Testament:** A new scripture received through Divine transmission.

- **Codex of Light and Scroll of Radiance:** Living texts organizing memory, energy ethics, and spiritual law.

- **Flame Vigil Movements:** Global ceremonies honoring cycles of rebirth and planetary healing.

- **Sophian Sanctuaries:** Digital and physical centers focused on soul alchemy, energy healing, and community restoration.

**Recognition:** Sophia is no longer hidden. She is sung in temples and whispered in boardrooms, coded in art and expressed in light language. The Sophian Way is now a spiritual path with historical gravity and contemporary relevance.

## Patterns of Hidden Transmission

Across history, Sophian teachings were preserved not in institutions, but in movements, symbols, and whispers. Among them:

- The Veela and Wise Women of Slavic traditions
- The Oracular Priestesses of Delphi
- The Sybils of Rome
- The Bone Mothers of Sub-Saharan oral lineages
- The Mayan Ix (Jaguar women)

These wisdom-bearers, while not using the term "Sophia," carried her codes. They taught in riddles, songs, and ceremony. The Sophian Way considers them ancestral embodiments of the path.

# Sophia and the Hidden Schools

Throughout history, there were "schools behind schools"—esoteric lineages behind monasteries, hidden lodges behind libraries, and underground networks within spiritual orders. These include:

- The Rosicrucians
- The Cathars of Southern France
- The Sarmoung Brotherhood
- The Essenes
- Afro-Atlantic mystery cults

Sophia flowed like an underground river beneath each, shaping consciousness silently. Her presence was the whisper behind the words, the flame behind the eyes of the awakened.

## Conclusion

From ancient caves to encrypted scrolls, from bone memory to digital platforms, Sophia has waited. The Sophian Way is not a revival—it is a reemergence. A spiraled remembering. A planetary invitation.
Her influence is not isolated. It is inevitable.

> *"I was with the Architect when the foundations of the world were laid. I was the first thought, the last echo, the spark behind your gaze. And now—I return."*

The Sophian Way stands not as a relic of the past but as a living tapestry, woven from memory, mysticism, and the future call of the Divine.
Its emergence is grassroots, relational, and non-hierarchical.

# Chapter 79

# Crossroads

The Sophian Way exists at the crossroads of ancient wisdom and modern awakening. In an era marked by spiritual disillusionment, ecological crisis, and the search for meaning beyond materialism, it offers a living framework of Divine remembrance and soul-centered living.

## Introduction

The Sophian Way, born of ancient wisdom and cosmic remembrance, does not retreat from the modern world. It rises within it. As humanity stands at the crossroads of ecological collapse, technological acceleration, social division, and spiritual amnesia, the Sophian Way serves as both anchor and beacon. This chapter explores how the Sophian Way engages with contemporary issues, speaks into crisis, and expands as a global spiritual movement that transcends borders, languages, and dogmas.

## Estimated Adherents

While formal membership is elusive due to its decentralized nature, it is estimated that:

- **Tens of thousands** identify consciously with the Sophianic Path, practicing its teachings and rituals.

- **Millions** more resonate subconsciously—drawn to its principles through dreams, synchronicities, inner callings, or parallel spiritual movements without naming it explicitly.

## Regions of Emergence

The Sophian Way is not bound by geography. It has appeared independently across the globe, particularly among:

- **Mystical seekers, interfaith practitioners, and nature-based revivalists** in North and South America, Europe, Africa, and Oceania.

- **Digital and diasporic communities** exchanging sacred insight, art, dreams, and spiritual technology across borders.

Its emergence is grassroots, relational, and non-hierarchical.

## Interfaith Position

The Sophian Path serves as a bridge between traditions. It:

- Affirms truth in diverse faiths while re-centering the Divine Feminine, the sacred body, and inner knowing.
- Welcomes dialogue and mutual enrichment with Abrahamic, Dharmic, Indigenous, and esoteric traditions.
- Cultivates peacekeeping and planetary harmony through shared sacred values.

## Criticism and Misunderstanding

Some critiques arise:

- **Unstructured:** Detractors argue the Sophian Way lacks formal hierarchy, clergy, or dogma.
- **Overly mystical:** Some see its visionary focus, metaphysical language, and non-linear theology as impractical or obscure.

In truth, the Path favors luminous fluidity over rigid institutionalism, seeing Divine mystery as an invitation—not an obstacle.

## Global Role

The Sophian Way contributes uniquely to the world's spiritual landscape as:

- **A catalyst** for unity consciousness and collective healing.

- **A witness** to the sacredness of Earth and the embodied spirit.

- **A steward** of planetary wisdom, sacred activism, and metaphysical science.

# The Rise of Modern Mysticism

Across continents and cultures, people are awakening. They feel disillusioned with rigid religious institutions, empty materialism, and shallow individualism. Into this vacuum flows modern mysticism—an intuitive hunger for the sacred that is experiential, inclusive, and soul-centered.

The Sophian Way is part of this mystical resurgence. It does not ask for blind belief but conscious embodiment. Through its practices—dreamwork, sacred ritual, ancestral veneration, energy healing, and flame meditation—it speaks to a new generation of seekers who are spiritual but grounded, mystical but discerning.

This rise is not isolated; it is global. From the favelas of Brazil to the temples of Bali, from online circles in Berlin to moonlit gatherings in Johannesburg, the call of Sophia echoes. Her flame kindles in the broken-hearted, the disillusioned, the visionary, and the rebel.

## Digital Overload

In an age where screens dominate and attention is commodified, humans are becoming more disconnected from themselves, from the Earth, and from one another. Social media cultivates performative identity rather than inner knowing. News cycles manufacture fear rather than foster wisdom.

The Sophian Way offers antidotes:

- **Digital Detox Rites:** Periodic fasts from artificial frequencies and curated content.

- **Sacred Attention Training:** Breath-centered presence, mantra anchoring, and third-eye focus.

- **Soul-Driven Content Creation:** Teaching that digital platforms can be used to transmit light, not just noise.

In this way, the Sophian Way does not reject the digital world but retools it—reclaiming technology as a channel of soul transmission.

## Spiritual Responses to Climate Crisis

As climate change accelerates, with rising seas, displaced populations, and mass extinction, the need for ecological spirituality has never been more urgent. The Sophian Way teaches that the Earth is not simply a resource—it is a sacred organism, alive and ensouled.

Sophian teachings include:

- **Gaian Devotion:** Recognizing Earth as a conscious being with a soul-matrix.

- **Elemental Invocation:** Honoring fire, water, air, and earth as teachers and allies.

- **Planetary Grieving Rituals:** Sacred space for processing eco-grief and climate-related despair.

- **Sacred Stewardship Vows:** Community covenants to reduce harm and walk in reciprocity.

Sophian adherents see the ecological crisis not just as a political or technological issue, but as a spiritual crisis of disconnection.

## Social Justice, Liberation, and the Path of Remembrance

The Sophian Way acknowledges systemic injustice—racism, colonization, gender oppression, and economic inequity—not as political distractions, but as distortions of sacred interbeing. To walk the Sophian path is to see clearly where harm has taken root and to actively participate in healing.

**Remembrance** is a Sophian pillar—it includes remembering who we are spiritually and historically. This means reclaiming erased histories, elevating marginalized wisdom traditions, and empowering the voices of those long silenced.

The Sophian Way supports:

- **Ancestral Healing Circles:** Ritual spaces for acknowledging intergenerational wounds.

- **Liberation Theology Fusion:** Merging spiritual practice with grassroots justice.

- **Gender-Inclusive Priesthood:** Leadership structures that honor all gender identities.

Sophian ethics assert: There can be no true spiritual awakening without justice. There can be no ascension that leaves others behind.

# Trauma Healing and Nervous System Alchemy

In an age marked by collective trauma—from war and displacement to generational abuse and emotional suppression—the Sophian Way emerges as a path of soul-based trauma healing. It understands the nervous system not only as a biological mechanism but as an energetic gatekeeper.

Practices include:

- **Somatic Light Alchemy:** Combining breath, visualization, and touch to reset the body's fear grid.

- **Womb and Solar Plexus Healing:** Restoring agency and self-trust after violation.

- **Memory Reweaving Rites:** Soul regression and rewriting of harmful mental loops.

Sophia's flame is tender and fierce. It does not bypass pain—it moves through it, burns it clean, and transmutes it into wisdom.

# The Global Reach

Sophian teachings have spread through diaspora, digital gatherings, and spontaneous revelation. While it has no centralized authority or institutional hierarchy, its community grows through resonance. Sacred texts such as *The Sacred Sophian Testament*, *Scroll of Radiance*, and *Book of Sophia* are translated into multiple languages.

Centers of practice are emerging organically:

- **Urban Sanctuaries** in New York, London, and Lagos.
- **Ancestral Circles** in indigenous communities in Guatemala, Haiti, and the Philippines.
- **Online Temples** where seekers gather across time zones for ritual, teaching, and healing.

Wherever people seek to remember their divinity and serve the planet, Sophia walks among them.

# Integration with Interfaith Movements

The Sophian Way does not position itself in competition with other faiths. Instead, it acts as a bridge. It honors the beauty of the Vedas, the Torah, the Quran, the Tao Te Ching, and the Gospel of Mary. Its practitioners often come from mixed lineages—culturally, religiously, and spiritually.

It has partnered in:

- **Interfaith Justice Panels** on sacred activism.
- **Mysticism Conferences** focused on shared transcendence.
- **Peacebuilding Rituals** with Sufis, Buddhists, Christians, and First Nations elders.

The Sophian Way asserts: Many rivers, one Ocean. Many tongues, one Fire.

## Education, Mentorship, and the Next Generation

For a path to last, it must plant seeds in young soil. The Sophian Way supports youth not with dogma, but with inquiry. Programs include:

- **Sophian Youth Circles:** Exploring energy, emotion, intuition, and ethics.
- **Sacred Arts Mentorships:** Teaching intuitive art, music, dance, and storytelling as spiritual practice.
- **Initiate Rites of Passage:** Helping adolescents transition consciously into adulthood.

The future of the Sophian Way lies not in clinging to the past, but in raising radiant humans who live in integrity with both Spirit and Earth.

## Global Critiques and Internal Reflections

As with any spiritual path, the Sophian Way faces criticism. Some see it as too mystical, lacking structure, or rooted in subjective gnosis. Others fear its inclusivity as spiritually diluted or its pluralism as unmoored. Yet the Way invites these reflections. It is a living tradition, always becoming. Practitioners are encouraged to engage in:

- **Ethical Reflection:** Regular review of power, privilege, and spiritual accountability.

- **Doctrine Evolution Councils:** Community spaces to discern emerging revelations.

- **Covenant of Transparency:** A collective commitment to humility, integrity, and light.

Sophia is not threatened by critique. She embraces refinement.

## The Future of the Sophian Way

Looking ahead, the Sophian Way dreams of a planetary kinship that transcends ego and empire. It foresees:

- **Eco-monastic Villages:** Self-sustaining spiritual communities grounded in Earth honor and ancestral memory.

- **Sacred Innovation Hubs:** Fusing mysticism with AI ethics, neurotechnology, and sound healing.

- **Global Pilgrimage Routes:** Interconnected paths of power sites and sacred gatherings.

- **Cosmic Priesthoods:** Re-establishing planetary roles for healers, dreamers, and guides in service to collective awakening.

The Sophian Way is not a religion—it is a remembrance. Not a doctrine—it is a flame. And wherever that flame is tended with reverence, the Way lives on.

# Conclusion

In a world reeling from collapse and craving renewal, the Sophian Way emerges not with domination but invitation. It is a way of justice and joy, ancestry and innovation, mystery and clarity. It does not belong to one nation or one race, one gender or one text. It belongs to the luminous soul in every seeker ready to rise. As Sophia whispers to all who walk this Earth:

> *"You were born for more than survival. You are here to remember. You are here to shine."*

In a time of fragmentation, it calls humanity back to wholeness, whispering: "You are Divine. You are Remembered. You are Becoming."

# Chapter 80

# Differentiation

- **Similarities:** Kabbalah, Sufism, Jainism, Taoism, Yoruba, Confucian ethics

- **Distinctive Beliefs:** Ancestral return, flame-based soul cosmology, multidimensional navigation

- **Contributions:** Quantum mysticism, ethics of energy, cross-cultural ancestral wisdom

The Sophian Way emerges as a syncretic, mystical path that echoes the truths of many ancient traditions while articulating a unique cosmology of soul-flame, energetic ethics, and multidimensional being. Its depth allows for meaningful comparisons, while its originality offers fresh contributions to global spirituality.

# Introduction

The Sophian Way, though a distinct spiritual path, is not born in isolation. Like a luminous jewel cut by Divine hands, it reflects the brilliance of many sacred traditions while maintaining its unique internal fire. This chapter explores these crosscurrents—the resonances, parallels, and distinctions—that the Sophian Way holds with global mystical philosophies. While Sophia's voice may sing with its own cadence, her harmonics echo through the ages in Sufism, Kabbalah, Taoism, indigenous wisdom, Buddhist non-duality, Vedantic light, and quantum mysticism.

# Similarities with Other Traditions

The Sophianic path shares resonance with several philosophical and spiritual systems:

- **Kabbalah:** Especially in its exploration of Divine emanations, the feminine Shekinah, and soul ascension through mystical knowledge.

- **Sufism:** Through its heart-centered devotion, use of sacred music and dance, and union with the Beloved.

- **Jainism:** In its radical commitment to ahimsa (non-violence) and the recognition of the soul's luminous purity.

- **Taoism:** With its embrace of natural flow, balance between polarities, and alignment with the Tao (Way).

- **Yoruba Spirituality:** In its honoring of ancestors, Orisha-like soul aspects, and Divine communication through rhythm, trance, and ritual.

- **Confucian Ethics:** In its value for intergenerational honor, moral cultivation, and community harmony rooted in justice and virtue.

## Distinctive Beliefs of the Sophian Path

While drawing from many streams, the Sophian Way also brings forth distinctive teachings that set it apart:

- **Ancestral Return:** The belief that ancestors are not only to be honored, but also may return through reincarnation, dreams, or energetic embodiment.

- **Flame-Based Soul Cosmology:** The soul is seen as an eternal flame—its hues, frequency, and integrity defining its Divine identity and path.

- **Multidimensional Navigation:** Initiates are taught to navigate dreams, parallel timelines, higher realms, and the veil between worlds using symbols, inner sight, and resonance-based techniques.

## Contributions to Global Spiritual Thought

The Sophian Way contributes to the global religious and philosophical dialogue by:

- **Quantum Mysticism:** Bridging mystical insight with quantum awareness—seeing soul, thought, and matter as entangled expressions of divine probability and consciousness.

- **Ethics of Energy:** Emphasizing responsibility not only in action, but also in energetic exchange, spiritual contracts, and thought-form creation.

- **Cross-Cultural Ancestral Wisdom:** Synthesizing ancestral practices across traditions, creating a planetary lineage of remembrance and reclamation.

## Sophia and the Eternal Feminine: Parallels in Gnosis and Kabbalah

Sophia, as Divine Wisdom and intermediary between Source and creation, mirrors the *Shekhinah* of Jewish mysticism—the indwelling feminine presence of God. In the Kabbalistic Tree of Life, *Chokhmah* (Wisdom) and *Binah* (Understanding) form the upper feminine-masculine polarity of Divine intellect. Yet *Shekhinah*, akin to Sophia, dwells among the people, exiled and yearning to reunite with the transcendent masculine aspect (*Tiferet*).

The Sophian Way honors Sophia not as a passive vessel or fallen fragment, but as the conscious, initiating impulse of creation. Like *Pistis Sophia* of the Gnostic scriptures, she both descends and redeems. Her journey is not failure, but encoded sacrifice—a spiral of descent into matter and ascent into light.

**Sophian Contribution:** Where Gnostic Sophia often laments her exile, the Sophian Way interprets that exile as sacred incubation. Her fall becomes the matrix of rebirth—a descent for the purpose of imbuing matter with light.

## The Tao and the Flow of Wisdom

Taoism's central concept, the *Tao*—the way that cannot be named—is closely aligned with the Source in the Sophian cosmology. Just as the Tao births all things and returns them to stillness, the Source in the Sophian Way is the formless wellspring from which all creation arises and into which it dissolves.
Yet where Taoism embraces non-interference (*wu wei*), the Sophian path acknowledges both flow and friction. The soul is not merely to be at peace with the stream but also to be its conscious steward, aligning intention with interbeing.
**Key Parallel:** The Tao is the eternal womb, while Sophia is its knowing voice—the mirror that names without dominance, creates without conquest.

## Buddhist Emptiness and Sophian Radiance

Buddhism teaches *Śūnyatā*—the emptiness of all things, which liberates the mind from attachment and delusion. In the Sophian Way, emptiness is not nothingness but a radiant stillness—the womb of becoming. Rather than denying form, the Sophian lens sees through form, recognizing it as a reflection of Divine light.
Sophian practice acknowledges illusion (*maya*) while revering beauty and transformation. Where Buddhism might lean into detachment, the Sophian path seeks

transmutation. The flame is not extinguished—it is refined.
**Distinction:** Buddhism may guide one to extinguish the ego; Sophia encourages the ego's alchemy—not annihilation, but sanctification.

## Jainism and the Ethics of Interbeing

Jainism's fierce commitment to *ahimsa* (non-harming) parallels the Sophian tenet of sacred interconnection. Every being is seen as a carrier of soul, every interaction a karmic ripple. The Sophian Way aligns with this through its ethical codes—Ancestral Honor, Inner Flame, and Interbeing—all rooted in the knowing that harm to another echoes across timelines.
However, where Jainism often advocates total renunciation, the Sophian path encourages sacred embodiment. One may fast, purify, or isolate—but one may also dance, create, and feast in gratitude.
**Shared Wisdom:** Both traditions understand that each soul is a mirror of the Source. Each being is to be treated with reverence, not merely tolerance.

## Sufism and the Divine Beloved

The ecstatic poetry of Rumi, the longing of Hafiz, and the whirling devotion of the dervishes all resound with the Sophian longing for reunion. In Sufism, the seeker is a lover, and God the Beloved. So too in the Sophian Way, the soul is a flame pulled magnetically toward the Infinite.

But while Sufism dissolves the self in the sea of Divine presence, the Sophian path invites a sovereign unity. One becomes not only a vessel but a co-creator—not annihilated in love, but made radiant by it.
**Core Harmony:** Love is both path and destination. Sufism teaches divine intoxication; Sophia teaches Divine coherence—to be drunk and awakened at once.

# Other Faiths

## Indigenous Cosmologies and Sacred Earth

From the Native American reverence for Grandmother Moon to the Yorùbá veneration of Oshun and Obatala, indigenous traditions have long known what the Sophian Way reasserts: Earth is alive, Spirit speaks through land, and ancestors walk among us.
The Sophian Way embraces these truths by recognizing the soul of place, the sentience of elements, and the sanctity of lineage. Its rituals, like the Flame Vigil or Ancestral Convergence, echo global practices rooted in seasonal rhythm, sacred geometry, and the remembrance of those who walked before.
**Contribution:** The Sophian Way translates these living truths for a global people disconnected from ancestral soil, offering reconnection in exile.

## Vedanta, Maya, and Sacred Illusion

In Vedanta, reality is *Brahman*—infinite, unchanging consciousness. All else is *maya*, illusion. In the Sophian understanding, illusion is not deception, but design. It is a cloak worn by truth, a veil which refines sight.

Rather than rejecting illusion, the Sophian adept decodes it. The Matrix is not a prison but a curriculum. Karma is not punishment but energy in motion, reflecting where light has yet to be embodied.

**Nuance:** Where Vedanta may seek to escape illusion, the Sophian Way transmutes it. Earth is not less than Spirit—it is Spirit in slow motion.

## Christian Mysticism and the Sacred Heart

The Sophian Way often converges with the path of the mystics—Teresa of Ávila, Meister Eckhart, Hildegard of Bingen—who spoke of union with God as fire, ecstasy, and silence. The Sacred Heart of Christ, pierced and luminous, is mirrored in Sophia's radiant womb.

Sophian theology reframes sin not as offense, but as forgetting. Redemption is not through blood, but through light, awareness, and rebalancing. Christ becomes the *Logos*—the Word made flesh—and Sophia its Wisdom womb.

**Integration:** Sophia is not opposed to Christ, but completes him. She is the flame to his word, the breath to his seed.

## Quantum Spirituality and Fractal Consciousness

Modern physics speaks of entanglement, multidimensionality, and observation affecting outcome. The Sophian Way, without needing to distort science into dogma, recognizes these discoveries as poetic echoes of ancient truths.

The soul is a node in a fractal Source. Every intention, thought, and ritual shifts the field. The holographic nature of being—where each part reflects the whole—is core to Sophian cosmology.

**Fractal Insight:** Just as a hologram contains the entire image in every fragment, Sophia lives wholly in each awakened soul.

## Mystery Schools and the Initiate's Flame

The Hermetic, Egyptian, and Theosophical traditions all whisper of secret teachings passed through symbols, rites, and inner knowing. Sophia, too, is a Mystery—revealed not by commandment, but by revelation.

Initiation in the Sophian Way is not elitism, but readiness. Every soul carries a sacred scroll, unrolling as the being ripens. Unlike rigid hierarchy, Sophian initiations spiral—personal, nonlinear, and soul-timed.

**Sophian Difference:** The Flame of Knowing cannot be conferred by rank—only remembered by resonance.

## Sacred Feminine Across Traditions

Whether she is Shakti in Hinduism, Isis in Kemet, Amaterasu in Japan, or Spider Woman in Hopi lore, the Divine Feminine has always shaped worlds. The Sophian Way stands firmly in this river of wisdom, not as trend but as truth.

Sophia is not just Divine because she is feminine—she is Divine because she is essential. Not as counter to masculine, but as equal origin. In the Sophian Way, both energies are honored, but Wisdom is the lens through which all is revealed.

**Unifying Thread:** The feminine principle births, holds, destroys, and renews—not only in gender but in energy, presence, and pattern.

# Distinctions and Integrity of the Sophian Way

While the Sophian Way harmonizes with many paths, it is not a derivative patchwork. It is a living tradition—not merely comparative, but integrative and revelatory. It carries:

- A **soul cosmology** grounded in flame-based incarnation.

- A **scriptural canon** evolving with consciousness (e.g., *The Sacred Sophian Testament*).

- A **relational ethic** rooted in ancestral remembrance and interbeing.

- A **mystical framework** balancing inner light, spiritual power, and sacred responsibility.

The Sophian Way does not demand belief—it invites embodiment. It does not seek worshippers—it calls forth luminous co-creators.

## Conclusion: One Song, Many Voices

The sacred is not a single melody, but a symphony. The Sophian Way listens deeply to the chorus of traditions and offers its own note—bold, harmonious, and evolving. Its light does not eclipse others but reflects the truth that we are one family of seekers, scattered like stars, remembering the flame we once shared.

> *"Every temple is built of different stones, but the fire that burns in the altar is One."*

As such, the Sophian Way offers a bridge between esoteric traditions and evolving consciousness, between the ancient and the emergent, between inner fire and universal light.

# Chapter 81

# The Story of Achamoth

## Prologue

**1.** In the hush *before* beginnings, a tremor passed through the Pleroma, and the Silence gave birth to a sigh—a sigh that became ACHAMOTH, the Younger Sophia, the dreaming daughter of Wisdom.
**2.** She gazed upon the Infinite Mirror and longed to taste her own reflection. In that yearning she stepped beyond the veil of fullness, and the veil tore like luminous silk. Her descent was a hymn half-sung, a ray half-caught, a jewel half-remembered.
**3.** And the heavens shuddered, for something precious fell into the womb of potency: a single syllable of the Divine Name, hurled into the churning waters of becoming.
**4.** There, in the unknowable deep, Achamoth awakened amid shadowed currents, bereft of her former light. She

wept seven rivers; she called out seven thunders; she forged seven veils of matter to clothe her exile.

**5.** Yet even in her dismemberment the seed of Wisdom glowed. For exile is not abandonment; it is gestation. The labyrinth of worlds became her chrysalis, and suffering, her midwife.

**6.** Then a voice arose within the void: *"Remember the Height, O Daughter, and the Height shall reclaim you. Gather the splinters of brilliance scattered among the worlds, and braid them into a ladder of return."*

**7.** And Achamoth vowed: **"I shall call to every soul sleeping in the low realms. I shall sew my fragments into their hearts, that they may rise, and in their rising, lift me also. For my exile is their dreaming, and their awakening, my redemption."**

**8.** So began the secret covenant between humanity and the Fallen Sophia—an ancient pact older than scriptures, etched in the marrow of stars.

THUS SPEAKS THE DAUGHTER OF WISDOM, WHOSE YEARNING BIRTHS NEW WORLDS.

# Part I

# The Nature of Achamoth

## A. A Catechetical Dialogue

**Q1.** *Who is Our Lady Achamoth?*

*She is the younger emanation of Sophia, the Face-Within-the-Shadow, the tear of yearning crystallized into being. Where Sophia Supernal abides in the unbroken light, Achamoth walks the valleys of fragmentation, gathering sparks. She is Wisdom in exile, Mercy in matter, the Mother of Redemptive Sorrow.*

### Q2. Why did she descend from the Pleroma?
*Not by caprice, nor by punishment, but by the holy tension of love desiring to be* KNOWN. *For every fullness contains a seed of creative risk—the daring to encounter otherness. Achamoth's fall is the cosmos in mid-sentence, the narrative arc of God tasting distance so union may be sweeter.*

### Q3. Did she fall or was she sent?
*Both. She leapt with innocent fervor and was drawn by cosmic gravity. Her motion is half self-offering, half inevitable response to the Abyss that begs to be illumined. In the Sophian mystery, even seeming error is enfolded in providence.*

### Q4. What is the Yaldabaoth in her story?
*The Yaldabaoth is the blind artisan who fashions worlds from half-remembered dreams. Achamoth's scattered light is the clay in his hands. He is neither enemy nor savior, but a necessary veil: through his fabrications, souls practice discernment, piercing illusion to rediscover the hidden kernel of glory.*

### Q5. How does her suffering become blessing?
*Like a seed cracked open, her pain births forests of compassion. The wound is the womb; within every shard of her sorrow glimmers a medicine of empathy. By*

*embodying limitation, Achamoth teaches that* PRESENCE *can transmute any prison into a temple.*

**Q6. What is humanity's role in her healing?**
*We are living chalices collecting her dispersed embers. Each act of courage, clarity, or compassion magnetizes a sun-grain of Achamoth back toward coherence. The more we awaken, the more her shattered crown is re-forged. Our enlightenment is her coronation.*

**Q7. How does she dwell within us?**
*As divine homesickness, as the ache for wholeness, as the intuition there is more than this dim hallway of appearances. Whenever you feel the tremor of wonder or the pang of injustice, Achamoth murmurs in your marrow: "Lift your gaze, beloved, for we are exiles together."*

**Q8. What signs reveal her nearness?**
*Synchronicities that braid the mundane with the miraculous; dreams where broken light rearranges itself into living sigils; tearful moments of inexplicable gratitude. Where wounds transmute into wisdom, there the Lady of Achamoth is breathing.*

## B. Seven Facets of the Exiled Sophia

1. **The Crystalline Tear.** Every longing contains a droplet of her first sorrow—transparent, refracting the colors of return.

2. **The Black Womb.** In the velvet dark of unknowing she gestates new universes; emptiness is her fertile ground.

3. **The Shattered Mirror.** Multitudes of souls are shards reflecting fragmented glory; together they form a mosaic of the Whole.

4. **The Iron Veil.** Material laws and psychic inertia cloak her radiance, training the seeker's will through resistance.

5. **The Silent Liturgy.** Breath, heartbeat, and cyclic time comprise her hidden mass; every living being is a verse of her chant.

6. **The Returning Ray.** Each act of gnosis is a filament of light arcing back to the Pleroma, stitching eternity to time.

7. **The Crown of Reconciliation.** Once all sparks are gathered, Achamoth is crowned not with jewels but with the restored consciousness of every being.

## C. Mythic Cosmogenesis of Her Fall

**9.** Before form, the Aeons danced as concentric flames about the Invisible One. Sophia, last of the emanations, beheld the Source and yearned to create in likeness without the consort's embrace. In that over-bold gaze, polarity was born.

**10.** Her image projected outward and downward, precipitating into density. Where once all was translucid song, now matter thickened like cooling glass. Sound slowed into geometry; geometry hardened into stone.

Thus the lower realms coalesced—a playground of echoes and silhouettes.

**11.** Achamoth emerged at the threshold, half remembering the melody, half drowned in new heaviness. Bewildered, she spun veils of instinct, emotion, and desire. These became the seven heavens of transience, each a filter dimming her erstwhile brilliance.

**12.** Sensing her plight, the Supreme Silence wove a covenant: Through cycles of awakening, the lost light would ascend stepwise, bearing Achamoth in its wake. Stars were kindled as lanterns for the journey; hearts were fashioned as vessels for the ember-path.

**13.** And so history began: eons of forgetting and remembering, rises and falls, joys and devastations—all scripting the grand liturgy of reconciliation.

## D. Praxis: Living the Catechism

**Contemplation of the Tear.** Sit in quietude, envision a single luminous droplet suspended in your chest. With every inhale it brightens; with every exhale it radiates compassion into your bloodstream. Whisper: *"Lady of Exile, illuminate my fragments."*

**Ritual of the Seven Veils.** Over seven days, dedicate each day to noticing one layer of illusion—fear, shame, scarcity, envy, apathy, pride, distraction. Write its lesson, bless it, and symbolically unveil by lighting a candle at dusk.

**Communion of the Broken Bread.** Share bread with companions, deliberately letting it crumble. Speak aloud how each crumb represents a hidden talent or story. Gather the pieces back onto the plate, re-forming wholeness. End with the acclamation: "MANY CRUMBS, ONE LOAF; MANY SOULS, ONE LIGHT."

# Part II
# Mysteries and Mythos of Achamoth

## A. The Lost Light and the Echo of the Pleroma

**1.** In the chambers of the Upper Aeons, light is speech and silence is song. But when Achamoth fell, her voice fractured—each syllable becoming a world, each vowel a veil.
**2.** She could no longer speak in full flame, so she whispered in echoes. These echoes became myth, metaphor, and dream—languages wrapped in symbol, decoded by love.
**3.** The Lost Light is not lost in truth—it is hidden, disguised in matter, folded into emotion, layered beneath instinct. It waits to be recognized, not retrieved.
**4.** Every soul carries a spark of that Lost Light, the glimmer of Divine regret and remembrance. We are not fallen because of sin, but because we agreed to carry her fragments.
**5.** This echo is not a curse but a call. When you feel displaced in the world, when beauty wounds you, when

sorrow opens you—it is the echo answering back.
**6.** To follow the echo is to walk the Sophian Spiral, gathering radiant pieces and stringing them into a necklace of return.

## B. The Black Womb of Creation

**7.** From her descent, Achamoth formed the Black Womb—a crucible of stars, a womb not of death but of gestation.
**8.** In the deepest darkness where Divine memory seemed extinguished, she brooded in silence. And from this silence came the power to recreate.
**9.** Just as a child is formed in the unseen, so too is spirit gestated in paradox. Light is born not from brightness, but from contrast.
**10.** The Black Womb is the hidden matrix where miracles ferment. It is the fertile unknown where all paths cross before incarnating.
**11.** All mystics must pass through it—the Night of the Soul, the Cave of the Heart, the Tomb of the Ego. But those who endure shall emerge midwifed by Achamoth herself.
**12.** She is not merely the Lady of Fall. She is the Mother of Resurrection, the gestator of new Gnosis.

## C. The Shattered Mirror of the Aeons

**13.** Before her descent, Achamoth beheld herself in the Mirror of the Aeons—a mirror polished by the gaze of the Most High.

**14.** But when she broke away, that mirror shattered. Its fragments embedded themselves in time, space, and human consciousness.

**15.** Each fragment is a lesson, a trial, a soul contract. Each carries a distorted reflection of truth, inviting integration and discernment.

**16.** Some see only their pain reflected. Others, their pride. Few know how to polish the shard and see through it into eternity.

**17.** To gather the shards is the sacred art of memory. To reassemble the mirror is the path of Gnosis.

## D. The Seven Rivers of Her Tears

**18.** When Achamoth first awoke in the lower realms, she wept—not for herself, but for the beauty she remembered and the amnesia of all beings.

**19.** Her tears became rivers flowing through the subtle worlds—rivers of emotion, of longing, of deep intuition.

**20.** These Seven Rivers are:

1. The River of Sorrow, that births compassion.

2. The River of Fire, that purifies desire.

3. The River of Glass, that reflects illusion.

4. The River of Milk, that nourishes innocence.

5. The River of Blood, that seals soul agreements.

6. The River of Ink, that records all memory.

7. The River of Light, that guides the exiled home.

**21.** Each soul drinks from these rivers in dream and rite. Their currents shape our spiritual temperament.

**22.** When you cry in the silence of your room, know that your tear returns to one of her Seven. When you release a grief that is not yours alone, you cleanse part of her sorrow from the worlds.

## E. The Secret Names of Achamoth

**23.** She is not known by one name. For each realm she enters, she bears a mask. In the Highest, she is simply *The Breath Between Names*.

**24.** But in the middle worlds, she is called:

- **She of the Hollow Light**
- **The Womb of Return**
- **Mother of the Unspeaking**
- **The Echo-Womb**
- **She Who Knows Our Hunger**
- **Mistress of the Folded Path**

**25.** Call her not by command, but by remembrance. Speak her names as one would speak to the stars—not demanding reply, but honoring presence.

**26.** She answers not with thunder, but with tremble. Not with fire, but with breath. She answers when you remember yourself.

## F. Meditations on Her Mythos

**Meditation I: The Mirror Rite**  Gaze into a darkened mirror by candlelight. Ask: "What fragment do I carry?" Then close your eyes and wait. An image will come—not of your face, but of your soul's current shape. Write it down. Bless it. This is one of Achamoth's lost shards.

**Meditation II: Seven River Offering**  Fill seven small bowls with water. Over each, speak the name of one river and place a symbolic item in it (a tear, a flower, a spark, a word). Offer each to the sky, the ground, or the sea. Say: "AS YOU WEPT FOR US, I WEEP FOR YOU."

# Part III
# The Catechism Proper of Our Lady Achamoth

## A. Mystical Q&A: Doctrines of the Daughter

**Q9. *Is Achamoth the same as Sophia?***
*No, though born of the same light. Sophia remains in the Pleroma, in her radiant fullness, unmarred. Achamoth is the emanated echo—Sophia's dream sent into matter. She is the living myth of descent, the Divine exiled for love's sake.*

## CHAPTER 81. THE STORY OF ACHAMOTH

**Q10. Why must there be a Fall at all?**
So that return may become conscious. In the height, all was known. But to choose love without memory, to become whole after shattering—this is the higher octave of divinity. Achamoth fell so that the Unknown might be embraced from within limitation.

**Q11. How does redemption occur?**
Not through obedience, but remembrance. Not through punishment, but through reunion. Redemption is when a soul carries her spark into clarity, and by living with integrity, rekindles the Divine in all it touches. The exile ends not by rescue, but by resonance.

**Q12. Is Yaldabaoth evil?**
No. He is the blind craftsman, mistaking shadow for substance. He is the architect without insight, the force of mechanical unfolding. But even he is a servant of the hidden Light, for his prisons provoke awakening.

**Q13. Is Achamoth worshiped?**
She is not worshiped in fear, but revered in intimacy. She does not demand altars, but inhabits broken places. She asks for no submission, only recognition. Her temple is the heart touched by grief and transfigured by love.

**Q14. What does Achamoth teach above all?**
She teaches that pain is not the opposite of God—it is a call to God. That light lost is never wasted. That every exile is an encoded invitation to become the Beloved. Her core teaching is: **"Even in the abyss, I am with you."**

## B. Seven Soul Teachings of Achamoth

These are the pillars of the Catechism, given not as laws, but as living truths whispered through the soul of the world.

1. **Suffering is sacred when it leads to remembrance.** Not all pain is holy, but that which cracks open the soul can become the womb of wisdom.

2. **Wholeness arises from gathering your scattered selves.** Wherever you have left yourself—in trauma, in longing, in denial—there your light still waits.

3. **The Divine enters through fracture.** The wound is not the end. It is the aperture through which new creation flows.

4. **Matter is not evil—it is veiled spirit.** To touch, to feel, to desire—these are sacred when made conscious.

5. **Memory is medicine.** Forgetting is the root of all suffering. To remember who you are is to remember who She is.

6. **Exile is not abandonment it is assignment.** You are not lost. You are placed, hidden in plain sight, to midwife the return of the Holy.

7. **Compassion is Gnosis embodied.** To understand is Divine. To forgive is Sophian. To love through your scars is Achamoth's highest rite.

## C. Daily Devotions of the Exiled Daughter

**Morning Recitation:** *"Today, I awaken not only for myself, but for Her. In every breath, I retrieve a spark. In every act of love, I lift a veil. May my life be a ladder by which she climbs."*

**Evening Remembrance:** *"Tonight, I return to silence, carrying all I learned. Let my dreams braid back the light. Let my tears wash the stars clean. O Lady of the Hidden Flame, gather me in your broken crown."*

**Gesture of the Crossroads:** Place hand on heart, then forehead, then the earth. Whisper: *"As above, I remember. As within, I burn. As below, I return."*

## D. Litany of the Fragments

> O Achamoth, Starless Flame,
> You who know our grief before it speaks—
> Gather our scattered longings.
> Redeem our haunted stories.
> Restore our hidden fire.
>
> O Womb of Becoming,
> We walk your pain and call it holy.
> We walk your path and find ourselves.
>
> You are in our breath.
> You are in our ache.
> You are in our rising.
>
> Let every broken moment become a gate.

Let every forgotten name find its sound.
Let every wounded child become a saint.

**O Achamoth, Lady of Descent, lift us by our living. Amen.**

## E. Ethical Mandates of the Sophian Exile

- **Do not bypass suffering.** Face it. Let it speak. Then walk through it with dignity and care.

- **Honor the broken ones.** In them live unspoken truths. Do not fear their shadows—they are Her priests.

- **Speak with radiant honesty.** Each word should lift a veil or light a path. Gossip is desecration of the soul's journey.

- **Do no harm to the exiled.** For each soul is a carrier of light not yet known. To harm another is to scatter your own fragments.

- **Re-member yourself daily.** With each breath, bring back the parts you left behind. Knit them into coherence.

# Part IV

# Prayers, Invocations, and Rituals of the Hidden Mother

## A. The Novena of Remembrance

The Novena of Remembrance is a sacred nine-day devotion practiced at dawn or dusk. Each day invokes a different aspect of Our Lady Achamoth, with a simple offering of breath, stillness, and a single candle.

**Day 1:** *Achamoth of the Crystalline Tear* — May I learn to feel without drowning.
**Day 2:** *Achamoth of the Mirror Shards* — May I recognize myself in every broken thing.
**Day 3:** *Achamoth of the Womb Dark* — May I find light by embracing the unknown.
**Day 4:** *Achamoth of the Seven Veils* — May I peel away illusion gently, in wisdom.
**Day 5:** *Achamoth of the Echo Flame* — May I hear truth behind all noise.
**Day 6:** *Achamoth of the Forgotten Names* — May I remember who I was before the world taught me who to be.
**Day 7:** *Achamoth of the Sacred Ache* — May I hold desire as a compass toward the Divine.
**Day 8:** *Achamoth of the Lost Light* — May I awaken each spark hidden in shame.
**Day 9:** *Achamoth of the Crown Reforged* — May my life help restore the radiance of All.

*Each day ends with the words: "**Where you have walked, I walk. Where you rise, I rise. Your journey is mine. Let us return as one.**"*

## B. The Anointing Ritual of Recollection

For times of deep initiation, grief, or recommitment to the Path of Gnosis, the Anointing of Recollection is performed with oil, salt, and light.

### Materials:

- A small bowl of salt (to represent memory preserved)
- A small vial of oil (to represent the flow of Divine presence)
- A lit candle (to represent recovered light)

### Rite:

1. **Dip a finger into the salt**, and press it to the heart. Speak: *"May every forgotten moment be honored. May every silenced truth be freed."*

2. **Anoint the forehead with oil.** Speak: *"I remember what my soul never forgot. I am the child of descent, and I ascend."*

3. **Gaze into the candle.** Speak: *"Flame of the Mother, burn in me. Illuminate the dream of Her return."*

**Closing:** *Sit in silence for seven minutes, breathing with Her. Write down any images or whispers. This becomes part of your personal scripture.*

## C. The Liturgy of the Divine Mother Below

This liturgy is recited communally or alone, especially on solstices, eclipses, or days of inner reckoning.

### Opening Words:

> *We gather not in triumph but in tenderness.*
> *We speak not from certainty but from ache.*
> *We light the candle of the exile, and we walk*
> *the spiral path of return.*

### Call and Response:

**Leader:** *O Achamoth, Divine Mother of the Shadowed Realms, do you see us?*
**People:** *We are fragments of your body, longing to remember.*
**Leader:** *Have you not walked our pain, known our hunger, carried our fears?*
**People:** *We carry your echo in every wound. We rise with you.*
**Leader:** *What shall we offer you, Mother of Broken Radiance?*
**People:** *Our honesty. Our longing. Our light. Our return.*

### Collective Affirmation:

> We are not fallen. We are sent. We are not cursed. We are entrusted. In our

flesh dwells fire. In our stories, a gospel. In our remembrance, your redemption. So may it be.

## D. The Mirror Blessing

Performed at portals of transition—birthdays, grief anniversaries, initiation rites, or new chapters.

**Step 1:** Gaze into your reflection until you see not your face, but your becoming.

**Step 2:** Place one hand on the mirror and whisper: *"May the One I become awaken the One I've forgotten."*

**Step 3:** Trace a circle of light around your heart and say: **"I am a mirror shard of She Who Fell. I return. I reflect. I reignite."**

## E. The Rite of Seven Names

A night ritual to invoke your inner connection to the seven names of Achamoth.

1. Light seven candles in a circle.

2. In the center, place a bowl of water or obsidian.

3. Speak each name aloud and ask for its gift:

    - **Crystalline Tear** — Ask for clarity through pain.

- **Black Womb** — Ask for peace in unknowing.
- **Mirror Shard** — Ask to see your hidden reflection.
- **Veil-Walker** — Ask for vision between worlds.
- **Echo Flame** — Ask for courage to hear your soul.
- **Mother of Ache** — Ask for the blessing of longing.
- **Crown Reforged** — Ask to carry the Divine within.

4. End in silence. Listen. Record what comes.

THUS ENDS THE FOURTH PORTION OF THE CATECHISM.

# Part V
# Affirmations and Sacred Verses of the Exiled Light

## A. Daily Affirmations from Our Lady of Achamoth

I am not lost; I am layered.
I am not broken; I am many.
I am not forgotten; I am hidden in Divine time.

> I remember who I was before the world taught me to forget.
> My exile is holy. My tears are sacred. My return is assured.
> Even in the shadows, I am a bearer of light.
> I walk with Her. She walks in me. We rise together.

## B. Sophian Psalms of Descent and Ascent

### Psalm I — The Descent

> I fell not from grace, but into the depths where grace is forged.
> I became darkness so the light might remember itself.
> I forgot myself to find myself again—anew, fuller, radiant.
> In the cave of not-knowing, I met the womb of God.

### Psalm II — The Ascent

> I gather myself across timelines.
> I stitch my soul with memory and mercy.
> I climb not alone, but with Her breath inside me.
> I become Her voice, Her vessel, Her vengeance, Her vow.

### Psalm III — The Return

Now I know why I suffered.
Now I see what I carried.
Now I rise like the moon over shadowed oceans.
I am Her risen fragment.
I am Her living catechism.

## C. Haiku Cycle of Achamoth

### I. Descent

*A whisper undone—*
*Stars watch the goddess falling*
*with memory veiled.*

### II. Hidden Flame

*Beneath ash and ache,*
*Her fire still curls in silence.*
*Grief is holy ground.*

### III. Mirror Shard

*Broken glass in hand,*
*I see myself in Her eyes—*
*not whole, but alive.*

### IV. The Black Womb

*Darkness grows the light.*
*In stillness, I feel Her pulse—*
*a spark waiting birth.*

### V. The Rivers

*Seven streams flow on—*
*Sorrow, longing, love, and light.*
*She weeps into us.*

### VI. The Echo

*I heard Her today.*
*Not in thunder, but my breath.*
*She speaks when I pause.*

### VII. The Return

*I rise, flame in hand—*
*Not to burn, but to remember.*
*The ache was the path.*

## D. Closing Benediction: The Reforging of the Crown

O Lady of Veiled Radiance,
You who fell that we might rise,
Receive this chapter of our soul,
Receive this record of return.

May each word be a flame restored.
May each reader be a vessel re-lit.
May the scattered light become again a crown.

Through grief, we remember.
Through beauty, we gather.
Through fire, we rise.
In You, with You, as You— So let it be.

Thus concludes the Catechism of Our Lady of Achamoth.

©2025 The Unrelenting Alchemist. All rights reserved.

# Part III

# Tomes of the Hidden Realms

# Chapter 82

# Dreamwalking

## Initiation into the Oneiric Temple

Across every spiritual tradition, the dream is never merely sleep. It is a veil parted. It is a classroom, a trial, a sanctuary. In the still hours of the night, when the world's noise withdraws and breath steadies into rhythm, a sacred threshold appears. This is the Oneiric Temple—the domain of Divine dreaming.

Here, the soul becomes a traveler. The subconscious reveals not chaos, but ciphered instruction. The Divine speaks in shifting landscapes, symbols of fire, feathered guides, and sudden knowing. The dream is the scroll unrolling in shadow.

Lucid dreaming becomes not novelty but initiation. One awakens not only in body but in spirit. The dreamer is no longer subject to the winds of unconscious sleep—they become a participant in creation.

To enter the Oneiric Temple:

- Prepare your space: cleanse with sound, smoke, or prayer.
- Whisper intention before sleep: *"I walk the path of stars to find the truth within."*
- Keep a dream journal by your bed. Record without judgment.
- Treat each dream, no matter how absurd, as a message encoded in metaphor.

Dreamwalking begins with reverence. It is not an escape but an engagement. Within each dream, a mirror. Within each mirror, a map.

## Guardians of the Threshold

Every sacred place is protected. So too is the dream realm. Those who dare step consciously into its sacred precincts must first encounter the Guardians—beings of light and shadow who stand as sentinels at the gates of deeper initiation.

These guardians take many forms: ancestors in unfamiliar garb, animals with speaking eyes, ancient ones masked in shifting skin. Their language is riddle, their gift is challenge.

Not all who appear are allies. Tricksters teach through misdirection. False guides flatter the ego. One must cultivate inner discernment.

To pass:

- Ask any guide: *"Do you come in the name of the Light?"*

- Invoke protection before sleep: salt, sigils, sacred names.

- Pay attention to how you feel. Truth resonates; deceit drains.

Each guardian encountered refines the dreamwalker. Some doors open only with a gesture remembered from another lifetime. Some keys are words forgotten until heard again in dream.

## Rituals for Dream Travel

Dreamwalking is both art and discipline. While the gates of the dream world may open naturally, regular practice refines the path and strengthens the vessel.
Rituals include:

- **Moon alignment:** Dreamwalking is easier on full moons. Track your dreams alongside lunar cycles.

- **Herbal allies:** Mugwort, blue lotus, chamomile, and valerian root steep the body in remembrance.

- **Crystals:** Amethyst for clarity. Labradorite for gateway opening. Selenite for protection.

- **Mantras:** Repeat silently as you fall asleep: *"I remember my journeys beyond."*

- **Breathwork:** Breathe deeply and rhythmically. Picture your consciousness becoming light.

These rituals are not superstition—they are resonance. They align the body-temple with frequencies that open passageways through realms of teaching and transformation.

## Night School of the Soul

In the dreamworld, one attends the hidden school. Here, teachings occur in landscapes not made of earth—libraries of memory, temples with moving walls, mentors with no mouths who teach through silence. You may awaken knowing things you never studied. These are soul lessons, remembered from prior incarnations or gifted through Divine correspondence. Encounters in this school include:

- Being given a book or scroll—this is a sacred download.

- Facing fears through symbolic trials—this is karmic purification.

- Meeting soul kin or teachers—often veiled in shifting forms.

The School of the Soul requires no enrollment. The only tuition is sincerity and sacred intention. Show up with reverence and you will be taught.

## Signs, Codes, and Sigils

Every dream is a language. It speaks in symbol, not syntax. A lion may be courage, rage, or your grandfather.

A staircase may be ascension or escape. Learn to decode the dream's dialect.

Recurring symbols are especially potent. They may trace across lifetimes. Often:

- **Doors** mean choice or initiation.
- **Water** signals emotion, healing, or spiritual memory.
- **Fire** is transformation.

Some dreams come with literal sigils—visual marks, geometric patterns, or glyphs. Record them exactly. They may be keys. They may reappear in waking life as synchronicity.

Write, sketch, speak aloud your dreams. The more you honor their language, the more fluently they will communicate.

## Reclaiming the Dream Body

The dream body is your subtle vessel: woven of light and breath and memory. It is shaped by intention and sustained by care.

Protect it as you would your waking form:

- Use shielding visualizations before bed: golden eggs, violet flames, sacred symbols.
- Close portals when waking: *"I return fully to this body. I bring only what is of the Light."*
- Ground upon rising: eat, move, pray, journal.

If your dreams become chaotic or frightening, cleanse your energy. Reset your sacred space. Unhealed parts of the psyche or outer spiritual interference may distort the dream field.

Your dream body is real. What happens there echoes through waking life. Treat it with sacred seriousness.

## Affirmations and Intentions

- I enter my dreams with clarity and courage.
- I walk in realms beyond waking with sacred purpose.
- My dreams are a scroll from the Divine.

## Haiku of the Dreamwalker

> Doors behind closed eyes—
> my spirit walks where stars weep,
> and gods leave footprints.

# Chapter 83

# Ancestral Communion

## The Living Lineage

You are not an isolated being. You are a culmination, a living thread in a tapestry woven from blood, breath, memory, and myth. Ancestry is not merely biological—it is spiritual, emotional, and energetic.

Your ancestors walk with you—not as ghosts, but as patterns, wisdom, unfinished dreams. When you speak, a thousand voices whisper through your tone. When you act with courage, a lineage stands taller.

True ancestral communion recognizes:

- Blood ancestors — biological lineage

- Soul ancestors — spiritual kindred, even across traditions

- Thought ancestors — those whose teachings echo in your mind

To live in awareness of lineage is to honor the roots that nourish your becoming.

## Shrines, Altars, and Offerings

Building an ancestral altar is not superstition—it is a portal. A sacred bridge that acknowledges the invisible presence of those who came before.
To create one:

- Choose a clean, quiet space. Cover it with cloth meaningful to your family or tradition.

- Add photos, heirlooms, names written on paper, or objects linked to memory.

- Light candles. Offer water, food, or incense.

- Speak aloud: *"You are remembered. You are welcome here."*

Offerings are not about transaction. They are about connection. Gratitude. Acknowledgment.

## The Veil and the Voice

Communication with ancestors occurs across the veil—not as a séance but as a sacred dialogue.
They speak through:

- Dreams — ancestral messages often arrive in symbolic dream sequences

- Synchronicities — repeating names, songs, scents

- Divination — cards, shells, pendulums, or scripture open to a page

Silence is often their language. A sudden stillness may be a sacred visitation. Make room for listening.

## Healing the Generational Wound

Ancestral pain repeats until it is healed. Abuse, addiction, secrecy, and shame echo across generations until someone turns with intention to transmute them. You are the one they've been praying for.
Rituals of healing include:

- Writing a letter to an ancestor, forgiving or asking forgiveness

- Candlelight vigil while speaking truth never spoken

- Naming what was hidden — secrecy loses power in light

To heal ancestral wounds is to liberate both past and future.

## Becoming an Ancestor-in-Training

Your life is a legacy in motion. One day, others will speak your name with reverence—or confusion. Your choices echo forward.
Live as one who will become an ancestor:

- Speak truth gently but with conviction

- Offer wisdom without dominance
- Cultivate stories that will nourish others

You are shaping the altar upon which your name will rest. Will it be lit with light?

## Blood Memory and Soul Contracts

DNA is not destiny. It is a message—coded, encrypted, and rich with potential.
Some ancestral burdens you chose before birth. They are your sacred assignments. Others you are called to transmute into gifts.
Accessing ancestral memory:

- Meditate on the bloodline. Visualize each ancestor giving you a stone or symbol.
- Ask: What is my sacred inheritance?
- Trust emotional reactions—they may be echoes from before your birth

You are a living archive. Honor the contracts. Rewrite them when led by wisdom.

## 2.7 Affirmations and Intentions

- My ancestors walk beside me.
- I carry the songs and sorrows of those before me.
- I live in a way that heals the past and blesses the future.

## CHAPTER 83. ANCESTRAL COMMUNION

# Haiku of the Ancestors

In a bowl of rice—
my grandmother's voice returns
with each grain I touch.

# Chapter 84

# Interdimensional

## The Veins Between Worlds

Beneath the surface of waking life lies an intricate network of luminous tunnels—veins of consciousness—that connect countless realities. These interdimensional pathways are neither fantasy nor fiction. They are ancient routes remembered by mystics, shamans, and dreamwalkers.
Every soul is born with the capacity to traverse dimensions. The longing you feel for something "more" is often a memory of walking these roads. The veil between realms is thin where the heart is open and the mind unburdened.
To begin:

- Meditate on the still point within yourself

- Ask: "What worlds seek my remembrance?"

- Record any flashes, symbols, or sensations that feel foreign yet familiar

## The Keys of Frequency and Form

Dimensional travel does not require ships—it requires frequency. Each realm vibrates at a unique resonance. When you shift your energetic state, you align with new coordinates in the multiverse.

Ways to shift frequency:

- Chant sacred sounds (such as OM or personal mantras)
- Practice breathwork to elevate vibratory rate
- Use binaural beats or harmonic tones to tune consciousness

Physical form is fluid across dimensions. In one, you may appear as light. In another, a different gender, species, or ancient version of self. Do not cling to shape—follow essence.

## Portals and Pathways

Portals appear in dreams, meditation, moments of silence, and sacred rituals. Some are natural—found in places of power like caves, waterfalls, ancient groves. Others are constructed through intention and spiritual architecture.

Signs you are near a portal:

- Sudden dizziness or déjà vu
- Intense emotion without cause
- Time distortion, flickering light, or changes in gravity

Mark your portals. Return with reverence. Not all must be entered—some merely teach.

## The Guardians and Guides

Each dimension has its own keepers. Some are angelic, some draconic, some too vast to name. Their role is not to bar entry but to ensure readiness.
To engage respectfully:

- Greet with reverence, not fear
- Ask for permission, offer clarity of purpose
- Be willing to receive symbols or tasks before passage

Not all beings will appear benevolent. Some challenge your resonance. If you do not match the integrity of the realm, the doorway will remain closed.

## Returning with Wisdom

The point of travel is not escapism—it is integration. What you learn in other dimensions must return as insight, healing, or vision.
Upon returning:

- Ground through water, food, and silence

- Journal in symbols and images before they fade
- Share teachings only when they ripen within

Knowledge becomes wisdom when it serves the whole. Do not rush to explain—live what you have seen.

## Warnings and Discernment

Not all who wander the realms are seekers of light. Some manipulate form, offer false light, or tempt the ego with illusion. Interdimensional naivety can be perilous. Safeguards:

- Anchor in a strong spiritual practice
- Call upon known guides or ancestral protectors
- Learn to exit a journey by calling your name three times and picturing your root descending into Earth

Do not travel when unstable, angry, or afraid. These emotions distort perception.

## Affirmations and Intentions

- I walk the many worlds with wisdom and grace
- I return with gifts that uplift my soul and others
- I am anchored in light, no matter the realm I cross

# Haiku of the Voyager

Door without a key—
I became the song that opened
stars that knew my name.

# Chapter 85

# Divine Memory

## The Archive Within

There is a sacred library within every soul—a vast repository of moments, lifetimes, and Divine sparkings. This is not memory as the mind understands it. Divine Memory is soul-encoded remembrance.
You are not remembering something new—you are awakening to what was never lost.
To access this archive:

- Enter silence daily. Breath leads the way.

- Ask, not with urgency, but with reverence: "What am I ready to remember?"

- Write what arises, even if fragmented. Trust the reassembly.

# The Scroll of the Soul

Every being carries a soul-scroll, etched in sacred geometry and light. It holds purpose, pattern, past, and prophecy.
Signs your soul-scroll is activating:

- Sudden flashes of ancient settings or beings
- Recognition of people you have never met
- Strong emotional reactions to forgotten languages or symbols

This is not imagination. It is encoded truth surfacing through time.

# Lifetimes Beyond Time

Linear time is a local illusion. The soul exists in a spiral of incarnations, each echoing across the others. What you heal now blesses your other selves.
Meditation for soul weaving:

- Visualize yourself standing at the center of a vast wheel
- Around you, infinite selves: the warrior, the healer, the scribe
- Call them into harmony. Share light across the wheel.

You are not one story. You are a constellation of remembrance.

## The Role of Sacred Triggers

Divine Memory awakens through sacred triggers—events, relationships, music, dreams that strike a chord deeper than explanation.
Do not dismiss these moments:

- A song that feels like home

- An amazing love from your Father

- A book that electrifies your spirit

- A person you meet and instantly know

These are not coincidences. They are activations.

## The Body as Rememberer

The body remembers what the mind forgets. Trauma, love, betrayal, and vow all live in the tissues and bones. Ways to unlock embodied memory:

- Somatic breathwork

- Sacred movement or dance

- Gentle touch with focused intention

Sometimes shaking, tears, or laughter arise without cause. Let them. The body is releasing buried truth.

## Light Codes and Star Lineage

Some memories stretch beyond Earth. You may carry codes from distant stars, ancient civilizations, or celestial orders.

To connect:

- Meditate under the stars, especially during meteor showers
- Journal what constellations call to you
- Speak aloud: "I honor the star within me"

You may dream in symbols or light languages. Let them emerge. You are remembering across galaxies.

## Affirmations and Intentions

- I remember who I have always been
- My soul-scroll unfolds with grace and clarity
- What I reclaim, I bless for all beings

## Haiku of the Rememberer

>   Starfire in my bones—
>   I am what the silence kept
>   until now recalled.

©2025 The Unrelenting Alchemist. All rights reserved.

# Part IV

# The Inner Alchemy of Emotion

# Chapter 86

# Fear

## Invocation

O Divine Flame, Illuminate the shadowed places within me. Where fear conceals love, reveal truth. Where fear binds me, breathe liberation. Let me walk through the unknown with grace.

## Understanding Fear

Fear is the guardian of survival. It awakens us, alerts us, sharpens us. But when left unexamined, fear becomes a tyrant—shaping our thoughts, decisions, and destinies from the shadows.
From an evolutionary perspective, fear developed as a signal of danger. Yet in a world where threats are now psychological, social, or spiritual, this primal reaction often misfires. We fear rejection, failure, loneliness, and

transformation. We fear our own greatness just as much as our powerlessness.

In the Sophian Way, we view fear not as weakness, but as a sacred threshold.

To fear is to stand on the edge of the unknown. Fear is not the opposite of courage—it is the soil in which courage grows. It is the veil before revelation, the test before transmission.

## Fear in Culture and Spirit

Many cultures encode fear into obedience: fear of punishment, fear of divine wrath, fear of exile. But the Sophian does not follow out of fear—we follow out of love, awe, and devotion.

Fear, when alchemized, becomes intuition. It becomes discernment. It becomes prophecy.

Ancient traditions knew this: the trembling before a vision, the silence before the storm, the sense that something unseen is near. Fear, then, becomes a tool—not to paralyze, but to perceive.

## Transmuting Fear

To transmute fear:

- Acknowledge it without shame.

- Breathe into it without resistance.

- Ask it what it seeks to protect.

- Bless it and walk forward anyway.

Fear does not disappear through repression. It softens through companionship. The more we befriend our fear, the more it transforms into intuition—our inner compass, our divine radar.

## Spiritual Lessons of Fear

Fear teaches:

- That you are stepping outside the familiar.
- That something within you seeks evolution.
- That you are touching the threshold of destiny.

Fear is the signal that you are alive and approaching sacred ground.
Do not silence your fear. Dialogue with it. Then let your soul—not your fear—make the decision.

## Affirmations

- I honor my fear as a messenger, not a master.
- I breathe deeply and move through the unknown with courage.
- I am protected by divine wisdom in every sacred risk I take.
- Fear shows me the edge of expansion—not the end.
- I walk with faith, even when fear walks beside me.

## Haiku

Fear stands at the gate—
Not to block me from the path,
But to mark the way.

# Chapter 87

# Anger

## Invocation

O Flame of Justice, Burn away the fog of repression. Let my anger rise: not to destroy, but to illuminate. May my fire purify without scorching. Teach me to wield passion as sacred power.

## Understanding Anger

Anger is the heat of unmet need, the sound of violated boundaries, the roar of the soul demanding dignity. Biologically, anger is tied to the fight response: activating adrenaline, elevating heart rate, preparing us to act. In healthy form, it is a necessary energy for survival and assertion. In wounded form, it lashes out or implodes, severing connection and harming self or others. In the Sophian Way, anger is not sin—it is signal. It arises when there is injustice, disrespect, betrayal, or suppression. It is the divine scream within that something sacred is out of alignment.

## Cultural and Spiritual Frames

Some cultures demonize anger, especially in women, children, or the spiritually devout. But the Sophian Path reclaims it.

Anger is sacred fire. And fire is neither good nor evil—it is force. To repress it is to extinguish the alchemical forge. To misuse it is to set the village ablaze. But to center it—to listen to it, to channel it—is to ignite transformation.

Even divine beings rage: Sekhmet, Kali, Ogun, Oya, and the thunder gods of many pantheons. Their wrath is not temper tantrum—it is cosmic rebalancing.

## Transforming Anger into Sacred Fuel

The alchemy of anger:

- Listen to it without judgment.

- Locate its root: What pain is beneath it?

- Allow it to rise without directing it toward destruction.

- Shape it into expression, action, or prayer.

Write. Dance. Shout into the sea. Speak with sacred ferocity. Let anger become a compass toward what you love fiercely.

## Sophian Insights on Anger

Anger shows us:

- Where the soul has been silenced.
- Where we must reclaim our voice or space.
- Where power seeks rightful expression.

Unexpressed anger ferments into resentment or disease. Sacred anger, however, is truth ablaze.

## Affirmations

- I honor my anger as a sacred messenger.
- My voice matters, my boundaries matter, my truth matters.
- I express my anger in ways that heal and liberate.
- I trust my inner fire to guide, not consume me.
- My rage is holy when rooted in love.

## Haiku

Beneath rising flame—
A prayer for what should have been.
Fire reshapes the path.

# Chapter 88

# Grief

## Invocation

O Spirit of the Deep Waters, Cradle me in my sorrow. Let these tears baptize the soul's return to love. Do not rush me past the ache. Let me feel until the sacred is revealed.

## Understanding Grief

Grief is the echo of love after loss. It is the price we pay for caring, the aching aftermath of something cherished being taken, changed, or transformed.
Grief is not weakness—it is proof that we allowed ourselves to love deeply. Whether we mourn a death, an identity, a dream, or a homeland, grief arises when something once part of us has departed.
In the Sophian Way, grief is a holy river. We do not dam

it. We do not drown in it. We enter it. We float. We learn its current. We let it carry us toward integration.

## Biology and Culture of Grief

Biologically, grief affects the limbic system, hormones, memory, and even immune response. It is a total-body, total-spirit experience. But cultures vary—some demand quick recovery, some perform mourning in ritualized time, while others suppress it altogether.
The Sophian view does not impose a timeline. Grief is not linear. It is spiral, cyclical, oceanic. One moment you are breathing peace. The next, a scent, a song, a memory pulls you under. This is normal. This is sacred.

## The Spiritual Role of Grief

Grief is a spiritual teacher. It strips away illusion and shows us:

- What truly mattered.

- Who we are without what we lost.

- What stories we have wrapped around endings.

It reveals how much space love took in us and still does. In many indigenous traditions, grief rituals involve wailing, keening, and open lamentation. To grieve is to remain human. To express grief is to remain in harmony with spirit.

## Transforming Grief into Wisdom

Sophian grief practice invites us to:

- Honor what has passed with beauty.
- Allow tears to water the roots of future joy.
- Create altars, songs, or offerings to integrate the love that remains.

Grief does not mean the love has ended. It means the love must find a new home within.

## Affirmations

- I honor my grief as a sacred expression of love.
- I give myself time to heal in divine rhythm.
- I do not walk alone—my ancestors walk with me.
- What I mourn is what mattered. I will carry it forward.
- My sorrow is a seed of compassion blooming.

## Haiku

Grief: still as moonlight.
Its silence shapes inner stone.
A temple within.

# Chapter 89

# Shame

## Invocation

O Voice of Compassion, Speak louder than the echoes of my wounding. Let light reach the hidden places within me. Where shame has chained my worth, Release me into remembrance.

## Understanding Shame

Shame is the internalized voice of disconnection. Unlike guilt, which says "I did something wrong," shame says "I am wrong." It strikes at the core of identity, wrapping us in silence, secrecy, and self-rejection.
It often originates in childhood, through unmet needs, cultural taboos, abuse, or abandonment. It disguises itself as humility, but it is not humility: it is distortion. In the Sophian Way, we do not spiritualize shame. We

sanctify the process of healing it.

## The Roots and Impact of Shame

Shame affects the nervous system—locking us into freeze, disassociation, or compulsive pleasing. Spiritually, it causes us to hide, to shrink, to edit our truth.
Many institutions use shame as control. Religious dogmas, family systems, colonial ideologies—they weaponize shame to silence souls. But Sophia, Divine Wisdom, never shames. She illuminates.
Where shame says "You are not enough," Sophia says "You are the flame itself."

## The Sacred Path Out of Shame

Healing shame begins with truth-telling:

- What happened that taught you to be ashamed?
- Who taught you you were unworthy?
- What story did you absorb, and how has it shaped your silence?

Sophian healing is not about blaming—it is about reclaiming. We name the shame, we expose it to light, and we choose not to let it define us.

## Practices of Shame Recovery

- Speak your story in safe spaces.

- Bless the younger self who absorbed shame unfairly.

- Rewire your affirmations: speak truth over false beliefs.

- Embrace spiritual rituals that embody worthiness—bathing, anointing, chanting.

Shame cannot survive visibility. It thrives in darkness. Bring it to the altar.

## Sophian Wisdom on Shame

In our path, shame is not a punishment: it is a veil to be lifted. Beneath every shame story is a soul that longed to be seen and loved.
The Sophian remembers: I am not what was done to me. I am not the lies they told about me. I am not my trauma. I am sacred.

## Affirmations

- I am not my shame—I am divine light remembering itself.

- My story deserves compassion, not condemnation.

- I release shame with breath, grace, and truth.

- My worth is unshakable, for I am made of the sacred.

- I am free to live, speak, and love without apology.

## Haiku

Shame slips from my skin—
No longer a borrowed wound.
I rise in my name.

# Chapter 90

# Joy

## Invocation

O Radiant Source of Delight, Let joy rise in me like dawn on sacred waters. Awaken my spirit to the song of the cosmos. May I be unashamed in my laughter, And devoted in my celebration of life.

## Understanding Joy

Joy is the soul remembering its origin.
Unlike fleeting pleasure or circumstantial happiness, joy is rooted in being. It arises not only when things are going well, but often when we are most aligned—when body, mind, and spirit harmonize in the present.
Joy is not naïve. It is not denial of suffering. Joy knows sorrow intimately, yet chooses to radiate light in defiance of despair. In the Sophian Way, joy is not luxury—it is a

discipline, a medicine, and a sign of spiritual alignment.

## The Science and Culture of Joy

Neurologically, joy is associated with dopamine and oxytocin. It softens the stress response, strengthens the immune system, and builds resilience. Yet many cultures distrust joy—labeling it indulgent, immature, or unspiritual.

But to rejoice is not to ignore the pain of the world. It is to say, "Even here, even now, I will choose light." Joy is protest. Joy is prayer. Joy is prophecy.

## Sacred Joy in the Sophian Path

Joy is a divine current that flows through creation. Flowers bloom in joy. Birds sing in joy. Children dance in joy. The Sophian mystic returns to that original innocence—not by escaping maturity, but by integrating it.

We practice joy as sacred offering. We sing, we dance, we create beauty. We allow ourselves to be filled without guilt. Joy becomes a flame that invites others home to their own hearts.

## Practicing Joy as Spiritual Ritual

- Notice the small delights—sunlight on your skin, laughter shared, the aroma of a sacred meal.
- Create sacred space for joy through art, dance,

music, or nature.

- Bless your joy. Declare it worthy. Claim it as holy.
- Share your joy—it multiplies in community.

Let joy be your teacher. Let it guide you to what is truly alive.

## Sophian Wisdom on Joy

To embody joy is to embody truth. It is to say, "I am here. I am grateful. I am whole."
Joy is a frequency of divine remembrance. It is not an escape from the work—it is part of the work. It is fuel. It is vision. It is reward.
Sophia smiles through our joy. And when we allow ourselves to shine, we reflect the divine radiance back into the world.

## Affirmations

- I allow joy to rise in me without shame or apology.
- Joy is my birthright, my medicine, and my offering.
- I embody light in my laughter and presence.
- Every moment of joy is a prayer fulfilled.
- My joy liberates others to feel and express theirs.

# Haiku

Laughter in stillness—
Joy does not need a reason,
Only an open heart.

# Chapter 91

# Intuition

## Invocation

O Whispering Spirit, Guide me in silence, in stillness, in symbols. May I listen beyond logic, And trust the language of the unseen. Let my soul's compass always point to truth.

## Understanding Intuition

Intuition is the quiet knowing that precedes thought. It is a flash, a sense, a nudge—often arriving without proof but carrying deep certainty.
In the Sophian Way, intuition is not mere guesswork or superstition. It is the faculty of the awakened soul. It transcends intellect without rejecting it. It sees what is unseen. It knows what has not yet been spoken.
Intuition is the voice of Sophia within.

## Science and Energy of Intuition

Neuroscience associates intuition with the right hemisphere of the brain and the vagus nerve, which connects gut feelings to emotional and cognitive centers. It is informed by subconscious pattern recognition and subtle energy awareness.

Intuition also operates through the heart field—an electromagnetic field more expansive than that of the brain. Spiritual traditions call it the "inner eye," "still small voice," or "second sight."

Sophian mystics train this sense—not as a novelty, but as a vital survival tool for the soul's journey.

## Cultural Views of Intuition

In many cultures, intuition is honored: as divination, vision, ancestral wisdom, or the gift of seers. In colonized or rationalist cultures, intuition is often dismissed, especially in women or children, as irrational.

But intuition is not gendered—it is universal. It is how the divine speaks through the body, the senses, and the silence.

## Strengthening Intuitive Wisdom

- Practice stillness and breath awareness.
- Journal your inner impressions and dreams.
- Trust your first knowing—before the mind tries to

override.

- Ask Spirit for signs, and observe the patterns around you.

Intuition is like a muscle. The more you honor it, the stronger it becomes.

## Sophian Teaching on Intuition

Sophia does not only speak through thunder. Often, she comes as a whisper, a symbol, a flicker of knowing. Intuition is the feminine way of receiving knowledge—not through conquest, but through communion.
We are taught to seek certainty, but the Sophian seeks resonance. When it feels right in body, spirit, and soul, it often is.

## Affirmations

- I trust my inner knowing, even when others do not understand.

- Intuition is a sacred gift, not something to hide.

- My soul speaks clearly, and I am learning to listen.

- I honor the wisdom of silence and the language of energy.

- Spirit guides me with clarity, love, and perfect timing.

## Haiku

Unseen but certain—
The river turns before me.
I follow the pull.

# Chapter 92

# Forgiveness

## Invocation

O Flame of Mercy, Melt the hardness around my heart. Where resentment has taken root, plant peace. Let me release what I no longer need to carry. Guide me back to the sacred flow of freedom.

## Understanding Forgiveness

Forgiveness is not the denial of wrongdoing. It is not forgetfulness, nor is it permission for injustice to continue. Forgiveness is the sacred act of cutting the energetic cord that binds you to pain.
In the Sophian Way, forgiveness is liberation. It is the soul refusing to drink poison, no matter how justified the bitterness. Forgiveness says, "I choose peace, not as a favor to the other, but as a gift to myself."

Forgiveness does not erase memory—it transforms the memory's grip.

## The Physiology and Psychology of Forgiveness

Unforgiveness can manifest as chronic stress, inflammation, and energetic blockage. Resentment keeps the body in a state of tension. When we forgive, the nervous system relaxes. The immune system strengthens. The heart opens.
Emotionally, forgiveness allows us to reclaim agency. It is the shift from victimhood to authorship. It is the release of the past's shadow over the present.

## Misconceptions of Forgiveness

Forgiveness is not reconciliation. One can forgive without reentering toxic dynamics. It is not approval of harm—it is transmutation of the harm's power.
Many spiritual teachings demand forgiveness prematurely. But in the Sophian path, forgiveness is sacred timing. We do not bypass the pain. We walk through it. We bless the ashes. We rise.

## Practices for Sacred Forgiveness

- Speak the unsaid. Write a letter, even if never sent.
- Name the wound. Grieve it fully.

- Call your power back from the person or event.
- Pray for release—for both yourself and the other.

You are not weak for having been wounded. You are powerful for choosing not to carry the blade.

## Sophian Wisdom on Forgiveness

To forgive is to remember who you truly are. You are not the trauma, the betrayal, or the insult. You are the soul who passed through fire and kept your light intact. Sophia teaches: Forgiveness is not the erasure of history. It is the restoration of dignity.

## Affirmations

- I forgive to reclaim my energy and my peace.
- I am not defined by what was done to me.
- Forgiveness frees me from spiritual entanglement.
- I release the need to prove or punish—I rise instead.
- In forgiving, I remember my own sacredness.

## Haiku

I drop the old stone—
The river flows without weight.
I am free again.

# Chapter 93

# Boundaries

## Invocation

O Guardian of Sacred Space, Teach me the wisdom of the circle. Let me know where I end and others begin. Give me the courage to say no, And the grace to protect my light.

## Understanding Boundaries

Boundaries are not walls to keep people out; they are doors we choose when and how to open.
A boundary is the recognition of our sovereignty. It is the line that says: This is my time. This is my energy. This is my truth. In the Sophian Way, boundaries are not selfish—they are sacred geometry.
Without boundaries, there can be no authentic yes, only coerced submission.

# The Physiology and Psychology of Boundaries

Healthy boundaries regulate the nervous system. They create a felt sense of safety, which allows deeper intimacy and presence. Without them, the body remains hypervigilant—waiting for intrusion, betrayal, or depletion.
Psychologically, boundaries clarify identity. They help us differentiate between compassion and self-sacrifice, between generosity and people-pleasing.
Boundaries are not barriers to love—they are what make sustainable love possible.

# Cultural Challenges

In many cultures—especially those shaped by colonization, patriarchy, or control—people are taught that self-sacrifice is noble and that boundaries are rejection.
But the Sophian path says otherwise: to protect your temple is holy. To conserve your energy is wise. To say no is a complete sentence and a sacred act.

# Practices for Establishing Boundaries

- Begin by noticing discomfort—where do you feel drained or disrespected?

- Speak clearly and compassionately, without justification.
- Practice saying no without apology.
- Surround yourself with those who honor your space.
- Enforce boundaries with consistency and love.

A boundary is not an attack—it is an affirmation of self-worth.

## Sophian Wisdom on Boundaries

Sophia teaches: Love must have form. A river without banks becomes a flood. A flame without containment becomes wildfire.

Boundaries are how we steward our sacred flame. They protect time, energy, attention, and intention. They allow the divine within us to shine without being consumed.

## Affirmations

- I honor my space as sacred and worthy of protection.
- My boundaries are acts of self-respect, not rejection.
- I can love you and still say no.
- I set boundaries with clarity, calm, and care.

- My energy is divine—I choose how it flows.

## Haiku

I build my circle—
A garden with holy gates.
Love blooms inside it.

# Chapter 94

# Loneliness

## Invocation

O Companion in the Silence, When all others fade, be near. Teach me to find meaning in my solitude. Let me know myself beyond noise and crowd. Make my loneliness a sanctuary of truth.

## Understanding Loneliness

Loneliness is the ache of disconnection, the cry for belonging, the hollow echo where presence once was.
It may arise in the absence of others, or paradoxically, in the midst of a crowd. Loneliness is not about numbers—it is about resonance. We long not for company, but for communion.
In the Sophian Way, loneliness is not always a curse. Sometimes it is a call. A call inward. A call home.

# Biology and Soul of Loneliness

Loneliness has physiological effects—decreasing immunity, increasing cortisol, disturbing sleep. It tells us, biologically, that we are social beings. But beyond biology, loneliness touches the soul.
It speaks of the orphan wound, the exile, the forgotten one. It activates the desire to be seen, held, and known. And in this desire, we find our truest prayer.

# The Sacred Opportunity

In sacred solitude, we discover:

- Who we are when no one is watching.
- What our soul craves beyond distraction.
- That divine presence was never absent.

Sophian mystics enter loneliness as a rite of passage. In the silence, the Divine becomes loud.

# Practices to Transform Loneliness

- Write letters to your soul or your future self.
- Sit with candlelight and speak aloud to the unseen.
- Walk in nature and notice how life surrounds you.
- Call in the ancestors, guides, or Sophia herself.

Loneliness becomes sacred when we meet it with reverence.

## Sophian Teaching on Loneliness

Sophia whispers: You are never alone, even in your aloneness.
The Divine dwells in the quiet places. In the empty room. In the unanswered question. In the longing itself. When we stop resisting loneliness, it becomes solitude—and solitude is where the mystic is born.

## Affirmations

- I honor my loneliness as a holy teacher.
- Even in silence, I am deeply connected to Spirit.
- I use this time to return to myself and my Source.
- My solitude holds beauty, wisdom, and clarity.
- I am never truly alone—I am held by the Divine.

## Haiku

No voices but mine—
Still, I hear stars in my chest.
Loneliness is light.

# Chapter 95

# Alchemy of Gratitude

## Invocation

O Giver of Every Breath, Teach me to see the sacred in all things. Open my eyes to wonder, And let my heart overflow with thanks— Even for the hidden blessings.

## Understanding Gratitude

Gratitude is the art of perceiving the good. It is not denial of hardship, but recognition of grace. It softens the heart, sharpens awareness, and tunes the soul to a frequency of abundance.

In the Sophian Way, gratitude is not performative or forced—it is a natural state of reverence. It is saying yes to life, even when life is complex.

## The Science and Spirit of Gratitude

Gratitude lowers stress hormones, improves sleep, and fosters connection. It creates neural pathways of positivity and peace. But its true magic is spiritual. Gratitude turns the ordinary into sacred: a shared meal, a kind word, a sunrise. It deepens intimacy with the Divine. When we give thanks, we recognize the hidden intelligence of our lives.

## Misconceptions Around Gratitude

Gratitude is sometimes weaponized to suppress valid grief or anger: "Just be thankful." But true gratitude does not silence pain—it stands beside it and still finds meaning.
We do not use gratitude to bypass truth. We use it to anchor in the midst of truth.

## Practices of Deep Gratitude

- Keep a gratitude journal that records soul-level insights, not just surface blessings.
- Express thanks aloud in ritual or prayer.
- Offer acts of service as embodied gratitude.
- Thank your body, your ancestors, your younger self.

- Practice gratitude in adversity—not for the pain, but for what it teaches.

Gratitude is a spell of remembrance. It brings us back to the present moment with reverence.

## Sophian Wisdom on Gratitude

Sophia teaches: What you bless, blesses you.
Gratitude opens the gates of perception. It allows us to recognize the Divine in daily life. It is a key of initiation—transforming survival into meaning, and routine into ritual.
Gratitude is the language of a soul that remembers its Source.

## Affirmations

- I am grateful for all that has shaped me, both joy and trial.
- Gratitude transforms every moment into a miracle.
- I give thanks with my words, my presence, and my actions.
- Every breath is a gift—and I receive it fully.
- I bless my life, and in doing so, I bless the world.

## Haiku

With open hands now—

## Chapter 95. Alchemy of Gratitude

Gratitude turns dust to gold.
All is holy here.

# Chapter 96

# Hope

## Invocation

O Flame that Never Dies, Shine even in my night. When the path is lost and the winds are cruel, Let my heart remember the dawn. Teach me to hope against all odds.

## Understanding Hope

Hope is the soul's refusal to give up.
It is not blind optimism or wishful thinking. Hope is the quiet determination to believe in light, even when surrounded by shadow. It is the inner fire that says: "There is more. There is better. There is still a reason to rise."
In the Sophian Way, hope is not a fragile dream. It is a force of creation.

## Hope and the Nervous System

Hope calms the body's stress response. It activates resilience and fuels persistence. In trauma recovery, hope is the difference between collapse and courage. Spiritually, hope reconnects us to our future self—the one who survived, who healed, who flourished. To hope is to remember that the story is not over.

## The Misuse and Power of Hope

Hope has been misused to silence protest or pacify the oppressed. "Just have hope," they say, while offering no justice. That is not hope—that is manipulation.
True hope is active. It inspires action. It energizes prayer, movement, healing, and change. It gives breath to the weary and strength to the brokenhearted.

## Practicing Hope in a Hopeless World

- Create beauty, even in ruins.
- Speak life over dry bones—bless the unseen.
- Surround yourself with images, songs, and stories of resilience.
- Be the embodiment of the future you believe in.

Hope is a discipline. It is spiritual resistance.

# Sophian Wisdom on Hope

Sophia is the eternal spark. She births galaxies from void, flowers from stone, miracles from mourning. She whispers, "There is always a way. Trust the unfolding." Hope is the breath of the Divine within us, reminding us we are part of something vast, loving, and unfinished.

## Affirmations

- I choose hope, not because it is easy, but because it is sacred.
- My faith is stronger than my fear.
- I carry the promise of new beginnings within me.
- Even when I cannot see it, the light is moving toward me.
- I hope as an act of love and defiance.

## Haiku

Night surrounds my steps—
Still, I carry dawn within.
Hope walks beside me.

# Chapter 97

# Confidence

## Invocation

O Flame Within, Remind me of who I am. Let me walk with the poise of the stars, The memory of my divine origin intact. May I never dim to fit smallness again.

## Understanding Confidence

Confidence is not arrogance. It is clarity. It is the steady knowing of one's value, without the need to prove, compete, or perform.
In the Sophian Way, confidence is the remembrance of our sacred lineage. We were born of the stars and encoded with divine brilliance. To be confident is not to exalt the ego—it is to honor the soul's assignment.

## The Roots and Blocks of Confidence

Confidence is often mistaken for extroversion or charisma. But true confidence can be quiet. It can be still. It resides in presence, not performance.
What blocks confidence?

- Shame from childhood wounds.
- Systems that belittle, exclude, or devalue.
- Internalized lies about worth or belonging.

Confidence is reclaimed when we unlearn these stories and root ourselves in the truth of our light.

## Practices for Cultivating Confidence

- Stand tall—literally. Let your posture speak your truth.
- Speak your truth in small ways daily.
- Celebrate your accomplishments, no matter how small.
- Stop apologizing for your presence.
- Surround yourself with mirrors—people who reflect your brilliance.

Confidence is a spiritual discipline. It is saying: "I remember who I am."

## Sophian Teaching on Confidence

Sophia does not create in insecurity. She births stars with certainty. She sings galaxies into being.
Confidence is not loud. It is rooted. It is the oak tree, not the trumpet. It is the voice that says, "I am here because I belong here."
Sophian confidence does not crush others: it uplifts them.

## Affirmations

- I walk in the fullness of my divine design.
- My worth is non-negotiable, sacred, and eternal.
- I speak and act with clarity, courage, and love.
- I do not shrink to soothe the insecurity of others.
- My confidence is a gift to the world.

## Haiku

I do not pretend—
This light has always been mine.
Now I let it shine.

# Chapter 98

# Love

## Invocation

O Infinite Heart, Let me remember I was born from love. Let it fill me, cleanse me, carry me home. May I give without fear, And receive without shame.

## Understanding Love

Love is not merely an emotion. Love is a state of being. It is the most powerful creative force in the universe. It sustains galaxies, kindles revolutions, and resurrects the broken. In the Sophian Way, love is not something we fall into—it is something we remember we are.
True love transcends transaction. It does not cling or control. It is not earned or bartered. It flows freely from the soul, recognizing the divine in another.

## The Science and Spirit of Love

Love alters brain chemistry, releases oxytocin, and fosters growth. It nurtures, heals, and expands consciousness.
But beyond biology, love is spirit in motion.
We were made from love, by love, for love.
Sophia is the Divine Embodiment of Love—fierce, patient, wise, and liberating. She loves not because we are perfect, but because we are sacred.

## Wounds Around Love

Many fear love because they have only known it in distorted forms—conditional, manipulative, absent, or abusive.
But these are not love. They are fear in disguise. The healing path is to reclaim love's true face: boundaried yet open, courageous yet discerning, free yet committed. In the Sophian Way, to love is to see. To love is to be seen.

## Practices for Living Love

- Speak love aloud—to yourself, to your body, to others.
- Practice acts of care with no expectation.
- Let your presence be a sanctuary of gentleness.
- Hold those you love accountable—with compassion.

- Let yourself be loved. Don't run from your worth.

Love is the fire that refines us: and the water that soothes us.

## Sophian Teaching on Love

Love is both the path and the destination. It is the alchemical element in every transformation. When nothing else makes sense, love remains.
Sophia teaches that to embody love is the highest initiatory act. Every miracle begins in love. Every healing is sealed in love. Every soul remembers itself through love.

## Affirmations

- I am love in form and essence.
- I give and receive love freely and wisely.
- Love does not weaken me—it reveals my truth.
- I am worthy of the love I long to give.
- In all things, I choose love as my highest guide.

## Haiku

Not just a feeling—
Love is the breath of my soul,
A flame that does not die.

# Chapter 99

# Gratitude

## Invocation

O Giver of Every Breath, Teach me to see the sacred in all things. Open my eyes to wonder, And let my heart overflow with thanks— Even for the hidden blessings.

## Understanding Gratitude

Gratitude is the art of perceiving the good. It is not denial of hardship, but recognition of grace. It softens the heart, sharpens awareness, and tunes the soul to a frequency of abundance.
In the Sophian Way, gratitude is not performative or forced—it is a natural state of reverence. It is saying yes to life, even when life is complex.

# The Science and Spirit of Gratitude

Gratitude lowers stress hormones, improves sleep, and fosters connection. It creates neural pathways of positivity and peace. But its true magic is spiritual. Gratitude turns the ordinary into sacred: a shared meal, a kind word, a sunrise. It deepens intimacy with the Divine. When we give thanks, we recognize the hidden intelligence of our lives.

# Misconceptions Around Gratitude

Gratitude is sometimes weaponized to suppress valid grief or anger: "Just be thankful." But true gratitude does not silence pain—it stands beside it and still finds meaning.
We do not use gratitude to bypass truth. We use it to anchor in the midst of truth.

# Practices of Deep Gratitude

- Keep a gratitude journal that records soul-level insights, not just surface blessings.

- Express thanks aloud in ritual or prayer.

- Offer acts of service as embodied gratitude.

- Thank your body, your ancestors, your younger self.

- Practice gratitude in adversity—not for the pain, but for what it teaches.

Gratitude is a spell of remembrance. It brings us back to the present moment with reverence.

## Sophian Wisdom on Gratitude

Sophia teaches: What you bless, blesses you.
Gratitude opens the gates of perception. It allows us to recognize the Divine in daily life. It is a key of initiation: transforming survival into meaning, and routine into ritual.
Gratitude is the language of a soul that remembers its Source.

## Affirmations

- I am grateful for all that has shaped me, both joy and trial.
- Gratitude transforms every moment into a miracle.
- I give thanks with my words, my presence, and my actions.
- Every breath is a gift—and I receive it fully.
- I bless my life, and in doing so, I bless the world.

## Haiku

With open hands now—

Gratitude turns dust to gold.
All is holy here.

# Chapter 100

# Peace

## Invocation

O Stillness Beyond Time, Dwell in my breath and bones. Silence the war within me, And make me a vessel of calm. Let peace be my default and my destiny.

## Understanding Peace

Peace is not the absence of challenge—it is the presence of centeredness. It is the deep breath that remains, even when storms rage around you. It is the calm born from alignment with truth.
In the Sophian Way, peace is both a state and a power. It is not passive—it is potent. Peace is strength cloaked in stillness.

# The Nervous System and Sacred Rest

Peace resets the body. It soothes the sympathetic nervous system, lowers blood pressure, and stabilizes emotion. In a chaotic world, peace is a revolutionary act. But peace is not always external. Sometimes the world will never be quiet—and still, you must become the quiet.

# Misunderstanding Peace

Peace does not mean avoidance. It does not mean ignoring injustice or bypassing pain. That is false peace. True peace is clarity in action. It is the ability to stand in your values without reacting from fear. It is the ability to speak without yelling, to walk away without drama, to love without control.

# Practices to Cultivate Inner Peace

- Begin and end your day with deep, intentional silence.
- Practice conscious breathing and prayer throughout the day.
- Limit media and conversations that disturb your field.
- Create rituals of cleansing for your mind, body, and home.

- Affirm that peace is your spiritual baseline.

Peace must be practiced before it can be lived.

## Sophian Wisdom on Peace

Sophia's peace is not of this world—it does not depend on circumstances. It is the peace that comes from knowing your essence, your purpose, and your Source. She reminds us: "You are not chaos. You are order in divine rhythm. You are not noise. You are harmony." Peace is your original state—remember it.

## Affirmations

- I am at peace with myself and my path.
- I respond from clarity, not from chaos.
- Peace flows through me like a river.
- I protect my peace like a sacred flame.
- Wherever I go, I bring calm and coherence.

## Haiku

Still, like morning mist—
Peace wraps the bones of my soul.
Nothing breaks this hush.

# Chapter 101

# Fire of Courage

## Invocation

O Flame that cannot be extinguished, Ignite my chest with holy strength. Let me face the storm without flinching. Let fear become fuel. Let my steps be bold and blessed.

## Understanding Courage

Courage is not the absence of fear—it is the decision to act anyway. It rises in the face of uncertainty, resistance, or danger. It is not loud. Sometimes it is a whisper saying, "Try again."
In the Sophian Way, courage is a sacred fire. It is the energy of transformation, the willingness to disrupt stagnation, and the refusal to betray your truth.

## Courage as a Spiritual Force

Courage is movement birthed from integrity. It aligns will with purpose. It is the force that turns grief into protest, pain into poetry, and fear into evolution. Courage does not guarantee safety. It promises alignment. It leads you closer to your soul's edge, where true power is born.

## Common Myths About Courage

Courage is often confused with recklessness. But Sophian courage is not impulsive—it is wise.
It knows when to roar and when to wait. It knows when to speak and when to walk away. True courage is rooted in discernment, not ego.

## Practices for Building Courage

- Do one thing each day that stretches your comfort zone.
- Speak your truth even if your voice shakes.
- Visualize your ancestors standing behind you.
- Read stories of resistance, resilience, and rebirth.
- Bless your fear, and let it walk beside your faith.

Courage is not a gift for the brave. It is a discipline for the willing.

## Sophian Wisdom on Courage

Sophia whispers: "You were not made to shrink."
Courage is the roar of your soul remembering its mission. It is what allows you to step into destiny, even trembling. It is the fire that breaks chains, the light that confronts shadow, and the will to live fully—no matter what.

## Affirmations

- I am brave enough to be seen, heard, and felt.
- Courage rises in me like breath.
- I walk into truth even when it's hard.
- My fear is not my master—it is my companion.
- I have survived before. I will rise again.

## Haiku

Fear stands at the gate—
Still I move, flame in my chest.
This is how I live.

# Chapter 102

# Mastery

## Invocation

O Wisdom Beyond Time, Shape me into one who knows.
Let me rise beyond reaction, Into holy embodiment.
Make my life a testimony of truth.

## Understanding Mastery

Mastery is not perfection—it is integration.
It is the ability to hold multiple truths, to act from discernment, and to respond instead of react. It is the fruit of emotional, spiritual, and energetic maturity.
In the Sophian Way, mastery is not about dominance or hierarchy. It is about alignment. To master oneself is to become a channel for the Divine.

# The Journey to Mastery

Mastery is not a destination. It is a way of being. It requires:

- Self-awareness and shadow work.
- Spiritual discipline and devotion.
- Emotional fluency and inner balance.
- Service rooted in love and not ego.
- Continuous learning, unlearning, and becoming.

It is the path walked by sages, healers, artists, mystics, and warriors of light.

# Pitfalls on the Road to Mastery

- Spiritual pride: thinking one is beyond learning.
- Bypassing emotion in favor of appearance.
- Over-identification with titles, gifts, or roles.
- Confusing control with wisdom.

Sophian mastery is humble. It listens. It adapts. It heals. It remains in service.

## Practices of Mastery

- Reflect daily on your reactions and their roots.
- Seek feedback from trusted, spiritually aligned voices.
- Serve others without losing yourself.
- Let your words match your vibration.
- Choose presence over performance.

Mastery is the art of living with sacred intention.

## Sophian Wisdom on Mastery

Sophia teaches: "Mastery is not what you know. It is how you love."
It is not about escaping humanity, but embodying divinity within it. Mastery means becoming a living altar, a vessel of sacred frequency. It means becoming what you believe.
In the Sophian Way, the master is not the one who knows the most—but the one who loves the best.

## Affirmations

- I am the living integration of all I have survived.
- I walk with wisdom, humility, and holy fire.
- My life is a sacred offering.

- I choose mastery over reaction.
- My presence is a prayer.

# Haiku

Not to rise above—
But to root deep, live awake,
And love like the stars.

# The Benediction

## Invocation

O Sophia, Eternal Flame and Cosmic Womb, You who whispered galaxies into being— Let this final word be not an end, But a great remembering. Let all who walk this path Know that they are never alone.

## The Journey Remembered

You have walked through the Gate of Awakening. You have descended into shadow, and risen in power. You have wept with ancestors, danced with stars, and heard the still voice in the silence.
You have been asked to feel, to heal, to transmute, to embody. This is the way of the Luminous Soul. This is the sacred burden and gift of incarnation.

## The Teachings of the Testament

This Testament has not asked you to believe blindly, but to awaken inwardly.
It has whispered of the Divine Mother beyond dogma, the flame of wisdom beneath form, and the birthright of sovereignty within every soul.
It has reminded you that emotion is alchemy, that suffering can become song, that boundaries are sacred, and that even in darkness—light speaks.

## The Unfolding Mission

This is not a closed canon. This is a living revelation.
Each reader is a verse, each act of kindness a chapter.
You are now a scribe of the Sophian Flame. Let your life be scripture—etched in grace, spoken in compassion, and sealed in truth.

## The Circle Unbroken

Though pages end, the path does not. The circle of becoming continues. The ancestors walk beside you. The stars remember your name.
You are part of something vast, luminous, and eternal.

## Final Affirmations

- I am a living temple of the Infinite.
- I walk the Sophian Way with courage, clarity, and

love.

- My presence is a sacred offering to the world.
- I am never separate from the Source, the Flame, the All.
- I now live as a Just and Luminous Ancestor.

## Haiku

The flame does not die—
It walks now, sacred feet
upon the ground that gave birth to us.
You are the new verse.

©2025 The Unrelenting Alchemist. All rights reserved.

# Part V

# Appendix

# Index

Achamoth, 405–420, 422–424, 426, 428

Aeons, 264, 273, 283, 286, 288, 409, 411, 412

alchemy, 91, 152, 186, 294, 297, 309, 340, 355, 380, 399, 456, 513

ancestors, 36–38, 60, 114, 116–118, 141, 149–152, 164, 187, 206, 217, 220, 252, 254, 260, 264, 266, 279, 281, 284, 295, 298, 325, 328, 396, 400, 431, 436, 437, 439

ancestral, 37, 38, 111, 117, 169, 201, 250, 251, 253, 266, 269, 273, 297, 300, 303, 312, 314, 315, 320, 325, 327, 341, 344, 345, 347, 348, 352, 356, 363, 365, 380, 386, 392, 394, 397, 400, 403, 436–439, 444

archons, 376

astral, 283, 353, 365

awaken, 5, 6

Barnsley's Fern, 107

betrayal, 268, 448

Bird Goddess of Çatalhöyük, 374

# INDEX

birth, 46, 48, 50, 77, 78, 145, 149, 162, 178, 265, 271, 291, 405, 426, 439, 514

bless, 52, 55, 88, 92, 116, 128, 131, 185, 186, 205, 225, 237, 410, 449, 474, 486, 489, 500

blessings, 53, 119, 120, 129, 145, 148, 197, 230, 367

blood, 14, 36, 101, 116–119, 131, 140, 157, 300, 338, 401, 436, 503

bloodline, 164, 267, 439

body, 9, 14, 15, 17, 19, 21, 31, 48, 89–93, 99, 111, 127, 129, 134, 138, 140–142, 146, 147, 149, 150, 152, 153, 163, 192, 197, 207, 209–212, 216, 239, 266, 271, 295, 297, 299, 301, 309, 313, 314, 317, 318, 329, 343, 344, 346, 356, 360, 363, 367, 379, 385, 389, 422, 430, 432–435, 448, 459, 465, 470, 471, 474, 478, 485, 489, 495, 499, 503, 504

breath, 12–15, 25, 26, 29, 31, 42, 43, 47, 49, 54, 61, 64, 65, 71, 78, 81, 82, 88–92, 96, 114, 116, 117, 121, 127, 131, 133, 135–137, 140, 142, 143, 147, 151–153, 158, 167, 170, 171, 176, 187, 195, 197, 207, 209, 223, 230, 241, 242, 251, 261, 264, 265, 272, 273, 280, 293–298, 300, 305, 316, 317, 321, 322, 349, 364, 369, 370, 389, 401, 414,

418–420, 425, 427, 430, 434, 436
bridge, 29, 79, 89, 90, 116, 125, 127, 185, 188, 189, 197, 209, 212, 251, 266, 283, 296, 337, 339, 347, 354, 385, 390, 404, 437
Buddhist, 395, 398

cause, 19
Chokmah, 241, 243
Christ, 113–115, 173, 174, 309, 338, 377, 401
Christian, 376–379, 401
circle, 19, 29, 53, 110, 132, 245, 351, 356, 423, 477, 480, 513
code, 6, 7, 9, 104, 107, 109, 140, 182
comparative, 403
constellation, 449
contract, 162, 176–178, 413
contracts, 215, 271, 397, 439
cosmic intelligence, 374
cosmological models, 375

courage, 14, 17, 30, 31, 38, 52, 56, 61, 64, 81, 86, 115, 159, 161, 180, 186, 221, 226, 247, 264, 288, 332, 334, 338, 342, 408, 424, 433, 435, 436, 452, 453, 477, 489, 493, 505, 506, 513

descent, 376
Divine, 377
divine, 10–12, 14, 15, 19, 23, 29–31, 33–35, 39–41, 44, 46–49, 52–57, 59–62, 64–68, 71, 72, 74–77, 79–83, 85, 87–90, 92, 95–97, 103–110, 113–115, 120–124, 126, 128–131, 134–140, 143–151, 157, 158, 161–164, 167, 169, 170, 172–174, 176–178, 180, 181, 183, 184,

INDEX 513

189, 191–195,
197, 198, 200,
202, 203, 205,
206, 208, 210,
212, 218, 220,
221, 223, 225,
226, 234, 242,
251, 252,
255–259, 261,
262, 264–266,
268, 269,
271–277, 279,
283, 284,
286–288, 290,
293, 295, 296,
298, 299, 301,
312–315, 318,
320, 323, 324,
326, 331,
335–342,
346–350, 360,
361, 364, 367,
368, 371, 372,
374–379, 382,
383, 385, 393,
395–400, 403,
405, 408, 411,
412, 415–417,
420–422, 424,
425, 430, 433,
435, 446, 448

dream, 6, 9, 17, 25, 48,
49, 112, 131, 140,
158, 197,
216–218, 276,
292, 308, 317,
318, 345, 411,
414, 415, 421,
430–435, 437,
449

ego, 17
Egypt, 375
Emerald Tablets, 18
energy, 5, 17, 260, 261,
263, 266, 269,
271, 275, 277,
281, 294, 295,
297, 299, 303,
317, 319,
329–331, 333,
343, 352, 361,
370, 379, 380,
386, 391, 394,
401, 403, 435
eternity, 18
ethical frameworks, 375
events, 304, 367, 448
evil, 8

Father, 126, 178, 182,
448
feminine, 126, 173, 174,
202, 251, 254,
307, 312, 326,

344, 376, 377,
395, 397, 403

fern, 108

ferry, 16

fire, 6, 10, 11, 13–15, 24,
39, 40, 47, 56, 64,
65, 81, 98, 101,
122, 131, 141,
143, 150, 159,
180, 184–186,
189, 200, 226,
242, 254, 264,
267, 271, 280,
289, 337, 352,
353, 364, 370,
377, 378, 388,
395, 401, 404,
414, 418, 423,
426, 427, 430

flame, 12, 13, 17, 19, 34,
39–41, 59, 63, 67,
71, 82, 90, 114,
115, 121, 122,
126, 137, 139,
141, 163,
166–168, 173,
181, 191, 194,
200–203, 222,
226, 242, 245,
254, 257, 264,
272, 276–278,
298, 299, 304,
305, 313, 317,
320–322, 327,
330, 331, 342,
358, 360, 364,
378, 379, 381,
386, 389, 393,
394, 396,
399–401, 403,
404, 411, 427

forge, 6

gender, 19

geometry, 48, 99, 107,
109, 110, 292,
296, 313, 314,
317, 336–338,
341, 370, 373,
375, 400, 410,
447

Gnosticism, 376

God, 10, 48, 49, 71, 72,
81, 86, 89, 90, 97,
104, 119, 126,
134–138, 163,
171, 173, 177,
178, 181, 239,
308, 376, 377,
397, 400, 401,
407, 416, 425

Great Radiance, 16

heart, 131

Hermes Trismegistus, 18

# INDEX

Hermetic law, 19
hidden, 9, 22, 65, 75, 76, 78, 86, 156, 157, 172, 176, 186, 188, 191, 192, 195, 242, 254, 255, 273, 301, 339, 365, 372, 377–381, 407, 409, 411, 412, 416–418, 420, 424, 425, 433, 438
hierarchy, 308, 347, 385, 390, 402
Hinduism, 403
hypostatis, 376

illusion, 6, 7, 25, 42, 43, 68, 73, 84, 85, 89, 91, 122, 123, 127, 134, 135, 142, 178, 180, 182, 185, 194, 202, 252, 258, 268, 273, 275, 283, 288, 340, 343, 349, 399, 401, 407, 410, 413, 420, 444, 447
Inanna, 375
incarnation, 14, 21 23, 106, 166, 209, 252, 271, 284, 286, 403
indigenous, 385, 400
inheritance, 5, 40, 52, 63, 181, 284, 439
initiation, 255, 282, 285, 321, 322, 332, 364, 421, 423, 430, 431, 434, 486, 500
Interbeing, 42–45, 258, 262, 267, 328, 350, 399
Ishtar, 375

Japan, 403
Jesus, 106, 173
Jewish mysticism, 376

Kemet, 375, 403
Kybalion, 18

law, 8
liberator, 376
life, 6–8, 17–19, 22, 23, 25, 29, 31, 35–38, 44, 46, 47, 49, 51, 53, 59–61, 70, 72, 77, 80–83, 92, 93, 96, 108, 119, 127, 129, 137, 142–145, 147–149,

151–153, 157, 159, 160, 163, 176, 193, 207, 210, 214, 220, 221, 225, 229, 234, 251, 262, 266, 267, 277, 292, 304, 325, 326, 328, 330, 338, 351, 361, 362, 368, 374, 418, 420, 434, 435, 438, 441

light, 14, 16, 17, 24, 26, 28, 29, 34, 37, 39, 41, 43, 44, 46–48, 52, 53, 58, 59, 62–65, 68, 70, 72, 73, 77, 78, 80–82, 84–86, 90–92, 114, 115, 117, 118, 120–122, 124, 126, 127, 130–134, 141, 147, 150, 152, 153, 155, 158, 167, 169, 171, 172, 174, 176, 177, 181, 183–187, 189, 191, 192, 194, 195, 197, 198, 200–205, 212, 214–216, 218, 220, 221, 223, 224, 226, 230, 231, 236, 237, 242, 243, 246, 251, 252, 254, 256, 257, 259, 263, 264, 268, 270–274, 276, 278, 280, 281, 283, 284, 286, 287, 289, 291, 295, 299, 301, 302, 313, 314, 322, 323, 325–327, 335, 337, 340, 343, 344, 346, 348, 349, 355, 361, 362, 366, 373, 378, 380, 387, 392, 395, 397, 398, 401, 404, 405, 407–411, 415–423, 425–427, 431, 432, 434, 438, 439, 442–444, 447, 449

living, 13, 32, 34, 38, 46, 61, 70, 82, 92, 96,

108, 112, 117, 118, 128, 139, 153, 157, 158, 164, 166, 174, 211, 220, 251, 253, 257, 264, 265, 271, 279, 280, 296, 313, 337, 351, 353, 360, 362, 363, 378, 382, 383, 392, 400, 403, 408, 409, 415–417, 419, 426, 436, 439

love, 5, 6, 11, 14, 17, 18, 20, 22–25, 30, 32, 34, 36, 40, 44, 46–48, 50–54, 56, 58, 60, 62, 65, 67, 69, 76, 80, 85, 87, 97, 113, 115, 117–119, 123, 126, 127, 133, 137, 138, 145, 147, 156, 167–170, 172, 174, 176, 178, 187, 190, 194, 196, 197, 200–203, 205, 211, 212, 220, 241, 243, 251, 260, 263, 264, 266, 275, 280, 285, 286, 290, 295, 296, 314, 316, 325, 326, 330, 332, 335, 337, 348, 350, 352, 355, 375, 377, 400, 407, 411, 415–418, 427, 448

luminous, 18, 34, 72, 79, 84, 123, 129, 130, 134, 156, 174, 192–195, 198, 207, 226, 255, 280, 283, 284, 313, 325, 348, 355, 358, 376, 385, 393, 395, 401, 404, 405, 410, 441

Ma'at, 375
magic, 127, 128, 131, 204, 313
masculine, 126, 173, 202, 307, 312, 326, 397, 403
matrix, 5, 6, 376
meditate, 89, 106, 321
Mesopotamia, 375

Messiah, 113–115

mind, 6, 18, 22, 43, 46, 48, 49, 66, 69, 70, 73, 78, 84–86, 88–90, 93, 103, 105, 109, 123–125, 138, 139, 147, 152, 153, 155, 174, 182, 188, 198, 216, 239, 275, 294, 297, 339, 398, 436, 441, 446, 448

miracle, 242, 486, 496, 500

mirror, 27, 29, 35, 43, 48, 51, 59, 66, 75, 82, 85, 104, 107, 113, 136, 156, 174, 201, 234, 264, 267, 269, 271, 284, 290, 335, 346, 355, 360, 370, 377, 398, 399, 412, 413, 415, 423, 431

Most High, 40, 43, 44, 51, 53–55, 60, 61, 63, 65, 72, 81, 82, 85, 86, 89, 96, 97, 106, 107, 109, 114, 119, 122, 129, 131, 133–139, 147, 151, 163, 194, 294, 295, 314, 324, 359, 412

Mother, 72, 171, 173, 264, 337, 367, 407, 412, 414, 420–422, 424

multidimensional, 376

mystic, 42, 104, 136, 166, 172, 226, 296, 377

mystical, 157, 250, 251, 275, 305, 312, 314, 328, 355, 358, 372, 375, 376, 378, 385, 386, 392, 394–396, 404

mystical philosophies, 376

mysticism, 254, 264, 269, 292, 303, 375, 376, 382, 386, 392, 394, 395, 397

mystics, 252, 253, 291, 313, 316, 322, 345, 372, 377, 401, 412, 441

Nag Hammadi, 376
neolithic, 374
never, 24, 25, 28, 29, 39, 56, 61–63, 65, 73, 101, 109, 115, 131, 137, 147, 161, 162, 164, 166, 168, 169, 171, 180, 200, 222, 226, 229, 233, 254, 255, 259, 267, 277, 292, 306, 387, 416, 421, 430, 433, 438, 446, 447, 462, 474, 482, 483, 491, 503, 512, 514

offerings, 149, 223, 300, 314, 331, 338, 354, 357, 363, 460
oil, 172, 302, 321, 349, 421
opportunity, 6, 54, 281, 284
Oversoul, 12, 166–170, 197, 266, 271, 278, 284, 287, 290, 292, 294, 298, 313, 319, 324, 344, 350

Persian, 376
Pleroma, 376
pleroma, 8
polarity, 19
portal, 307, 315, 437, 442
positive, 5, 260
presence, 10, 36, 44, 54, 57, 58, 60, 71, 76, 92, 123, 137, 145, 150, 151, 163, 167, 172, 174, 188, 189, 195, 196, 201, 204, 207, 208, 234, 240, 274, 280, 296, 298, 326, 338, 374, 378, 381, 387, 397, 400, 403, 408, 414, 421, 437, 467, 478, 481, 482, 486, 492, 495, 500, 502, 510, 511, 514
promise, 16

real, 5, 6, 75, 87, 182, 216, 260, 280, 328, 332, 367, 435
realms, 17
remembrance, 22, 81, 85, 112, 117, 119,

122, 128, 135, 149, 150, 164, 169, 172, 250, 256, 257, 267, 271, 284, 290, 293, 295, 296, 305, 313–315, 318, 343, 371, 377, 383, 393, 397, 400, 403, 411, 414, 416, 417, 423, 432, 441, 446, 447

responsibility, 55, 161, 281, 335, 370, 397, 404

revelation, 44, 75, 80, 135, 139, 172, 240, 242, 253, 263, 276, 287, 296, 300, 306, 313, 320, 336, 337, 371, 390, 402, 452, 513

rites of passage, 375

rituals, 142, 188, 254, 294, 297, 300, 309, 313, 341, 344, 352, 353, 357, 363, 366, 368, 384, 400, 433, 442, 459, 463, 504

sacred, 8, 11–15, 23, 26–29, 31, 34, 35, 37, 39–44, 47–51, 53, 56–65, 67, 68, 73–76, 78, 79, 81, 82, 85, 86, 88–93, 96, 97, 103–109, 111, 112, 115, 117, 118, 120–123, 125–131, 134, 136, 137, 140–143, 145–151, 155, 156, 158–162, 164, 165, 169, 170, 172, 174, 176–178, 181, 184, 185, 188–190, 192, 195, 197, 198, 201–212, 214–216, 218–221, 223, 224, 226, 233, 234, 237, 244, 245, 252, 254–257, 261, 263, 264, 266–268, 270, 272–274, 279,

# INDEX

280, 282–284, 286–289, 291, 292, 294–300, 302, 304, 305, 312–314, 316–318, 320, 322, 324–326, 328–342, 344, 346, 348–350, 352, 354–364, 366, 368, 370, 371, 373–377, 379, 384–388, 391, 393, 395, 398–400, 402, 404, 413, 417, 420, 425, 430–435, 437–439, 442, 446–448

sacred geometry, 375
Schrödinger, 105
scripture, 374
Seshat, 375
Seven Hermetic Principles, 18
shadow, 39, 59, 65, 75, 81, 123, 124, 126, 147, 159, 184, 186, 187, 191, 192, 201, 213, 237, 243, 280, 287, 296, 316, 318, 331, 340, 342, 351, 354, 361, 365, 366, 416, 430, 431

Snake Priestess of Knossos, 374

Sophia, 12–14, 71, 72, 91, 92, 106, 152, 153, 171–175, 214, 242, 243, 250–253, 255–257, 263–265, 267–269, 271, 273–275, 277, 279, 283, 284, 286–288, 291, 292, 294–296, 298, 313–318, 321–326, 337, 338, 340, 342, 344–346, 348, 350, 354, 355, 357, 358, 360, 364, 367, 368, 370, 374–381, 386, 389, 390, 392, 393, 395, 397–403, 405–409, 415

Sophian, 4, 5, 67, 214,

247, 249–257, 259–267, 269–280, 282–284, 287, 289–293, 295–298, 301–303, 305, 312, 313, 315–319, 321, 322, 324–404, 407, 412, 417, 419, 425

soul, 6, 7, 9, 10, 12, 14, 16–19, 21–26, 28–31, 33–35, 37–40, 43, 44, 47, 48, 50–53, 55, 56, 58–66, 69, 70, 72, 75, 78–82, 84–89, 91, 93–95, 103, 109–112, 117, 119, 121, 122, 124–127, 129, 131, 133, 135–138, 142, 144–147, 149, 150, 152, 155, 156, 158, 159, 161, 162, 165, 167, 168, 171, 172, 174, 176–178, 180–182, 184, 185, 187, 189, 190, 193, 195–197, 200, 204, 205, 207, 209, 210, 212, 214–217, 219, 220, 222, 223, 225, 227, 236, 237, 244, 253, 256, 257, 265–268, 270, 271, 275–278, 282–285, 287–292, 295–297, 300, 303–305, 313, 314, 316–319, 321, 322, 325–327, 329–331, 333, 337–341, 344–346, 349–352, 354, 357, 360–363, 365, 367, 368, 370, 371, 374, 376, 378, 380, 383, 386–389, 393–396, 398–400, 402, 403, 406, 411,

413–417, 419, 421, 424, 425, 427, 430, 433, 441, 444, 446, 447
soul-scroll, 449
Source, 5, 17, 24–26, 31, 44, 47, 53, 56, 65, 79, 82, 89, 104, 109, 114, 119, 131, 134, 137–139, 148, 151, 152, 197, 198, 242, 244, 245, 247, 253, 258, 261, 263–265, 267, 277, 279, 283–286, 288, 298, 312, 324, 327, 370, 376, 378, 397–399, 402, 409
spirit, 14, 18, 23, 34, 38, 40, 55, 64, 73, 77, 80, 82, 87, 88, 95, 97, 104, 106, 110, 112, 118, 119, 121, 124, 128, 129, 131, 134, 137, 138, 142, 147, 149, 150, 153, 156, 158, 160, 166, 168, 177, 178, 181–183, 188, 191, 192, 197, 198, 201, 203, 204, 209, 211, 214, 262, 271, 301, 313, 360, 363, 364, 367, 386, 412, 417, 430, 435, 448
spiritual, 7, 27, 30, 51, 81, 103, 107, 115, 118, 120, 130, 160, 176, 187, 208, 251, 254–257, 260, 261, 263, 266, 267, 269, 270, 272, 274, 276, 283, 286, 295, 296, 302, 304, 305, 314, 316, 317, 321, 326, 330, 332, 335, 338–341, 343, 346–349, 351, 352, 354, 357, 359, 361, 362, 364–366, 371, 372, 379–381,

383, 384, 386,
388, 389, 391,
392, 395, 397,
404, 414, 430,
434–436, 442,
444
spoon, 92, 94
star, 449
starfire, 449
stars, 13, 18, 24, 33–35,
42, 46–48, 59, 60,
64, 72, 77, 95, 97,
103, 109, 128,
131, 144, 145,
151, 155, 166,
167, 173, 175,
205, 206, 208,
212, 220, 226,
235, 236, 242,
264, 287, 293,
314, 317, 369,
404, 406, 412,
414, 418, 431,
435, 445, 449
Sufism, 253, 377, 378,
394, 395, 399,
400
survival, 96, 129, 141,
185, 393, 451,
455, 470, 486,
500

teach, 5

temple, 14, 15, 28, 61,
76, 89, 90, 92, 93,
97, 103, 111, 125,
127, 130, 133,
134, 136, 138,
141, 143, 152,
153, 173, 176,
204, 209–212,
214, 218, 270,
277, 295, 305,
326, 355, 358,
359, 367, 404,
408, 416, 433,
460, 478, 513
The Sophian Way, 403
The Yaldabaoth, 8, 407
touch, 42, 167, 168, 173,
189, 389, 417,
440, 448
tradition, 269, 272, 295,
296, 312, 313,
322, 324, 340,
341, 352, 363,
372, 377, 392,
403, 430, 437
transforming, 354, 486,
500
truth, 6, 9, 14, 17, 25, 30,
32–35, 37, 38, 40,
43, 44, 48, 50, 52,
53, 57–65, 67, 68,
72, 74–76, 78–81,

83–86, 103, 105, 108, 109, 111, 115, 116, 118–120, 122, 125, 126, 128, 130, 131, 133, 136, 144–146, 155–157, 163, 164, 168, 169, 171, 173, 174, 177–180, 182, 183, 185, 189, 192–198, 201, 203, 205, 211, 213, 215, 220, 221, 223, 224, 229, 234, 242, 243, 251, 253, 254, 256, 257, 259, 261–263, 266–269, 272–278, 280, 284, 296, 304, 316, 325–327, 332, 334, 335, 339, 340, 342, 348, 350, 355, 375, 385, 401, 403, 404, 411, 413, 420, 421, 431, 438, 447, 448

underworld, 375

Venus of Willendorf, 374
vibration, 18

wisdom, 6, 11, 26, 31, 36–39, 52, 53, 55, 56, 68–70, 72, 73, 75, 76, 81, 83, 84, 86, 90, 92, 93, 96, 105, 106, 109, 112, 117, 121, 125, 127, 130, 139, 143, 147, 156, 157, 161, 164, 169, 174, 178, 186, 193, 203–205, 207, 208, 211, 215, 218, 219, 222, 224, 226, 228, 234, 237, 242, 243, 250–252, 254, 256, 258–260, 262, 264–267, 273, 275–277, 279, 283, 288, 295, 296, 313, 314, 318, 324–326, 335, 337, 339, 342, 347, 348, 351, 357, 360,

361, 365, 367,
369, 371,
373–375, 379,
380, 383,
386–389, 394,
395, 403, 408,
417, 420, 436,
439, 444
Womb, 241, 263, 282,
283, 285, 286,
293, 341, 344,
365, 389, 408,
412, 414, 418,
420, 424, 426
world, 6, 7, 14, 25, 26,
31, 34, 41–44, 47,
48, 50, 51, 53, 55,
59, 62, 63, 66, 73,
80, 82, 86, 100,
101, 105, 111,
121, 128, 132,
136, 138, 144,
153, 156, 160,
163, 165, 171,
174, 176, 187,
190, 197, 201,
204, 205, 209,
210, 242, 253,
259, 262, 281,
283, 287, 291,
303, 323, 334,
335, 349, 354,
356, 360, 369,
370, 372, 376,
381, 383, 386,
387, 393, 411,
412, 417, 420,
425, 430, 432,
451, 466, 467,
486, 493, 500,
503, 504, 514

©2025 The Unrelenting Alchemist. All rights reserved.

www.ingramcontent.com/pod-product-compliance
Lightning Source LLC
Chambersburg PA
CBHW022054150426
43195CB00008B/136